D1594224

THE TRUTH OF IMAGINATION

Also by Andrew J. Welburn and published by St. Martin's

POWER AND SELF-CONSCIOUSNESS
IN THE POETRY OF SHELLEY

The disparity between 'objective reality' and human imaginative response. The natural landscape below is dwarfed by the humanized Sun and the imaginings he evokes. William Blake, *The Sun at His Eastern Gate*, from the illustrations to Milton's *L'Allegro*. Watercolour (Pierpont Morgan Library, New York).

The Truth of Imagination

An Introduction to Visionary Poetry

Andrew J. Welburn

British Academy Fellow in Romantic Studies, New College, Oxford

Foreword by Owen Barfield

St. Martin's Press   New York

© Andrew J. Welburn 1989
Foreword © Owen Barfield 1989

First published in the United States of America in 1989

Printed in Hong Kong

ISBN 0–312–03632–9

Library of Congress Cataloging-in-Publication Data
Welburn, Andrew J.
    The truth of imagination : an introduction to visionary poetry / Andrew J.
Welburn : foreword by Owen Barfield.
        p.   cm.
    Bibliography: p.
    Includes index.
    ISBN 0–312–03632–9
    1. English poetry—History and criticism.   2. Imagination in literature.   3.
Visions in literature.   4. Vision in literature.   5. Self in literature. I. Title.
    PR508.I45W45 1989
    821.009—dc20   89–10345
                                                                                          CIP

For Julia

Contents

List of Plates and Figures	viii
Foreword by Owen Barfield	ix
Acknowledgements	xiii
Introduction The Truth of Imagination	1
1 The Poetry of Vision	16

Part I
Neglected Visionary 51

2 Milton's Inner Journey	53
3 Milton's Christianity and the Birth of the Ego	79

Part II
Devil's Companions – Romantic Mythologies 97

4 Blake, Initiation and *The Book of Thel*	99
5 The Devil for a Companion: Goethe and Shelley	123
6 From *Prometheus Unbound* to *The Portal of Initiation*	149
7 The Two Lives of W. B. Yeats	165
Epilogue The Tower	202
Appendix 1 Ranters and Poets	217
Appendix 2 The Gnostic Lyric: Blake and Baudelaire	221
Appendix 3 Yeats, the Gyres and a Learned Jesuit	226
Bibliography	231
Index	235

List of Plates and Figures

PLATES

Frontispiece The disparity between 'objective reality' and human imaginative response. The natural landscape below is dwarfed by the humanized Sun and the imaginings he evokes. William Blake, *The Sun at His Eastern Gate*, from the illustrations to Milton's *L'Allegro*. Watercolour (Pierpont Morgan Library, New York).

1 William Blake, *Satan, Sin and Death*, from the illustration to Milton's *Paradise Lost*. Watercolour (Huntington Library, San Marino, California).

2 Samuel Palmer, *The Lonely Tower*. Etching (1868: The Paul Mellon Collection, Yale Center for British Art, Connecticut).

3 William Blake, title-page to *The Book of Thel* (Copy O). Relief etching (The Lessing J. Rosenwald Collection, Library of Congress, Washington, DC).

4 Rudolf Steiner – Arild Rosenkrantz, painting in the small cupola of the First Goetheanum (detail).

FIGURES

1 Imaginative Consciousness. The Shelleyan Mythic Polarities.

2 The Structure of Imagination in *Paradise Lost*.

3 The Eleven Scenes of *Die Pforte der Einweihung* as a Sonata-Movement.

4 Imaginative Polarities. Phases of the Moon.

5 Rudolf Steiner, Planetary Seals. A sequence illustrating the evolution and simplification of forms (Goethean metamorphosis).

6 Athanasius Kircher, The Gyres of the Moon. Engraving by Pierre Miotte from *Ars Magna Lucius et Umbrae* (1646).

Foreword

The question has been raised before now whether there really is such a category as Literature. Libraries have to decide somehow whether, for instance, Carlyle's *The French Revolution* is literature or history. And is *Thus Spake Zarathustra* literature or philosophy? There is nevertheless a class of reader, less numerous perhaps now than it was fifty and more years ago, whose taste is for literature as such, who like books, and books about books, and are inclined to say to such intrusive irrelevancies as history, philosophy, psychology, sociology etc., 'A plague on all your houses!' Any member of that fraternity who picks up this book, sees at once that there is very much in it besides literary criticism, and puts it down again murmuring 'not for me', will be making a great mistake. For he will be missing a body of critical commentary, on Milton, Shelley and W. B. Yeats in particular, and less extensively on Wordsworth, Blake and Goethe, which, if there were nothing else in the book, would represent a notable contribution to English literary criticism. Its author has in abundance just what we look for in that class of writing: an original angle of vision, well-supported by quotation and tempered by extensive acquaintance with the views of other critics, and above all that *warmth* – enabling depth – of penetration, which is only to be had when the final result has been 'begotten in the ventricle of memory and nourished in the womb of *pia mater*' not just analytically, but also *con amore*.

The fact remains that his personal relish for 'visionary poetry' has been used to enhance rather than obscure his awareness of poetry's wider function, the one that Matthew Arnold had in mind when he called it 'criticism of life'. That way of putting it has come to mean a good deal more than it did in Arnold's day, except perhaps to the late F. R. Leavis and his epigones. It is a pity that the term *philology* has become not much more than a synonym for linguistics or etymology. It used to mean so much more: at its widest, learning in general and then more specifically the kind of literature and literary criticism that concentrates especially on the nature and mystery of language. It is this kind that has noticeably expanded during the last thirty of forty years. The amount of attention that has been bestowed on what I will call the concept of language as revelation is to my mind very striking, and I should not like the job of compiling a bibliography of books and articles, both literary and philosophical, that have appeared on such topics as myth, allegory, metaphor, symbol and symbolism, imagination. Obviously they cover a wide variety of opinion and speculation, but if I were asked to lay my finger on a single predominant trend, I should have to point to an increasing realization that these phenomena cannot be satisfactorily apprehended without taking account of a substantial change of consciousness that has been taking place in the West over a long period; further, that a crucial point in that change occurred at about the time of the Renaissance, culminating in the scientific revolution and its sequelae. Perhaps it is some such awareness that underlies a still more recent trend in the general climate of opinion, noticeable in circles well outside the realms of philology in either its earlier or its later sense, which Theodore Roszak has called the Human Potentials Movement. It certainly involves an enhanced estimate of the potentialities inherent in the individual human being.

Having embarked on *The Truth of Imagination*, one's first impression is of surprise to find Milton, and not only Milton but especially *Paradise Lost*, in such unlikely company; to be told that a stronger bond joins him 'with the sceptical Shelley and the ambivalent Goethe than binds him to the forms of religious tradition'; to be told moreover that 'In *Paradise Lost* he turned from outer to inner struggles, and depicted with unsurpassed imaginative energy an inner journey, a descent into one's own soul and a vision of paradise.' Others have agreed that (contrary of course to the poet's intention) Satan is the real hero of the poem. Dr Welburn does not share that view; what he does maintain is, that in the figure of Satan

> Milton's myth-making power responds to the challenge of self-exploration with one of its profoundest achievements . . . a journey to the threshold of unconscious depths. He shows that long before Freud, a poet could handle themes of repression, and the making conscious of the unconscious, with imaginative assurance and truth.

The second reaction, if my own is anything to go by, is acquiescence. Full treatment of the subject, well supported by quotation and including a finely tuned appreciation of Milton's mastery of language, has justified the new perspective.

I fear all this may have given the impression that the book is mainly about Milton. No so. It is not even mainly about poetry, though it is presented largely in terms thereof. Essentially it is about the predicament of the human mind at its present stage of evolution; and it leads off with Milton because he was the first great English poet to appear after a crucial moment in the substantial change to which I have referred, and because true imagination, both in and out of poetry, is the first step on that inner journey. The moment can be located, the author points out, between Spenser's time and Milton's, and much can accordingly be learned by, for instance, studying the difference between their respective uses of allegory (*Sin* and *Death* in *Paradise Lost* are allegorical personifications). The other poets dealt with are all Romantics or post-Romantics, and it was in Romanticism that the new direction first began to be aware of itself.

But something more needs to be said about the change of consciousness and the direction its evolution is, or should be, taking. Even more recently than the last thirty or forty years signs have been appearing, especially perhaps in the realm of literary criticism, of agreement on a historical perspective. Namely, that it was a change from the survival of a former age, when the mind had participated in the sources and processes of the natural world, to the present one in which it is cut off from nature and thrown back on its own individual resources. To achieve its entelechy (and the alternative to doing so is corruption and death) it is necessary for the mind to restore its lost participation without losing its self-conscious autonomy. Such is the author's view, and here again it was the Romantics who made the first infant attempts towards such a restoration. It is because their successors (with the possible exception of Yeats) have abandoned the enterprise, that Shelley's claim for poets to be 'the unacknowledged legislators of the world' has met with little recognition.

A Foreword however should not try to be a synopsis and the reader will discover for himself that, when the word 'initiation' is employed, as it frequently is in the latter part of the book, it is the fullest achievement of that restoration to which it is alluding. In drawing attention to the significant contrast between Shelley's *Prometheus* and Goethe's *Faust* the author makes use of a critical comment thereon to be found in an early letter of Rudolf Steiner's. That is one instance of another feature distinguishing this book from any other serious contribution to literary criticism that I have come across. It makes full use of Steiner. As early as the Introduction we find a reference to 'what Rudolf Steiner called an Anthroposophy, human wisdom', and as late as near the end much trouble is taken to establish the fact that Yeats was acquainted with, if not inspired by, this Anthroposophy. The intervening pages are laced with references to Steiner, and a whole chapter is devoted to one of his mystery-plays, which are especially relevant on the subject of 'initiation'. I expect some readers to be put off by this feature. Mistakenly so. It is there because the author has discovered (knee-jerk sceptics will say, fancied himself to have discovered) what it is many years since I also discovered. Namely, that long before Freud or Jung or Yeats had been heard of, Steiner had mastered pretty well all there is to know about the Unconscious, the evolution of consciousness, and the 'inner journey' they entail. Aside therefore from literary anthroposophists, I envisage three classes of reader for this remarkable book: the sceptics already referred to, the open-minded who will be receptive to its merits in spite of the carefully preserved taboo on Steiner, and a third class who will be led by them to follow the author's footsteps in his discovery. What I find it harder to envisage is a single reader who will think more highly of it than I do myself.

Owen Barfield
Forest Row, Sussex

Acknowledgements

The chapters gathered here bring together ideas and writing from the last several years, often originating out of more specialist enterprises. Only gradually did the framework of a general introduction to visionary poetry emerge to contain them. It finally reflects my conviction, however, that despite the growing and intensive interest in the poets of the visionary tradition since Milton, the general force or overall significance to be attached to their work remains a matter of considerable cultural uncertainty. Many of their insights are lodged in the most prized lyric and other poetic achievements of our literature. At the same time, they must remain a challenge to our most basic presuppositions about knowledge and art. I aim only to help that challenge be more clearly felt, whilst clearing away some of the false assumptions often made about the conditions imposed by such poetry – particularly a false relation in which it is often supposed to stand both to extreme scepticism and to religious belief.

Some of the ideas go back to a period of detailed work on William Blake, including the writing of a thesis, during which time I received the invaluable advice and criticism of Professor J.B. Beer, who also kindly read and commented on much of the subsequent work on the Romantics. Professor Anne Barton likewise generously read and encouraged my work on Shelley, including parts of it which appear now in a broader context, and helped point me to wider issues of poetry and the imagination. Many more specific debts could be mentioned, not all of them very tangible, but of those most obviously relevant I recall an inspiring conversation with Professor Richard Ellmann about Yeats over lunch at New College, and a remark of the late G. Wilson Knight about the 'fall of the voice', spoken in the context of the *Essay on Man* but affecting ever afterward my appreciation of Milton. A stray remark from Kathleen Raine about 'The Second Coming' and the end of the twentieth century confirmed me in the direction my Yeats-studies were proceeding, and took on more meaning as I advanced. I should also like to thank Peter Kändler for his very open and extraordinarily well-informed advice on the activities of magical and secret societies at the time of Yeats and Rudolf Steiner. Owen Barfield anchored my sense of Steiner's manifold connections with the Romantic movement by drawing my attention to his correspondence with Helene Richter. But that is the least of the obligations I owe to one who has patiently perused much that I have written, advised and helped not least by his example and the approach to Romantic literature he has pioneered, and by his grasp of the deeper philosophical issues treated at length in his various books, though scarcely touched on in these introductory considerations of mine. I am grateful to him still further for agreeing to the difficult task of introducing the book. I would like to take this opportunity of also thanking Dr J. Batchelor for his friendly support and enthusiasm.

Less tangible instances to acknowledge are conversations with students and friends which eventually crystallized the direction of my argument. Some of the material forming these chapters was given as public lectures at 35 Park Road, London NW1. To the faithful audience with their questions and comments I am also obliged – particularly for some information, from one who knew them, about Iseult Gonne, W.B. Yeats and their enduring interest in Rudolf Steiner. Chapter 2 was written while I was for a short time a guest of the Freie Hochschule der Christengemeinschaft, Stuttgart. Material forming Chapter 5 appeared in two articles in *The Golden Blade* (1982–3). The book was completed while I was fortunate enough to have been elected a British Academy Fellow at New College, Oxford: I am grateful to the Academy for its generous support of my work, and to the Warden and Fellows of New College for their unfailing hospitality in welcoming me back.

For the illustrations, permission to reproduce works in public and private collections is acknowledged as follows: for William Blake's *The Sun at his Eastern Gate*, to the Pierpont Morgan Library, New York; for William Blake's *Satan, Sin and Death*, to the Huntington Library, San Marino, California; for William Blake's title-page to *The Book of Thel*, to the Library of Congress, Washington DC; for Rudolf Steiner – Arild Rosenkrantz, painting in the small cupola of the First Goetheanum (detail), to Godhard von Heydebrand, Photo Heydebrand-Osthoff.

Thanks go to Claudia Steffen of the Philosophisch-Anthroposophischer Verlag am Goetheanum and to Margaret Cooley of the National Gallery of Art, Washington DC for their prompt reply to queries; to my editors at Macmillan Press, Frances Arnold and Sarah Roberts-West for steering the book through the complexities leading from typescript to published work, and to Jill Lake for detailed sifting of errors and inconsistencies from my text. Still deeper thanks go to Mona, who typed it with loving interest; and to Julia, to whom it is dedicated, and without whose encouragement and help I could scarcely have faced the labours of correction.

For those to whom this 'Introduction to Visionary Poetry' is indeed a prelude to greater involvement with the work of the poets studied here, I may mention that I have treated some aspects of the material in more detail in a number of more specialized articles. Blake's Gnostic universe was examined in my article, 'Blake's Cosmos: Sources and Transformations' in *Journal of English and Germanic Philology* LXXX (1981) 1: 39–53 which also says something about his relationship to Swedenborg; and in my thesis, 'The Gnostic Imagination of William Blake' (Cambridge, 1980). The struggle of forces in Shelley's poetry was the theme of my book, *Power and Self-consciousness in the Poetry of Shelley* (Macmillan/St Martin's Press, 1986). I have written more on some aspects of Yeats' vision in my article, 'Yeats, the Rosicrucians and Rudolf Steiner' in the *Journal for Anthroposophy* (1988).

Finally, I must say a word or two about the system of references used in the following pages. As befits the character of a general work, these have been kept to a minimum: specialists will easily be able to track down any unfamiliar passages, and the general reader is more profitably directed to read the poems or critical discussions mentioned in full. Passages of poetry are cited from the editions recommended at the end of the volume. I am especially grateful to J.M. Dent and Sons for the freedom to use B.A. Wright's text of Milton, which attempts to stay particularly close to Milton's intentions. Any passage of criticism quoted with the name of its author are from the work of that author given in the recommended reading at the end. Where several books of a single author are cited there, or where the quotation comes from another book or article of that critic, a footnote gives the full reference for the reader's convenience. Likewise, quotations from works not directly literary, or not specifically recommended at the end of the book, are also referenced in footnotes to the text. I hope in this way to strike a balance between the need for references and the more basic need to encourage the reader to find his or her way into the literature.

All reasonable efforts have been made to obtain all copyright and reproduction permissions. If enquiries have failed to reach the correct source in any case the publishers will be pleased to make the necessary arrangements at the earliest opportunity.

I am certain of nothing but of the holiness of the Heart's affections and the truth of Imagination.

— Keats

If the Spectator could Enter into these Images in his Imagination, approaching them on the Fiery Chariot of his Contemplative Thought, if he could Enter into Noah's Rainbow or into his bosom, or could make a Friend & Companion of one of these Images of wonder, which always intreats him to leave mortal things (as he must know), then would he arise from his Grave, then would he meet the Lord in the Air & then he would be happy.

— Blake

We begin to feel our kinship with the cosmos, our integral relationship to the life of the totality. Anthroposophical reflection begins by making friends with the world. We come to know the world that repelled us on our first, external acquaintance. And such knowledge leads us to become more human.

— Rudolf Steiner

Imagination – here the Power so called
Through sad incompetence of human speech,
That awful Power rose from the mind's abyss
Like an unfathered vapour that enwraps,
At once, some lonely traveller. I was lost;
Halted without an effort to break through;
But to my conscious soul I now can say –
'I recognise thy glory'.

— Wordsworth

Introduction

THE TRUTH OF IMAGINATION

Keats' conviction of 'the truth of imagination' rings strangely in modern ears. Contemporary writers and critics alike are liable to express an interest in the 'theory of fictions' rather than in poetic truth. Many modern theorists write indeed from a standpoint where truth, it is taken for granted, is so elusive as to be useless or even inimical to the purposes of literature. We are in danger of losing touch with the goals and achievements of some of our greatest poetry as a result.

Keats' statement belongs within a potent tradition of thought and creativity that has been central to our culture and which may, when we can survey our own age from the vantage point of later times, be seen to have run underground rather than to have disappeared. It can be paralleled by the claims made by Blake for what he termed 'Vision', by the statements of Wordsworth and Coleridge, the latter especially ranking as our foremost theorist of the imagination's power. With Goethe, working within the broad European current flowing from the same source, the truth of imagination became science as much as poetry, and interest is now reviving in the extraordinary successes of the Goethean approach to such diverse phenomena as colour and plant-growth, as well as in their relation to the poetic insights of his all-embracing drama of *Faust*. In the twentieth century, W. B. Yeats struggled against doubts yet in the end upheld imagination as the deepest source of knowledge available to us; his path was prefigured by Shelley, and has its analogies in certain aspects of modern 'esoteric' thought with which Yeats was also closely involved. If I emphasize this to what may seem a surprising extent, it is because I think we shall be surprised to recognize in some unfamiliar places the problems which confront and even oppress us today, and see them from the perspective of unexpected possible solutions. The poets and visionaries to be discussed here shared many of the insights of our philosophers and theorists, especially about the difficulties of apprehending what they called 'truth', the instability and relativism of all our thinking presuppositions. Yet they still sought to satisfy the conditions of truth in the deepest sense, and their

answers have at least the merit of challenging the more comfort-
able and slipshod relativisms which many would put in their place
today.

In a general sense, the 'visionary line' in poetry reaches back to
Milton – whose work is still so sadly misunderstood as that of a
towering egotist, or alternatively as a mere poet of a pre-existing
faith. Neither view does justice to the exploratory and creative
aspect of his genius. Beyond him the tradition reaches back to the
wonderful large-scale romance of Spenser, the *Faerie Queene*, a
poem which itself commences with the quest for Una, the one
Truth in a world of errors and deception. In Milton and his
successors, the quest is internalized. Poetry becomes an effort of
consciousness, an openness attained by something like readiness
for an apocalyptic revelation in the case of Wordsworth or Shelley,
or by a transforming knowledge, a *gnosis*, whose effect is to
humanize both world and seer, as in the case of Blake.

What kind of truth can the imagination give? Indeed, can its
claim to truth be upheld at all in an age of doubt and science?
Poetic truth seems somehow to hover in the interstices (if there are
any) between science and religion, cosmology and psychology.
Keats spoke in the same breath of 'truth' and 'holiness' when he
addressed his friend Bailey, who was reading for the Church. But
we may suppose that his correspondent was shocked by the
appropriation to poetry of terms reserved to a religious vision, and
Keats was evidently describing the secular invasion of the sphere
hitherto accessible only to the mysteries of faith. It is a mistake too
to conceive of Blake as a poet embodying in his work a religious
system for which he demands any kind of belief. Not to invent
one's own religion, for Blake, meant to be enslaved by another
man's. Visionary poetry lays claim to the scope and power of
religion, and many have been misled by the biblical materials
utilized in Milton's *Paradise Lost* or in Blake's 'prophetic books' into
thinking that these poets asked of their readers a commitment in
faith. Yet it is not so. A stronger bond joins Blake and Milton with
the sceptical Shelley and the ambivalent Goethe than binds them to
the forms of religious tradition. For they all shared the determina-
tion to be true, at least in their life's work of poetry, to imaginative
experience wherever it might lead them, however unorthodox the
heresies their deepest intuitions might suggest.

In this book I shall argue that visionary poetry may be character-
ized neither as quasi-religion nor as quasi-metaphysics or specula-

tion but as commitment to the full range of human experience. Imagination is our concrete hold on the richness of experience. Science and religion alike offer drastic simplifications of experience, and attain thereby an energy of transcendence suggesting ultimate perspectives. Yet they do not take with them the whole man. They are content with the accord of the intellect, or the assent of faith. Visionary poetry also aspires to be a vision of ultimates: but it does so under conditions far more demanding, in terms of inner effort and perhaps of suffering. 'What is the price of Experience?' asks Blake's figure Enion in *The Four Zoas*, 'do men buy it for a song? / Or wisdom for a dance in the street?' The only answer she finds is that it is bought for not less than everything. What is risked in the highest poetry can be nothing short of one's whole existence, the meaningfulness of anything or everything. Knowledge of this kind is comparable to an initiation, a crisis of rebirth, and themes of death and regeneration are pervasive in the work of all the poets we shall examine.

It is doubtful how far our culture is prepared to purchase truth at such a cost. Visionary and especially Romantic poetry have also brought the familiar image of the solitary artist, estranged from common life by the demands of his vision; so Blake adds, 'Wisdom is sold in a desolate market where none come to buy, / And in the wither'd field where the farmer plows for bread in vain.' Perhaps such a stage is necessary and inevitable, though it is not essential to imagination as such. Or perhaps the poet is only more aware of the oppressive solitude and hopelessness generated by the modern naturalism. So thought Yeats, for whom poetry was a weapon in the struggle against the rationalist world view which, as he puts it, 'leaves man helpless before the contents of his own mind'. To become aware of estrangement was already a step back to an awareness of deeper communality, and Yeats' involvement with the emerging nation of Ireland showed that he could indeed touch those hidden roots; Blake's Albion began as a dim 'Giant Form' of England, and became in the end 'Universal Man'. If there is a truth of imagination, as Keats saw, it can be no 'paradise for a sect' but must be grounded on what is most deeply felt and most human in us all.

Is there such truth available? Or has the rise of rationalistic science defeated the possibility of integral vision, leaving our landscape dispeopled of its mythologies, the Muse in chains? The question is no light one, since poetic 'truth' here means not only conscious knowledge but our right relationship to the world and ourselves. If we can make friends with the world, and on some deeper level enter imaginatively into its processes, our knowledge may become what Rudolf Steiner called an Anthroposophy, a human wisdom; it may become what Blake called meeting the Lord in the air, a 'second coming' which is not a material miracle in the stratosphere but an awakening of consciousness, a revelation of man's own nature which alone has the power to make him essentially 'happy'. Each of the poets examined in this volume sought to define the conditions under which such awakening is possible, a consciousness correlative to the truth of imagination. Each won through to a solution, at least provisionally. And each of their solutions, I shall suggest, has a continuing relevance, and in part complements the others. None of their solutions can spare us the risks; nor, as Yeats contended, might we find the risks any the less if we chose to live instead in the subjection of the naturalistic, in bondage to forces within us and outside. At the end of Shelley's *Prometheus Unbound*, Demogorgon's message is that the battle had to be won and may have to be won again; Goethe's Faust goes forward in endless striving, a lifetime of error and defeat somehow more valid in the endless perspective of the *Final Scene* than would have been a victory on any lesser terms.

*　　　*　　　*

Boswell: Then, Sir, what is poetry?
Dr Johnson: Why, Sir, it is much easier to say what it is not. We all
　know *what light is; but it is not easy to* tell *what it is.*

(Conversation of 12 April 1776)

We have not, perhaps, advanced much further in ability to discuss the difficult subject of poetry, or the imagination generally, since James Boswell approached his eminent friend and literary hero for enlightenment. In fact, there has been agreement that the imagination cannot be described directly at all. We may assert in a general way, as does D. G. James, that 'in poetry the poet endeavours to convey his sense of the inner unity and quality of the object as embracing and transcending what is given in sense'. But if imagination is our ability to evoke for ourselves the wholeness and immediacy of the thing, it is obvious that no paraphrase, no translation, can catch the imagination actually in the poem, the picture, or melody. And yet there is something we can reflect on. Thus Jean-Paul Sartre says in his *Psychology of Imagination*: 'When the truly imaginative consciousness wanes, there remains a residue which is describable.'* Such is the situation for the poet as much as the critic or philosopher. Shelley insists that 'when composition begins, inspiration is already on the decline, and the most glorious poetry that has ever been communicated to the world is probably a feeble shadow of the original conception of the Poet'.

The attempt to depict the imagination therefore presses toward the sense of an 'Energy' (Blake), traditionally a breath or wind (Milton, Wordsworth, Shelley, etc.). Inspiration was originally the in-breathing of such a power, conceived as prior to achieved form, and finally inducing that feeling of inadequacy in the achieved form to the power of the vision which is characteristic of visionary poetry in particular. Such poetry progresses by touching the limits of the imaginable, and its climaxes are frequently collapses which serve to define an obscure confrontation with ultimate powers. In our brief introduction we can examine the imagination under the two heads of the image, and transcendence of the image. We must say something too of poetic truth in relation to the truth of science, and also to more esoteric enterprises.

'SIMPLE, SENSUOUS AND PASSIONATE'

Milton understood the nature of the image clearly in the practice of poetry. He attained to theoretical insight too, though seeming a little uncertain how to evaluate his own idea. For, he says, poetry is 'subsequent, or indeed rather precedent to logic', being 'less subtle and fine, but more simple, sensuous and passionate.'

We may find that modern reflections are able to help on the issue of priority. But for the moment we must examine the terms of the pronouncement. 'Simple' means primarily non-analytical, since the aim of poetry is to catch the whole tone or significance of an experience, not to reduce it to its elements; 'sensuous' refers to the concreteness, the immediacy of poetic experience which leads it to clothe itself more naturally in the language of perception rather than of thought, or which lends to thought itself in poetry the

*J.-P. Sartre, *The Psychology of Imagination* (London, 1972) p. 16.

directness of the senses; 'passionate' designates the emotional resonance which is intrinsic to all human utterance, and which in poetry becomes a sustaining force and moving power. Each of these features belongs of right to meaningful language, though it is in poetry that they are developed or heightened for their own sake.

What kind of truth attaches to poetry which possesses these characteristics? Let us take some instances from Milton himself. We shall see how Milton arrives at a 'truth' through poetry, and we may take the opportunity to point out in what manner this truth differs from the assertions of theology and of what might now be regarded as psychology. At the end of *Samson Agonistes*, for instance, there is the fine chorus-passage expressing the sense of mystery and overshadowing Providence behind the happenings the Chorus (and the audience) have witnessed. Divine Providence is, of course, an article of faith for many Christians; but Milton does not demand that we accord him belief before we can understand his poem. Most prominent is the emotive tone, emphasized in context as the aftermath of catastrophe when the Philistine temple falls in ruins around Samson:

> All is best, though we oft doubt,
> What th' unsearchable dispose
> Of highest wisdom brings about,
> And ever best found in the close.
> Oft he seems to hide his face,
> But unexpectedly returns
> And to his faithful champion hath in place
> Bore witness gloriously; whence *Gaza* mourns
> And all that band them to resist
> His uncontroulable intent.
> His servants he with new acquist
> Of true experience from this great event
> With peace and consolation hath dismist,
> And calm of mind all passion spent.

This is great imaginative writing because, having shared the Chorus' vision of events, we know as fully as it is possible to know that their conviction is 'true experience', and why they say that 'All is best' in precisely this hushed voice. Imagination is the name we give to our faculty of entering with this completeness into experience, whether our own or another's. There is no gap between seeing and believing, no weighing of evidence or steps in argument. What we experience is undeniable. Whatever truth there is in the idea of Providence, there is at least this truth.

It was presumably thinking of such imaginative realization that Blake wrote:

> Truth can never be told so as to be understood, and not be believ'd.

Milton does not need to ask that we put our doubts aside, therefore, but can include them: 'we oft doubt', 'unsearchable', 'seems to hide', 'unexpectedly', etc. Indeed, the whole enterprise of visionary poetry can be undertaken by minds of a powerfully sceptical tendency, as in the case of Shelley; or be subjected to constant questioning, as in the case of Yeats. But in the issue of imagination itself is neither faith nor doubt, but a sense of actuality. Perhaps that is why Coleridge inclined to speak less of belief than of a 'suspension of disbelief' – though problems lie concealed in such a formula if we apply it too widely. We may compare a remark of Gustav Mahler that his music did not answer his questions but made them irrelevant.

Blake adds a complementary proverb on imaginative truth, and it may be taken as a statement of poetic tolerance:

> Every thing possible to be believ'd is an image of truth.

We may hold many opinions, and deny many more. In so far as we imagine our opinions, we apprehend how they really work or would work in life. (Often when we say that something is fine 'in theory' or 'on paper', what we mean is that it has been properly thought out but not imagined.) This process also works for opinions other than our own. In imagination there is no room for our personal views except where they have become imagination, and imagination is what enables us to see the truth in 'every thing possible to be believ'd'. Yeats was eventually to develop from this his doctrine of the Mask, based on our power to 'imagine ourselves as different from what we are, and try to assume that second self.' Whatever may be the popular notion of artistic 'self-expression', the imaginative writer or artist knows the struggle to overcome every trace of the subjective or merely personal if he is to break through to the level of imaginative truth.

There is a suggestion of the magical in the ability of imagination to enter the experience of another, to free us from our own views. Milton commands such magical power in his dazzling pair of poems *L'Allegro* and *Il Penseroso*, and we sense the exhilaration with which the poet knows his own virtuosity in creating contrary types – the 'pensive man' and the 'lively man'. 'Who is the speaker here,' asks Geoffrey Hartman, 'if not a magus, dismissing some spirits and invoking others? ... *L'Allegro* and *Il Penseroso* are ... romantic monologues. They show a mind moving from one position to another and projecting an image of its freedom against a darker, daemonic ground.'*

The twin poems, in octosyllabics, are remarkable for their vivid depiction of opposing temperaments, the one melancholy and thoughtful, the other spontaneously joyful and effervescent, and Milton brilliantly pits their contrasting qualities against one another. In a bold abandonment of any narrative or similar device for holding the poem together, he resolves his poetry into a series of pure imaginative impressions, strung along after an introductory address to the presiding spirit worshipped by each, the goddesses 'Melancholy' and 'Mirth'. The polarities are explored with conscious pleasure in these rather extreme personalities, imparting to the whole a certain 'theatrical' self-consciousness. Milton delights in his own exuberant tendency toward self-dramatization. The pensive man wants only gloomy, dark, quiet and chaste companions:

> Come pensive Nun, devout and pure,
> Sober, stedfast, and demure
> All in a robe of darkest grain,
> Flowing with majestic train,
> And sable stole of *Cypress* Lawn
> Over thy decent shoulders drawn.
> Come, but keep thy wonted state,
> With even step, and musing gate.†
> And looks commercing with the skies,
> Thy rapt soul sitting in thine eyes:
> There held in holy passion still,

*G. Hartman, 'False themes and gentle minds', *Philological Quarterly* 47 (1968) 1, p. 59.
†i.e. gait

> Forget thy self to Marble, till
> With a sad Leaden downward cast,
> Thou fix them on the earth as fast.

The active man, on the other hand, wants the company of Mirth herself – and as many friends as she can bring with her:

> Haste thee nymph, and bring with thee
> Jest and youthful Jollity,
> Quips and Cranks, and wanton Wiles,
> Nods and Becks, and Wreathed Smiles
> Such as hang on *Hebe's* cheek,
> And love to live in dimple sleek;
> Sport that wrinkl'd Care derides,
> And Laughter holding both his sides,
> Come, and trip it as ye go
> On the light fantastic toe ...

The imaginative effect depends in large measure upon the striking oppositions of visual impression in such parallel passages: the lonely detachedness of the *penseroso*, rather heavily detailing everything he wants in his sombre Nun, the lively man scarcely pausing to register one figure before he has gone on to the next; the melancholic's love of dark, rich textures in clothing – whereas Mirth does not seem to be wearing anything except smiles. But even more, the 'meaning' of the poems can be grasped in terms of pure intonation and movement, the first example yielding a certain doleful fall in the voice which hauntingly captures the mind of the thinker; the second expressed, for instance, in the switch from the breathless:

> Quips and Cranks, and wanton Wiles,
> Nods and Becks, and Wreathed Smiles

to the long syllables flung out in the next line:

> S̄uch as h̄ang on *H̄ebe's* ch̄eek

(Hebe, incidentally, being the goddess of Youth). And then come the doting (even slightly gluey) l's of:

> And love to live in dimple sleek.

This indulgent line slows the movement down momentarily, until the cracking pace is resumed once more. By such means Milton reminds us that the essence of an imagination, of the *meaning* of a poem, may lie in knowing the exact tone of voice in which to say a phrase, or the precise speed at which to speak a line. Likewise, outside poetry 'imagining' a situation often consists not in being able to picture it exactly, but in catching the mood, the tone or gesture of an experience (a picnic in a meadow on a summer's day, or entering a cathedral, etc., etc.).

Besides mirroring, and pleasantly exaggerating the moods, indulgences and characteristic attitudes of his ever-diverse pair, however, Milton demonstrates in one respect how imagination differs from reason. Rational thought can easily assemble qualities pertaining respectively to vivacity and pensive melancholia; indeed, it could list many important features that Milton has ignored. Yet it would not arrive, I think, at the twist which gives the portrayal of the *penseroso* its final convincing touch. For there is nothing more revealing of the melancholy mind, despite being logically opposed to the very idea of melancholy, than its ponderous idea of – humour. Best of all is silence, he first says, unless the nightingale ('Philomel') will deign to sing for him. Ah yes, we hear him chuckling to himself in his endearing if lugubrious tones, the nightingale:

> Sweet Bird that shunnst the noise of folly,
> Most musical –

or, what comes to the same thing (and note the doleful fall in the voice once more):

> – most melancholy.

Thus imagination enables us to enter into the very texture of another mind, as well as our own experience. We catch, with Milton's help, the exact shade of mild melancholy humour, or the breath of life of the devotee of Mirth. Potentially rather abstract concepts of the Active and Contemplative Life are given extraordinary immediacy, imaginative truth. There is no intruding 'theory' between us as readers and Milton's meaning – though of course we can relate the poems to Renaissance psychology, religious, astrological and other ideas if we wish. Historical clarification can help to prevent misunderstandings, stop us jumping to false conclusions or reading back modern notions into the words. But finally it is when Milton has filled out the old psychology with his vivid imagination that we actually understand the underlying truth behind its theories. And this truth is not theoretical. It is undeniable, because still humanly accessible across three hundred or more years.

There is a case to be made that there is just so much truth in any theory – scientific, theological or even philosophical – as finds its way into literature, or perhaps we should say into imagination. The thinker is always inclined, when he adopts new ideas, to attribute to them more meaning than they actually possess. If he is to have any enthusiasm for the latest hypotheses, the scientist must be prepared to suppose that they can be the means of solving a range of problems extending beyond the immediate context. Science moves forward in this way; constructive experimentalism only makes sense, after all, when there is something that can be put to the test. Initial assumptions are often extraordinarily wide. Only gradually are the proper limits of a concept defined, and it may be said that it is the final aim of analysis to make each concept mean as little as possible. It is when ideas are realized in imagination that the scientist – or anyone else – is enabled to contemplate the actual validity of the concept, since it is in imagination that idea is measured directly against possible experience, indeed becomes inseparable from it.

Hence it is that ideas often survive in the truth of poetry after their 'scientific' scaffolding has been abandoned: rather as the psychology of 'humours' (or four temperaments) lives on in the convincing imaginations of Chaucer, Shakespeare and Ben Jonson, for example, even when we no longer suppose that the human body is compounded out of four basic fluids. A modern analogue may well turn out to be Darwinism and evolution. Whatever the ultimate fate of Darwin's Victorian-materialistic version of evolutionary theory, the new type of narrative consciousness connected with what Gillian Beer has called 'Darwin's plots' will probably be far more significant.* We are still at the stage of deciding where the limits of the Darwinian theory lie – for example, in social theory and even in the theory of knowledge. But in the qualitative change brought about in our sense of the meaning and direction of our flux

---

*Gillian Beer, *Darwin's Plots* (London, 1983).

of experience among writers since Darwin lies the imaginative truth. In the end, the mechanisms of Darwin's evolutionary theory may come to seem as outmoded as the bodily–psychic fluids, and a future doctrine of evolution may be developed in different terms. But it will certainly build upon the new perception of time and development which is the imaginative truth, the undeniable experience of evolution.

Scientific truth, then, emerges out of the dialectic between a projected generality, the wide reach of the hypothesis, and the analysis of instances – all that working of the 'logical' mind which Milton contrasts with the 'simplicity' of the image. In the twentieth century the scientific enterprise has been subjected to intensive philosophical and critical scrutiny. There has been a whole series of anti-scientific movements, including such figures as Wittgenstein as well as phenomenologists, existentialists, and others. Science survives, of course, and can boast impressive results from its interpretations; it has tightened its grip, indeed, on cultural life in general. But the nineteenth-century claims of scientific objectivism to uncover 'the only truth' of things are a currency that has now been largely withdrawn. That there is 'a truth' of science seems certain. The issue of its relation to the truth of imagination, however, is today more than ever an open one.

The generalizing drive of the scientific method employs various techniques for levelling out the qualitatively unique aspects of experience which the poet strives to capture. It undertakes to reveal a world of stable, mathematically describable and predictable regularities. The philosopher Merleau-Ponty refers to the 'process of impoverishment' by which the manifold 'lived' experience of the body and perception is pared down in the scientific concept of the body and the object. The uniqueness of the place or the moment are redefined in an undifferentiated continuum of space–time. No possibility here of an epiphanic time which shows that 'All is best, though we oft doubt'.

It has been widely recognized by modern thinkers that the scientist does not really tell us what experience is like, so much as focus attention on certain limited features of experience. His approach undoubtedly suppresses a great deal of the sheer diversity and spontaneity of actual life. And, as the scientific historian Thomas Kuhn and his successors have shown, it is curiously difficult for the scientist to tell us why we should agree to adopt his particular framework or constructive limitation on the multiple aspects of the world – at least for so long as we consider truth as our single guiding star.

We come much closer to resolving the question if we inquire not into truth but into power.

The founder of modern scientism, Francis Bacon, announced the purpose of science to be 'the knowledge of causes, and secret motions of things; and the enlarging of the bounds of human empire, to the effecting of all things possible'. It makes immediate sense that we should choose the framework selecting scientific regularity, predictability and uniformity, on the assumption that we wish to gain power 'to the effecting of all things possible', since these are the very features of control. Science tests the validity of its ideas by their power to produce effects. Owen Barfield illuminatingly calls this sort of knowledge 'dashboard knowledge', comparable to that needed to drive the car rather than describe how it moves. Science has given us a tremendous amount of this 'dashboard knowledge' and, perhaps wisely, has held back from the problems of how the vehicle works – although now, in the discussions of methodology, we have at least an awareness of the issues and, most interesting, a beginning of scientific acknowledgement of the role of imagination. At any rate, it is easy to see the particular aims of a power-orientated knowledge and the usefulness of its paradigms; it is also easy to see the elements of 'impoverishment' if we take it as the only truth available.

General stabilities give us power to exploit nature, but they fail to find meaning in the always unrepresentative, ungeneralizable course of an individual biography, for instance. It is the strength of imagination that it can grapple with the unique, the ironic, even the grotesque as well as the sublime, or the ideal. It grasps the essence of what Blake calls the 'Minute Particular', not in the sense of the detail alone, but the atypical and irreducible, the unrepeatable. 'Chance' and 'subjectivity' make the course of life 'a parcel of nonsensical contingencies' (Sterne); it is only imagination which can tell us how to recover meaning from it, only imagination which can show, in the words of another novelist, how 'it all hangs together in the deepest sense' (D. H. Lawrence).

It is when we bring the issues into the human arena that they become at least morally clear-cut. We know that it is possible to make use of the physical and psychological regularities of human beings to exploit them by corresponding mental or physical means. Yet we know that such methods are precisely 'inhuman'. More than that, we know that the knowledge of such needs of body and mind is not the deepest knowledge available to us. Demanding proof of our friends' affections or generalizing the features of a loved face could betoken only a dehumanizing cynicism, or at the very least a damaged inability to enter into full relationship, a fear of the other suggesting trauma rather than strength. The world of materialist vision demands that we live upon such terms, in what Coleridge called:

> that inanimate cold world allowed
> To the poor loveless ever-anxious crowd.

All that he judged 'of higher worth' is ruled out of court if we imagine, not just abstractly assert, the world of the behaviourist. In the human case we cannot forget that the aspects of uniformity and exploitation are not the whole story. We can tentatively go further, and suggest that the 'scientific' approach to human problems will generally be mistaken, as it has shown itself in a great deal of town-planning, social organization and especially education in the twentieth century. It is only imagination which is equal to the encounter with humanity. Yet the same may be true, in the end, of all aspects of reality. The beauty of the forest and the mountain rivulet may be irrelevant to the project of the engineer constructing his dam: but it is as much a truth of the world as the water's rate of flow and the stress to be sustained by the concrete wall replacing it. Blake upheld some such doctrine when he said of natural beings not that they were less than human, but that they were 'Men Seen Afar'.

Some of the Romantics – notably Blake – denounced the rising scientism of the nineteenth century; others, such as Wordsworth, were uncommitted or undecided. Milton, writing in an earlier age, could still hedge, and leave open the issue of the sun-centred or earth-centred universe. It was Goethe above all, but also Shelley and to some extent Coleridge, who attempted to include it within their project of the imagination. They undertook to 'image that which we know' and restore it to its human meaning. It was Wordsworth who set it as the poet's goal here 'to carry sensation into the midst of the objects of science itself, and to contemplate these objects as an enjoying and suffering being.' But it was Goethe alone who demonstrated that scientific research could itself be carried on without the suspension of the imaginative faculties demanded in theory by the functional approach of science. The truth of science unfolds in union with the truth of poetry in his researches on colour and plant-metamorphosis. The human response to the meaning of human experience exists in harmony with the exercise of critical analysis and rigorous observation – as in his account of the 'sensuous moral' qualities of colour, to take but one example which has been fruitful in recent perceptual research. There are glimmerings of a new interest in Goethean science generally. It is another sign of a hoped-for reconciliation, though one that is hardly yet achieved, between the thinker and the Muse.

In order to comprehend the 'visionary' use of the imagination, however, we must take into account not only the power of the image, but also the difficult issues that arise when poetry touches upon the limits of imagery or representation. Indeed, it is characteristic of imagination that it plays upon these border regions and takes from them its sense of power unfulfilled. Coleridge in his Shakespeare-lectures of 1811–12 described the 'middle state of mind' on the edge of representational consciousness as 'more strictly appropriate to the imagination than any other, when it is, as it were, hovering between images ... As soon as it is fixed on one image it becomes understanding; but while it is unfixed and wavering between them, attaching itself permanently to none, it is imagination.' But it was Wordsworth who, because he loved nature, and the images of nature that lived on in his memory, yet struggled to include all of human perception, felt these issues with especial poignancy. It is accordingly to him that we turn in our first chapter.

1
The Poetry of Vision

> To relinquish all
> We have, or hope, of happiness and joy,
> And stand in freedom loosened from this world,
> I deem not arduous; but must needs confess
> That 'tis a thing impossible to frame
> Conceptions equal to the soul's desires;
> And the most difficult of tasks to keep
> Heights which the soul is competent to gain.
>
> – Wordsworth

'THE DEEP TRUTH IS IMAGELESS': WORDSWORTH AND THE LIMITS OF NATURE

William Wordsworth was no visionary, but a poet of nature and of 'natural piety' – though he did not deserve the round judgment passed by Shelley on his parody-Wordsworth or *Peter Bell the Third*:

> He had as much imagination
> As a pint-pot.

Wordsworth does possess imagination in a pre-eminent degree. But he chose to make the experiment of disciplining the imagination's visionary urge and confining himself within the bounds of nature.

By the nineteenth century, something of the vastness of physical nature had become known; man's place was being re-evaluated. The ages of faith appeared to be over, which meant that the themes of Spenserian romance, or myth, or miracle, were outmoded. Wordsworth attended St. John's College, Cambridge, and so was on nodding terms with Newton's statue, as well as being himself fascinated by mathematics in addition to poetry. Yet his nature was less that of a scientist than that of a plain man with open eyes. His poetry is to a striking extent simply a record of direct perception.

The reasons behind Wordsworth's attempt to purge the visionary imagination would lead us far to uncover, and still farther to interpret. Some of them were no doubt personal and psychological. Yet they have an immediate bearing on Wordsworth's relation to the 'visionary line'. John Beer has studied Wordsworth's attitude in depth, and has suggested in conclusion that some of his poetry is best seen as that 'of a man who has known some of the same visionary experiences as Blake, yet has withdrawn from them – not without an occasional spasm of fear'. Thus his need for the quiet permanencies of nature may have been a retreat from certain overwhelming manifestations of imaginative power which gripped him at times in childhood, and sometimes in later life. It is characteristic of Wordsworth's mind that even when he relates his visionary experiences most directly, as in the ode *Intimations of Immortality*, he regrets the loss of childhood intensity yet refuses to attempt to regain it. He insists on the compensations of his subsequent adult consciousness ('years that bring the philosophic mind') and the more balanced appreciation of nature he has attained without the transports and haunting passions of his youth.

His experiment of turning the light of imagination full upon nature, however, has been productive of a great deal in our modern sense of the value of the environment. So much so that without him the widespread appreciation today of natural beauty and perhaps the concept of nature-conservation would be largely unthinkable. Yet the acclimatizing of the imagination to natural reality is still more significant in its failure.*

That it was a failure is admitted by many of Wordsworth's interpreters, and has been argued in depth by Geoffrey Hartman in his indispensable account of the poet's development. For all his adherence to the forms of actual perception, in his conviction of the grandeur of natural landscape, argues Hartman, Wordsworth invests natural reality with a meaning for the imagination that is still more intense. At the highest moments of his poetry the visible, sensible universe falls away leaving him to face the exultation and terror of the homeless, the visionary imagination:

---

*A failure, that is, in the high sense that all attempts to attain the limits of man's reach are defined by their failure. Yeats' father once noted to his son that whenever we talk of a genius, we find ourselves trying to explain his failure.

                              in such strength
            Of usurpation, when the light of sense
            Goes out, but with a flash that has revealed
            The invisible world, doth greatness make abode,
            There harbours; whether we be young or old,
            Our destiny, our being's heart and home,
            Is with infinitude, and only there;
            With hope it is, hope that can never die,
            Effort, and expectation, and desire,
            And something evermore about to be.

                                        (*The Prelude* VI, 599–608)

Here 'usurpation' rather than 'failure' is Wordsworth's own word;
but he admits the overturning of the natural succession. The soul
at these climactic moments of *The Prelude* after all rebels against the
wish to be domiciled in the visible, tangible world and admits to
being at home only with infinity. Such, at these critical moments, is
the ultimate allegiance of the heart, and his recognition of it makes
of Wordsworth, if not a visionary poet, at least a 'borderer of
vision' – following an image suggested by his own problematic
play *The Borderers*.

   The climax of Book VI of *The Prelude* is a sort of apocalypse,
perhaps one of those experiences which remind us of Blake.
Specifically, we can compare it to Blake's own peculiar notion of a
'Last Judgment'. No more than Wordsworth does Blake conceive a
Judgment as mediaeval man supposed it would be, a *dies irae* ('day
of wrath') at the end of history, when everyone would be called
personally to account by God. For Blake, a Last Judgment occurs as
a process of inner awakening or knowledge (*gnosis*). It happens, he
says, whenever error is recognized and cast out. Knowledge serves
to bring about an inner liberation, so that there is always for Blake
both condemnation (of the error) and release (of the essential Man)
in any act of 'Judgment'. In short, Blake regards our condition as
one of delusion so long as we look at the content of our conscious-
ness, our inner and outer experience of the world, and suppose
ourselves to be defined in essence by that content. This, he says,
is to confuse the 'State' in which we find ourselves with the
'Humanity' which passes through many States. Liberation – a Last
Judgment – comes about when we recognize that we transcend the
actual or present content of our mind, that we have potentialities

for further growth or development, for new insights which were ruled out so long as we supposed what we know to be the only way of looking at the world. At such moments our former assumptions and prejudices harden into 'error'. Blake regarded the congealing of error as itself a productive phase of the Judgment, since the more exclusive and rigid our perception of any matter becomes, the nearer we draw to the moment when it will have to be 'cast out', its inadequacy to creative human experience having grown finally clear. Hence in *Europe, A Prophecy* it is Newton – somewhat surprisingly! – who initiates a Last Judgment. By bringing the mechanistic world-view to unprecedented clarity in the thought of his age, it is he who reveals at the same time the enmity between that view and the imagination, at least as Blake knew and valued it:

> A mighty Spirit leap'd from the land of Albion,
> Nam'd Newton: he seized the trump & blow'd the
>   enormous blast!
> Yellow as leaves of Autumn, the myriads of Angelic hosts
> Fell thro' the wintry skies seeking their graves,
> Rattling their hollow bones in howling and lamentation.

The vision which follows in Blake's poem is that of a Gnostic universe. The Newtonian scientific cosmos appears as an anti-divine creation, a system of 'sickening Spheres' to imprison man on earth. Man himself is a skeletal mechanism. Yet in response to the sharpening of the image, there arises at the same time the sense of the real power of the imagination. It is as if the world cracks open, and in *Europe* releases the Energy of the spiritual sun in man. This will finally sweep away the demonic powers, the 'spirits of wickedness in the heavenly places'. Confrontation with the forces of hindrance and rigidity, the 'incrustation' of error, leads directly to a confrontation with the dissolving and remaking imagination.

Wordsworth's personal apocalypse shares many of these features, yet takes in the end a different course. The events leading up to it may be briefly told. Wordsworth and his companions, on a walking-tour of Europe, are crossing the Alps – the actual crossing of the highest point on their route constituting the climax of excitement on the trip. Great anticipation surrounds this moment, especially on the day the party expect to finish their gradual climb and begin descending into Italy. On that day, however, things go amiss: the party is separated from its knowledgeable fellow travellers, first takes the wrong path and then finds itself proceeding downhill. No harm is done, except that the long-expected moment of reaching the highest point is snatched from Wordsworth and his friends. They hear, at first incredulously, from a local peasant, that they have crossed the Alps. Their way is now all downward.

The violence of this inner shock accounts for the rare happening in Wordsworth's imagination. The fact is forcibly thrust on his awareness that the psychic charge, the intensity of excitement attaching to the moment of crossing the Alps, has perilously little to do with the natural reality of the highest point. It belongs almost entirely to the imagination itself. In most of his work, Wordsworth's imagining is turned toward and fused with outer nature. But here it is forced to confront itself in naked intensity, the outer support being snatched away – and Wordsworth hardly knows how to deal with it:

> Imagination – here the Power so called
> Through sad incompetence of human speech,
> That awful Power rose from the mind's abyss
> Like an unfathered vapour that enwraps,
> At once, some lonely traveller. I was lost;
> Halted without an effort to break through;
> But to my conscious soul I now can say –
> 'I recognize thy glory'.

(The Prelude VI, 592–9)

Imagination appears as a pure supersensible power, undomiciled in nature and homeless except in infinity. The solid ground has gone out of Wordsworth's experience, and as he travels down the valley among the tumult of cloud and water, all seems on the verge of apocalyptic dissolution:

>   The immeasurable height
> Of woods decaying, never to be decayed,
> The stationary blasts of waterfalls,
> And in the narrow rent at every turn
> Winds thwarting winds, bewildered and forlorn,

The torrents shooting from the clear blue sky,
The rocks that muttered close upon our ears,
Black drizzling crags that spake by the wayside
As if a voice were in them, the sick sight
And giddy prospect of the raving stream,
The unfettered clouds and region of the Heavens,
Tumult and peace, the darkness and the light –
Were all like workings of one mind, the features
Of the same face, blossoms upon one tree;
Characters of the great Apocalypse,
The types and symbols of Eternity,
Of first, and last, and midst, and without end.

(The Prelude VI, 624–40)

Apocalyptic imagery again denotes a crucial encounter with the imagination, as in a Blakean 'Last Judgment'. But this experience does not lead Wordsworth forward into visionary clarification. It leads to no break with nature or concentering of imagination on its own energies. It remains a 'border' experience, not a new visionary beginning.

'Wordsworth does not sustain the encounter with Imagination,' points out Geoffrey Hartman. 'His direct cry is broken off ... It is not Imagination but his "conscious soul" he addresses directly in the lines that follow.' From the supersensible-apocalyptic Power he turns back to the content of the conscious mind, from the energy of creation to the created images. Later in his life Wordsworth's imagination began to fail him, and Blake would doubtless have said that Wordsworth failed to save his 'Humanity' by distinguishing it at such moments from its 'State'. He needed to have grasped the life of imagination on its own terms and to have deepened or developed it within. Instead he expected it to be fed with images from nature, and in the end nature proved inadequate. After all, the pattern of nature is always birth, growth and in the end decay. From nature the imagination can hope for nothing more.

Wordsworth's prime interest remained with nature. It is from that characteristic that his achievement in poetry derives its enduring quality. Yet experiences such as the 'Last Judgment' among the Alps served ultimately to reinforce his sense that 'natural' objects and images drew poetic significance from the aura of the invisible around them – the hidden workings of the supersensible imagination. Hence it was, in his own terms, that human experience could be felt to be invested with 'an obscure sense of possible sublimity'. Nature – the 'world out there' registered by the conscious soul – was underpinned by secret analogies, possibilities of further meaning, a 'dark inscrutable workmanship' sensed beyond the world we objectively know.

Modern critics and readers have sometimes equated this, the 'Wordsworthian profundity' or hidden depth, with the psychological concept of the Unconscious. And they have some right to do so. Yet the Wordsworthian vision calls in question the modern naturalism of Freud, just as it called in question the naturalism of Wordsworth's own time and his own tendencies. Can the aura of the imagination be so firmly relegated to the hinterland of the mind? Freud thought of the Unconscious as the repository of repressed or forgotten fragments of experience, a kind of psychic Sargasso Sea cluttered with the debris from consciousness that had been rejected by the waking faculties. Imagination, or fantasy (for Freud there could be no difference) might disport itself with these fragments, and reveal thereby the unconscious truths of man's nature. But it could claim no special outlook on reality. Indeed, it had to be tamed by the 'reality principle' and brought to abandon its illusory hopes.

Advances in the science of knowledge, particularly the emergence of developmental and structural analyses of the mind, have called many of Freud's assumptions in question. In psychology itself, many have abandoned the notion that the Unconscious can be derived entirely from originally conscious experience. There have been postulates of 'archetypes', or more interestingly of 'formative forces', structuring activities at work already in our perception of the world. The extraordinary complexities of language and its power to organize experience may also be in some sense innate, implicit in our approach to things rather than learnt piecemeal from it. In the history of science, discovery itself may have to be understood less as finding out how things are than as constructive modification of a paradigm, the working out of shared assumptions and the creation of new areas of meaning. In many domains of thought we have come to the point of gazing into that Wordsworthian abyss at the limits of nature – points where the mind no longer seems to be receiving patterns from without, but where its own activity creatively mediates the reality we see.

When Blake arrived at a similar insight, he cast it in the guise of a disturbing paradox or 'Proverb of Hell':

A fool sees not the same tree that a wise man sees.

But it has become in effect an accepted truth. Philosophers no longer believe in the strict distinction between perceiving and thinking about what we perceive. The constructive, meaning-productive aspect is already presupposed in perception. This entails, says Mary Warnock, 'both that we must think of perception as containing a thought-element, and perhaps, that we must think of thinking as containing a perception-element.'* It was Goethe who already spoke of a perceptive power of thought (*anschauende Urteilskraft*), and so projected a scientific, cognitive mode of the imagination – another Romantic insight which may now bear fruit.

The dark aura, or 'obscure sense of possible sublimity', then, may be less the shadow, the anti-image of our waking perception, than a mine of potential meanings and possible relations. Its darkness may be that of hitherto unrealized connections of thought which are nevertheless implicit in the very way we see the world. Shelley understood that poetry, through metaphor, brings to the clear surface of consciousness some aspects of meaning which have hitherto remained dark; it 'marks the before unapprehended relations of things and perpetuates their apprehension', as he says in the *Defence*. But in our own time it is Owen Barfield who has developed these thoughts in regard to poetry and language. He locates the aesthetic imagination in the 'expansion of consciousness' which is the apprehension of new meanings, relations and analogies. At the same time he has gone far beyond the Romantics in tracing the workings of imagination already in perception, in the concrete meanings which are preserved in the fragments of mythologies, above all in the changing consciousness of man in history. He has demonstrated in a remarkable way that it is possible to bridge the formidable divide between history and the sciences of language, meaning and even epistemology. He has explained the poet's constant straining at the limits of meaning as the root of the dynamics of knowledge: he quotes another saying of

---

*Mary Warnock, *Imagination* (London, 1976) p. 192. The fourth Part of this book, on 'The Nature of the Mental Image', is undoubtedly worth reading.

Blake, that 'If it were not for the Poetic or Prophetic character, the philosophic and experimental would soon be at the ratio of all things, and stand still, unable to do other than repeat the same dull round'; he adds that it is mystics and poets who have most readily grasped the nature of meaning, but that the meaning-apprehending imagination is implicit in even the most scientific knowledge.

Barfield helps us to see certain ways forward where we face the limits of nature, for in his view the relationship between the mind and the world-out-there is itself an evolving one. Where images from nature failed Wordsworth's conscious soul at the end of his life, it may be that nature can be transformed by a transformation of human thought. The perception of nature contains a thought-element, and it may be that the visionary poet's quest for the sources of meaning has its most important issue after all in the envisioning not of a new heaven but of a new earth.

Whatever forces we may ultimately discover to be active at the source of the imagination's power of relation, the demands made upon the consciousness which undertakes to explore it are considerable. This is admitted by all researchers alike. Wordsworth drew back from the vision of the 'homeless', unaccommodated power he intuited in the apocalyptic moments of *The Prelude*. But Milton earlier and Wordsworth's Romantic successors after him dared to enter into that abyss he felt opening, the 'infinite' womb and grave of the human spirit. Such an undertaking is an initiation, as we defined it at the outset, and is interpreted thus by the poets as well as by Rudolf Steiner, whose descriptions we shall sometimes call upon to illuminate the poems. But if Wordsworth drew back from the full force of visionary experience, his attempt to satisfy the imagination with images from nature and his failure to do so forms a highly significant pattern. For it demonstrates the failure of any attempt to bind man to his world by anything other than his will to know, and ultimately to transform it.

THE CONTRARY MYTHS

Two souls, alas, are housed within my breast,
And each will wrestle for the mastery there.
The one has passion's craving crude for love,
And hugs a world where sweet the senses range;

The other longs for pastures fair above,
Leaving the murk for lofty heritage.

– Goethe, *Faust*

Goethe is a more diverse poet than Wordsworth. Indeed he
delights in the conflicts of drama and a baffling many-sidedness.
He includes the restlessness of the human spirit in his vision, and
certainly will not limit his search for satisfaction to nature alone.
He registers also the longing for a transcendent freedom, together
with all the inner contradictions which make up his representative
man or Faustian quester. If Faust could ever be satisfied by the
images of nature in his 'conscious soul', that would be the moment
of Mephistopheles' triumph, his devilish task will be done:

> *Faust*
> If to the fleeting hour I say
> 'Remain, so fair thou art, remain!'
> Then bind me with your fatal chain,
> For I will perish in that day.
> 'Tis I for whom the bell shall toll,
> Then you are free, your service done.
> For me the clock shall fail, to ruin run,
> And timeless night descend upon my soul.

In some sense, every man enters into a wager or pits his
consciousness against the powers who undertake to master him, to
explain him (or explain him away), to define for him the bounds of
his being. The character of Faust is based upon the attempt to
prove that there is more to man's existence than can be explained,
or utilized – though it can be imagined, can be lived. This is the
ground of Faust's endless striving, akin to that of Wordsworth
among the Alps struggling to grapple with that 'something
evermore about to be.' And it is answered, in Goethe's vision, by
the promise of the angels in the power of love ('Wer immer
strebend sich bemüht, / Den können wir erlösen'). But the ques-
tions which present themselves before we trust ourselves to such a
vision are crucial and profoundly difficult ones. What kind of truth
is possible here? How can the conscious self maintain itself amid
the psychic pressures and burdens it must bear if it is to attain that
knowledge which might be available? Goethe offers his own
imaginative solutions to these problematic issues; but we can find

relevant explorations among the English visionary poets too, especially in Blake and Shelley. Indeed, we shall turn in a later chapter to consider parallels beween Goethe and the Shelley of *Mont Blanc* and *Prometheus Unbound*.

Scientific knowledge offers clarity within a framework of particular assumptions. Perhaps it is not a question for science to explain how the framework is related to reality; the scientist offers his pragmatic kind of truth, valid for certain purposes, and its justification is to be found in pragmatic terms. The framework itself seems to be in Yeats' sense a myth:

> I do not mean a fiction, but one of those statements our nature is compelled to make and employ as a truth though there cannot be sufficient evidence.

Rather the limiting framework is what enables us to evaluate the evidence in the first place. The modern school of Deconstructionist literary critics, whatever their limitations, have at least the merit of taking these difficulties seriously as applied to literature. They have taken seriously the confrontation with that shadow-realm of potential meanings, unpredictable and unapprehended relations, which so disturbed the natural man in Wordsworth; they have faced the difficulty of grounding the representation of things in things-as-they-are. They have accepted the inability of science to describe man, since any description turns out to be describing rather man's world – 'Man is the great absence'. Of course, it is possible to see these matters another way. It is possible to emphasize our ability as social beings to live out of a community of thought, rather than out of an unattainable pure objectivity. It is possible to see in the characteristic displacement of description to man's world the seed of a subtle anthropocentrism, perhaps even of an Anthroposophy in Steiner's special sense. And the conscious self might react to the threat against its autonomy, as in Barfield's thought, by taking upon itself a dynamic role, a drive toward transformation and urge to 'die and become' in the flux of meanings.

At any rate, to advance into these dimly lit domains is to become aware of the power of 'myths' to shape man's life and attitude to the world he dwells in. Two contrary myths in particular will occupy our attention in the studies that comprise this book: two archetypically powerful myths concerned with the nature of good

and evil but containing implicitly contrasting views of reality. They
have affected our cultural history, as well as our poetry. It is part of
Rudolf Steiner's significance that he spoke of them, not as relating
to things in themselves but as powers within the soul – as
temptations and dangers to the conscious self, daemonic forces as
hard to control as Mephistopheles in *Faust*; but also as spirits
'mighty to obey' in the pursuit of a higher truth. His explorations
were certainly anticipated, however, by the poets of the visionary
and Romantic imagination, and Steiner's thought has been aptly
summarized as a 'Romanticism come of age.'

We can approach the inner reality of the myths best by
considering opposite modes of the imagination. For in one respect
Sartre went widely astray in his analysis of imaginative experience.
He claims that imagination is always consciously derivative: it
represents our effort to 'hold on to the object' and retain it after
perception has ceased.* Whereas in reality nothing is so character-
istic of the imagination as the tendency to take over and occupy
the space of the mind, crowding out the objective content and
suspending the conscious faculties in reverie or day-dream. The
image may finally become an obsession if this tendency is not held
in check, or an hallucination displacing 'real' space and time to
usurp the place of natural reality. These are aberrations; but
aesthetic experience itself probably always depends to some extent
upon the undermining of consciousness, the contact with a
possibility of meaning not yet brought to mind with full aware-
ness. Sartre was motivated to deny such a stage, it has been
suggested, out of his desire to escape the 'superstition' of the
'occult' or the Unconscious. In the end, however, we must not be
content with evasion, but rather attempt to gain knowledge.

The tendency of imagination to which we have referred is
important because it corresponds to a deep drive in human nature
– the drive to break free from immediate surroundings, to
transcend present impressions and concentrate life and energy into
a single intensity. The very diversity of experience often tires
attention: one essential force of imagination is the urge to focus
desire on the simplifying, unifying image. The consciousness
which results from the tendency to do so is vivid, more vivid than
normal perceptual experience. Its vividness, however, has some-
thing of the compelling brightness of dream. The mind can have an

*J.-P. Sartre, *Psychology of Imagination*, p. 14.

unprecedented sense of its own autonomy in such states, giving rise to a god-like assertion of freedom from the shackles both of truth and of moral limitations.

That this tendency is potentially destructive perhaps does not need saying. We need reminding of it less because there have been in the twentieth century many poets who have celebrated the 'image' especially in its mode of dream-like, reality-disturbing beauty. Criticizing that mode, Yeats referred to a movement of mind that has 'more and more so separated certain images and regions of the mind ... that these images grow in beauty as they grow in sterility'. Symbolist beauty readily becomes decadent beauty, and its devotee also discovers all too soon that the worship demanded by the image must be ever more obsessive; its demands, like the freedom it half gives, are infinite. The one-sided imagination will not rest until it has succeeded in ousting reality altogether – nay more, until it has monopolized the space of attention, compelling the mind into a single intensity or *idée fixe*.

Modern writers have made their own discoveries here, and Freudian psychology has taken up the theme of the disruptive power of fantasy in 'complexes' and in psychotic states where the balance and integral organization of the conscious self is split. But in ancient mythology many of these ideas are already played out in an appropriately symbolic mode. It is easy to recognize the myth of Lucifer and the primal temptation to which Adam and Eve were subjected. 'For God doth know', says Lucifer in the Book of Genesis, standing by the forbidden tree, 'that in the day ye eat thereof, your eyes shall be opened: and ye shall be as Gods, knowing good and evil'. The Judaic emphasis on Luciferic temptation, and its war with the cults of the great goddesses of ecstasy who swayed the cultures of the Near East, throws into relief the other great doctrine of the Old Testament: the concept of divine creation. Reality was divinely made, and in its mere createdness, its character as 'finished work', points to a transcendent God. To imagine more of objects was the grossest sin – idolatry. Against the potency of the obsessive cults it was sufficient to pose reality. Nevertheless, the first man had yielded to Lucifer and the history of Jewish consciousness was precisely the history of the resulting inner struggle.

On a certain level, therefore, and despite the 'scientific' language which Freud adopted, the Jewishness of Freud's basic assumptions is obvious. 'Fantasy *versus* the reality-principle' is an old story. Its result as doctrine nowadays, as in Old Testament times, is to highlight the sense of history and to impose a certain pessimism. The myth enables us to contemplate the life of consciousness in its inner contradictions and complexities, to grasp our individuality as emerging from the struggle – but at the cost of acknowledging a primal guilt, trauma or complex, and of submitting the hopes of the imagination to the bounds of the existent.

The Jewish myth not only recognizes the Luciferic, but embodies a particular resolution of the psychic forces involved, a resolution favourable to a strong individual consciousness that is nonetheless burdened morally with an inevitable sense of guilt or inadequacy. The tendency of the imagination to undermine conscious realism is not only resisted: the resistance is made to generate a certain type of religious mentality. We begin to see how a myth can also be a living force, how it can also determine a form of life, a way of living together with one's fellows and with the world.

It would be a mistake to suppose, however, that the impetus of the 'Luciferic' can only be conceived and resolved in the Jewish manner. The drive to 'cut loose' from the contingent world can assume many forms: among the ancient Greeks it was certainly not regarded as demonic, but expressed itself in the purities of classical art and in the metaphysical urge of early philosophy. In a broader sense we may regard it as having fashioned the basic cultural attitudes of Hellenism, above all as having formed the bright world of the Olympian deities, the 'cloudy kings' as Keats referred to them. According to Steiner:

> All that arises in the course of history in the guise of wonderful programmes, marvellously beautiful ideas, by which it is always believed that somehow or other a return can be made to the Golden Age – all this has its origin in the Luciferic tendencies which flow into man. Everything by which he tries to loosen his connection with reality, to soar above his actual circumstances – all this points to the Luciferic.

In the visual arts it leads to idealization; in the arts of speech to the concept of levels of style, so that the 'high style' frees itself from the embarrassments and imperfections of 'low' life. The subject matter of tragic poetry receives a lofty treatment of which ordinary life is not considered worthy. Poetry, as Aristotle remarked, is at war with the mere contingencies of history.

No more than Judaism was Greek civilization able to allow the Luciferic urge to reign unchecked. Its resolution of the mythic forces, on the other hand, follows an exactly opposite route. Far from demonizing the Luciferic, the Greeks deified it – thereby removing it with equal effectiveness from the human sphere. The gods alone were able to live a life of pure essence, outside of contingency and the accidental distortions typical of nature. Man may not aspire so high. Those such as Icarus, Bellerophon, Sisyphus and Tantalus who according to myths attempted to cross the divide between mere mortals and the Olympian heights were destroyed. They could not sustain their flight and plunged to earth again; or they were punished by tasks of hopeless and mind-destroying absurdity, clear intimations of the psychic dangers. Those, like Semele, who had an immortal lover, looked upon divine glory but were consumed to ashes in its fire. In the 'Olympian ideal' we have once more a recognition and a defence-mechanism of the imagination. Again, a certain self-consciousness is fostered and at the same time held in check by the warnings of inner disruption contained in the myths.

Any poem which is 'visionary', i.e. which undertakes to create its own meaning, or to discover a pattern of truth rather than work within an accepted framework of ideas, must achieve an understanding and resolution of the Luciferic power. Milton's Satan contains much of the Luciferic drive in its positive and negative aspects, anticipating the Promethean heroes of Romantic poetry. In Shelley, Prometheus – who seized the fire of the gods to give to mankind and was bound in chains on the icy Caucasus mountains – becomes a central figure. The power of Lucifer is yoked to man's conscious self to create the imagination of a radical freedom. Indeed, Shelley goes far beyond the Greek myth or its Judaic counterpart to call in question the traditional moral valuations.

It is not that he is unaware of the signal dangers to inner balance. But he believes equilibrium can be maintained without the limitations enforced by the older myths: he believes that human self-consciousness can play the role anciently shared with God or the gods. He therefore explores a new possibility. Before the conscious self can make use of Lucifer's potency, it must be able to observe the workings of the Luciferic imagination with a certain reserve and inner detachment. Shelley therefore allows, in some of his poems, the urge to work itself out in unprecedented fullness, but saves himself from its dangers by a conscious distancing. Such a movement of mind is not, in the context of his greatest work, an end in itself; rather it will serve to allow him conscious control over inner forces when he comes to invoke them for deeper purposes. However, it permits us to examine the Luciferic imagination with him, at first in isolation from more complex themes. The poem in which we can best do this we might call indeed a portrait of Lucifer, who in the poem appears as 'the Witch of Atlas'.

The Witch of Atlas begins with a bold flourish, suspending reality in order to examine the mythic powers which shape our attitude. Yet it does so not in order to call in question the foundations of being or man's place. Shelley is simply, and self-consciously, giving to the Luciferic projection a totally free space in which to unfold. His self-consciousness expresses itself in a tone of playful irony, disparaging mere reality as he suspends it so as to transport us back to a condition:

> Before those cruel Twins, whom at one birth
> Incestuous Change bore to her father Time,
> Error and Truth, had hunted from the Earth
> All those bright natures which adorned its prime,
> And left us nothing to believe in, worth
> The pains of putting into learned rhyme.

> (*Witch of Atlas*, I)

At first all is dissolving, melting and disappearing. Slowly the Luciferic embodiment, the reality-scorning Witch, takes shape before our inward eyes. Or rather, takes such shape as defies all categories of shape whatsoever.

She was conceived, says the poem, in an ecstasy of dissolving joy on the part of her mother ('one of the Atlantides'), when she was kissed by the warm beams of the sun in a mountain cave and melted away. Her subsequent transformations playfully echo the meteorology which Shelley had used poetically in *Prometheus Unbound*:

> 'Tis said, she first was changed into a vapour,
> And then into a cloud, such clouds as flit,
> Like splendour-winged moths about a taper,
> Round the red west when the sun dies in it:

And then into a meteor, such as caper
  On hill-tops when the moon is in a fit:
Then, into one of those mysterious stars
Which hide themselves between the Earth and Mars.

(*Witch of Atlas*, III)

Meanwhile in the cave, as a result of the union, 'a dewy splendour' takes shape and motion as a 'lovely lady garmented in light / From her own beauty': the Witch herself. Beasts and 'savage natures' mildly adore her. The woodland deities pay homage. The mysterious, invisible presence of the 'universal Pan' came too – so it was said – and brought just a hint of naughtiness to the verse:

He passed out of his everlasting lair
  Where the quick heart of the great world doth pant,
And felt that wondrous lady all alone, –
And she felt him, upon her emerald throne.

(*Witch of Atlas*, IX)

Richard Cronin points out that the fantastic invention and playful tone works in a way quite contrary to conventional mythopoeia. It makes us more aware of the unreality of what is said, rather than striving to make the imaged concrete. Our attention is drawn more firmly to reality precisely at the moment it is left behind. *The Witch* brilliantly releases us from the actual into a cosmos of consciously Luciferic imagining, but at the same time leaves us with a dark and haunting sense of the reality from which it turns away.

The Witch is beautiful. Her beauty is that of the image which has succeeded in totally displacing the ordinary world, which fades as if into shadow:

– her beauty made
  The bright world dim, and everything beside
Seemed like the fleeting image of a shade:
  No thought of living spirit could abide,
Which to her looks had ever been betrayed,
  On any object in the world so wide,
On any hope within the circling skies,
But on her form, and in her inmost eyes.

(*Witch of Atlas*, XII)

In short, she is the ideal beauty which is potentially destructive of human life. Man's finite desire cannot attain her infinite loveliness, but falls back into absurdity or is crushed by the shock of the return to normality, the inevitable backlash of alienation. But here the potential destructive conflict with reality is neatly dodged, as the Witch weaves an improbable veil out of starlight, shifting the imagination to a plane like that of the well-known *Skylark Ode*. Shelley refuses to commit his consciousness, and deftly allows the Luciferic imagination to soar into realms of fantasy where no external constraints remain and infinite desire is realized.

The conditions of that dazzling Luciferic accomplishment, however, are a rejection of social intercourse and even of all fellowship with changing, transient beings. Even the oak-nymphs who live for centuries and the naiads whose fountains flow for millennia would, relatively soon, fade and die compared with the immortal Witch, and cause her regret: which must not be. Meanwhile from her heaven–haven of imaginative fulfilment she can look with equanimity on all the change and troublesome strife 'Which stirs the liquid surface of man's life'. Shelley gives her Olympian distance from human turmoil:

> And little did the sight disturb her soul. –
>   We, the weak mariners of that wide lake
> Where'er its shores extend or billows roll,
>   Our course unpiloted and starless make
> O'er its wide surface to an unknown goal: –
>   But she in the calm depths her way could take,
> Where in bright bowers immortal forms abide
> Beneath the weltering of the restless tide.

(Witch of Atlas, LXIII)

We cannot but be startled by the shockingly light tone of these sombre reflections, containing some of Shelley's most potent images of man's mental voyage as surveyed from the Luciferic realm of reality-defeating imagination. It leaves us ultimately baffled and unsatisfied by the Witch's wisdom. Again as in the *Skylark Ode*, there is an ironic contrapuntal movement beneath the bright surface of the poetry which directs our attention to the dark after-image.

The staggeringly inhuman force of the disjunctions, between the profound insight of the Witch and the pathetic inconstancy of suffering mankind, far from leading us to side with her, finally render us appreciative of our seemingly-so-contemptible human lot. Shelley's success in transposing his imagination into the Witch's serene infinity of invention is a highly original exercise in poetic clairvoyance, and to be appreciated fully requires the narrative context of her voyages in the miraculous boat, the strange Hermaphrodite who perhaps stands for the work of art itself, and the numerous tricks played among the people of Egypt and round the Mareotic Lake – in short, the brilliant inventiveness sustained into the final phrases of the poem unsubdued by the growing darkness of its human implications. Shelley's experiment in self-conscious vision thus reveals both the phenomenal power of the imagination, in its Luciferic aspect, to transcend actuality and, at the same time, its inadequacy to a fully human experience. The poet's self-consciousness leads to the gradual infiltrations, as if from the margins of awareness, of a negative penumbra, a creeping horror at the unassimilable aspects of reality the Witch all-too-blithely ignores.

The experiment of allowing the Luciferic to expand to its full proportions leads to confrontation with an opposite power: the force inherent in the imagination at this opposite pole is the sense we have of reality as alien, other, indifferent to human purposes or desires. This is especially the response of imagination to the world of science, the purely objective law-governed universe invented by rationalism; but even in science the imagination is active, bringing the world into relation with man as a knower. It is once more when we engage in asking ultimate questions that we are faced by the stark possibility propounded by the sceptic – namely, that the world is essentially unfathomable, and answers our hopes of knowledge and relationship with inner silence and vacuity. We may then find, in the words of Shelley, within our thoughts 'the chasm of an insufficient void'; and the imagination may shape another daemonic power, one which threatens to deny the validity of the human spirit altogether.

I have suggested that the Old Testament myth enabled the Jewish consciousness to concentrate its resources on the struggle with Lucifer, i.e. the genesis of inwardness. It removed the fear of the alien world by its incessantly repeated injunction not to look at the universe without thinking of its Creator. Greek thought was touched more directly by a sense of the uncontrollable 'otherness' of things, in its concept of Fate and its tragic intuitions in art and poetry. But in the archaic East, especially in the mythology of ancient Iran, the conflict between man's spirit and the hostile or inhuman power behind outer nature received direct expression. The result was a myth whose potency and influence rival that of the biblical story: the dualism of Light and Darkness, named in the prehistoric teaching of the Iranian prophet Zarathustra (or Zoroaster) as Ohrmazd and Ahriman. Long afterwards, his vision was written down in the book called the *Bundahishn*:

Ohrmazd was on high in omniscience and goodness: for infinite time he was ever in the light. The light is the space and place of Ohrmazd: some call it the Endless Light. Omniscience and goodness are the permanent disposition of Ohrmazd: some call them 'Religion'. The interpretation of both is the same, namely the permanent disposition of Infinite Time, for Ohrmazd and the Space, Religion and Time of Ohrmazd were and are and evermore shall be.

Ahriman, slow in knowledge, whose will is to smite, was deep down in the darkness: he was and is, yet will not be. The will to smite is his permanent disposition, and darkness is his place: some call it the Endless Darkness.

The *Bundahishn* was rediscovered in the West in the late eighteenth century, and studied eagerly by Shelley and others. But it was not necessary to wait for its recovery to acknowledge the presence of the dark power, or Ahriman. For the oriental dualism had led a prolonged if largely underground existence in the West, and indeed influenced Christianity at the time of its origins. It reappeared in full-blooded form in the Christianity of the Babylonian prophet Mani (3rd century AD). Subsequently the 'Manichaean philosophy' was taught through the Middle Ages by esoteric sects, culminating in the Cathars who were exterminated by the orthodox Christians in a bloody 'crusade' against heresy.

Zoroastrian and Manichaean dualism challenges the Old Testament estimate of the 'finished creation', and likewise has little to say about the inner struggle. It wars against Ahriman as the 'spirit of negation', on the grounds of truth as well as of humanity. Accordingly, it can be said to have taken on a new relevance in the age of the scientific Enlightenment. For the poets of modern times find themselves as much engaged in a struggle against the outward

denial of man's hopes and intuitions as in the struggle with
Lucifer's temptation. Their vision has been attained, of course,
through imaginative exploration and not through dead tradition.
In their search for poetic truth they have tried to establish how far
man's present consciousness could survive the full revelation of
the Ahrimanic. For Shelley, the result was the shaping in his mind
of another daemonic presence, whom he calls by his ancient name
of Ahriman, or elsewhere Demogorgon. He is a negative absolute,
a fabulous formless darkness, the 'abyss of how little we know' in a
universe that seems only partially apprehensible to human facul-
ties. Goethe too gave this Power a voice, ironic and destructive, in
his Mephistopheles, the Lord of Denial ('der Geist, der stets
verneint'). But it was perhaps Blake who most fully comprehended
the workings of the Ahrimanic spirit in the age of the Industrial
Revolution.

The 'dark Satanic Mills' are an obvious protest against human
exploitation. Yet the phrase has a resonance that derives from its
wider significance in Blake's poetry. For the 'Mills of Satan' is his
phrase for nothing less than the scientific cosmos, the system of
the 'terrible starry wheels' orbiting massively over our heads and
dwarfing human concerns by their vast imperturbability. Coleridge
was worried by the feeling that the stars might be God's relentless
spies; but Blake is troubled by the utter lack of concern with man's
affairs that the scientist posits for the starry spaces. He senses the
presence of an Ahrimanic spirit, with 'iron laws' inscribed in his
terrible book. This is Urizen, portrayed in a famous illustration as
'The Ancient of Days' measuring the deep with his compasses, or
as the tortured God in 'Elohim Creating Adam'. For Blake's vision
is of the type known as Gnostic, where the Ahrimanic spirit is so
powerfully apprehended that it usurps certain characteristics of the
Godhead. In his powerful inversion of the Genesis creation-story,
The Book of Urizen, Blake's Ahrimanic daemon figures as a typically
Gnostic 'Demiurge', a blind and self-deluded divinity creating an
oppressive universe.

The atmosphere is claustrophobic, for in Urizen's world all self-
expression is stifled and denied. Mankind survives only by learn-
ing the virtue of selfishness, in a ghastly parody of the Old
Testament promise:

> Six days they shrunk up from existence,
> And on the seventh day they rested.

And they bless'd the seventh day, in sick hope,
And forgot their eternal life.

(Book of Urizen 27, 39–42)

Urizen himself is appalled at the world he has made: but for the striking reason that, despite all their efforts and sufferings, men cannot in the end submit themselves totally to his rule. He realizes with agony that 'no flesh nor spirit could keep / His iron laws one moment':

Cold he wander'd on high, over their cities,
In weeping & pain & woe.
And where-ever he wander'd in sorrows
Upon the aged heavens,
A cold shadow follow'd behind him,
Like a spider's web, moist, void, dim,
Drawing out from his sorrowing soul
The dungeon-like heaven dividing
Where ever the footsteps of Urizen
Walk'd over the cities in sorrow.

(Book of Urizen 25, 5–14)

In *The Four Zoas*, the later Blake's huge mythic expansion of his earlier visions, the poet added to the chill presence of Urizen in the heavens a picture of human life on earth under his domination – his rule, which makes of this world already a place of death:

Scar'd at the sound of their own sigh that seems to shake the
                                                    immense
They wander Moping, in their heart a sun, a dreary moon,
A Universe of fiery constellations in their brain,
An earth of wintry woe beneath their feet, & round their loins
Waters or winds or clouds or brooding lightnings & pestilential
                                                    plagues.
Beyond the bounds of their own self their senses cannot
                                                    penetrate:
As the tree knows not what is outside of its leaves & bark
And yet it drinks the summer joy & fears the winter sorrow,
So, in the regions of the grave, none knows his dark compeer

Tho' he partakes of his dire woes & mutual returns the pang,
The throb, the dolor, the convulsion, in soul-sickening woes.

(*The Four Zoas*, Night the Sixth, 89–99)

The Ahrimanic reduction makes of the living earth a 'region of the
grave' to those in whose consciousness it attains priority. The
Ahrimanic spirit grasps only externals, only mechanism, compul-
sion, exploitation, separateness, self.

Blake's deepest insight into the power of Ahriman, however,
concerns the consequences for man himself. For he grasped the
difficult truth that a system of thought is not simply an instrument
for interpreting the world. In the course of explaining the world,
man is simultaneously defining his own setting, his own context.
In terms of the world he must explain himself. Hence for Blake the
real danger of the Urizenic outlook is that we identify ourselves
with the universe of matter-and-force our thinking has made, and
he subtly analyses the fear which impels us to do so. If man is
possessed of a spiritual nature, Blake suggests, yet finds himself in
a materialistic universe, he will be able to find no way of coming to
terms with his own spirituality; he will be able to ascribe no content
to it, since he knows only mechanism. The spiritual dimension will
yawn open therefore as a vacuum, like Shelley's 'insufficient void'
or Demogorgonic cave. A terror of the void will haunt him. In
Blake's vision, this fear attacks the creative or poetic spirit Los
when he labours to bring form to Urizen's cosmos, to give it
meaning and life. The abyss of 'Non-Entity' gapes ever wider
beneath him, a 'dismal Darkness beneath immensity':

Pale terror seized the Eyes of Los as he beat round
The hurtling demon; terrified at the shapes
Enslav'd humanity put on, he became what he beheld:
He became what he was doing: he was himself transform'd.

(*The Four Zoas*, Night the Fourth, 284–7)

To escape his fear, Los identifies himself with the material on
which he is working. It is to escape the fear of 'Non-Entity', the
vacuum which conceals our spiritual nature, that we take refuge in
the materialistic world-view. The real threat of Ahriman is thus not
that we misinterpret the world: the danger lies in the fact that our
world-view will also interpret us.

In the case of Luciferic and Ahrimanic tendencies alike, then, there comes a point at which the imagination refuses allegiance or resists a threat to the conscious self. A truth is defined or suggested which does not refer to a metaphysical absolute, a thing-in-itself or transcendent idea: visionary imagination finds its own inner boundaries. The Luciferic must be overcome through self-knowledge and the recognition of human failure and shortcomings, balancing his aspirations. The Ahrimanic terror must be overcome by the ability to enter into that 'void', which will become a womb of rebirth, an awakening to man's own essential being – his power to give meaning to the contingency and chaos of external perception.

The moment of imaginative balance, or centering of the imagination in itself, necessarily takes us beyond the images which flow out of the imagination. It points to the very power which enables all images to be formed. It has been consistently rendered in visionary poetry by the fading out of visual impressions and the filling of their place by the intenser quality of sound – music. This is the transition from Blake's Beulah or world of images to the state he calls Eden; it is the realm of Shelley's 'stops / Of planetary music heard in trance'; or the energy invoked by Wordsworth in his *Ode on the Power of Sound*, identified with the traditional force of apocalypse, the trumpet note which will dissolve the visible and tangible world into dust. At its highest reaches, poetry touches the limits of imagery and leaves an impression of music. In this way it attains to a kind of 'objectivity', like a harmonization or concord with the unseen – 'Harmonizing this earth with what we feel above', as Shelley expresses it in *Prometheus Unbound*. With music there can, of course, be no question of a reference to natural reality or 'world out there' to guarantee the rightness of the correspondence. And yet neither is music merely a matter of internal relations: it does seem to reach out beyond itself to express something essential and true above the mathematics of proportions between tones and rhythms.

We need not believe, with Walter Pater, that all art aspires to the condition of music. But one strand in our study of the visionary poets will be the recurring desire they show to ground the form of their work not in mimesis but in musical articulation. Poetry cannot be made into music without denying itself: but the principles of music can inform and transfigure poetry. One way of understanding the formal experiments of poets from Milton onwards might be to see how they modify inherited modes of epic, drama or reflective verse into manifold guises of lyric.

The understanding of Luciferic and Ahrimanic as contrary myths, and as actual powers in the soul, occupies a central place in the thought of Rudolf Steiner and in his artistic work. One reason for its centrality is that it brings together issues of knowledge and freedom – whose relationship had already formed the subject of Steiner's early philosophical investigations in his *Philosophie der Freiheit*, and which is crucial to his whole conception of man. For the very ground of the visionary knowledge to which imagination can lead is clearly nothing but human freedom, which is discovered in the balance between the polar energies of the demons, in a dynamic equilibrium between the tendencies of Luciferic and Ahrimanic. Here is the seed of Steiner's remarkable concept of the self, not as a 'thinking thing' but as development and transformation – taking up and extending ideas of Goethean 'metamorphosis'.

The twin powers appear explicitly in Steiner's poetic drama, *The Portal of Initiation*. But it may be better first to give some account of the extraordinary setting in which he intended the drama to be peformed. The original or First Goetheanum, designed by Steiner and realized in highly-carved, sculptured wood, was among other things a theatre, a 'house of speech', though indeed it also embodies Steiner's conception of 'musical' form and architectural metamorphosis, and the interior domes were covered in paintings whose subjects were closely related to the building's spiritual functions. The style of the whole can only loosely be related to the aesthetics of Expressionism in the way that has sometimes been proposed, useful though the notion may be as a point of departure. In the different media, representational, architectural, musical and dramatic, Steiner attempted to embody a certain vision, whose character is perhaps summed up in the sculptural group which was to have dominated the interior of the theatre, *The Representative of Humanity between Lucifer and Ahriman*.

The group was executed with the help of the English sculptor Edith Maryon, and since the fire which destroyed the still unfinished First Goetheanum it stands in a special display-room in the new or Second Goetheanum (completed 1928). This was amongst the first buildings to realize the free possibilities of concrete as a building material, and has been described by the architectural historian Wolfgang Pehnt as 'one of the most magnifi-

cent pieces of sculptural architecture of the twentieth century'.* In
it the tradition of dramatic festivals – the well-known *Faust*-
productions and the cycles of the mystery-dramas – has been
carried on.

Against background forms oddly suggestive of both fire and
rock, the twin daemons are represented: Lucifer as if rising upward
under the shade of his arched wings, his head contemplative and
his look indrawn; Ahriman, skeletal and grasping, below, a life
reduced to a basic horror. Next to them, and between them in the
sense of connecting the levels vertically, stands the Representative
of Humanity, powerfully upright and with a commanding gesture,
one arm raised and the other directed downward. And then –
since it would be of no avail to create a pattern of spiritual fixities –
we unexpectedly have the daemonic figures once again, above and
below the controlling gesture of the Representative, thus making
a dynamically complex whole. Above the raised hand with its
potent grip, Lucifer cascades downward in a sweeping fall as the
earth-scorning power of his wings fails him. Below the other hand,
shown in a painting on the smaller dome as the source of
down-streaming energy, lies Ahriman's shattered form in a cavern
below the whole group. Chains twist like nightmarish roots round
his rigid limbs. The work thus contrives to embody seemingly
contrary meanings: the presence of the daemons remains as an
assertion and a threat, while their second 'fallen' and 'shattered'
forms suggest not so much a narrative as a victory which has
constantly to be won. Yet the sculpture stands as an affirmation of
man's power to rule the potential 'anarchy of hopes and fears', the
daemonic forces essential to his freedom yet a threat to his very
existence if not controlled. The effect is sombrely impressive; the
Human- or Christ-figure shows a wisdom won by suffering in the
scarred brow. Yet the wisdom would be stern indeed, were it not
for a genial addition – the Spirit of Humour, a kind of seraph with
a mysterious pained smile, a transient witness almost disappearing
at the pinnacle of the group.

For Steiner, the triple constellation of forces is deeply enwoven
in cosmic reality. Lucifer and Ahriman are powers involved in
man's relation to the world around him, constantly threatening to
distort that relationship and to replace the mingled music, the
mottled texture of human consciousness struggling between ideal

*Wolfgang Pehnt, *Expressionist Architecture* (London, 1973) p. 148.

and bare truth, with their own simpler intensities. Each is necessary to man. The Ahrimanic is the only way out of the charmed circle of man's self-obsession, his Luciferic urge to be as God and make of the world only a reflection of his own glory – and the solipsistic imagination its own reward. And the Ahrimanic spirit must be acknowledged, since it is part of the conditions under which self-consciousness is achieved; it will make itself felt as a destructive backlash against the passion of the ideal if it is not, from the beginning, incorporated into the mind as a necessary pole of its development. Likewise the Luciferic urge is a salvation from the process of dehumanization which infects the external knowledge of the sciences. It is necessary to all art, in that it rescues objective reality for human experience, and invests it with that necessary aura of meaning which we call beauty. The result is still more significant for us. 'The search for truth', said Steiner, 'renders us ever more humble. Yet if man were simply to proceed in this way, becoming more and more humble, he would eventually arrive at his own dissolution . . . The peculiarity of the aesthetic life lies in this: it comprises truth, that is, selflessness; but it is at the same time an assertion of self-supremacy in the soul-life, giving us back to ourselves as a spontaneous gift.'

Steiner suggests a new mythology for the complex self-consciousness of modern man. It depends upon the achievement of a finely wrought balance between principles treated more one-sidedly in the older myths. But he believes at once in the stable strength and the sheer resilience of man. There is room for suffering Humanity, but also for the smiling, seraphic spontaneity of that Spirit of Humour.

LOVE AND DEATH

Steiner – like the English visionary poets who achieved their own resolution of the pressures he describes – was aware that the new mythology was not without precedent. Indeed, the essential step had been taken by a religion which overturned most of the accepted truths of ancient myth while it seemed to incorporate them: Christianity. By referring to the Christian spirit which informs the poetry of visionary writers, I shall not generally mean the beliefs they may have held. That relationship, between belief and imagination, is a difficult one: in the instances of Blake and

Milton we shall find that belief by no means easily equates with imaginative conviction. In the case of two other poets, commitment to a religious position in addition to imagination may be held to have involved them in special complications. Coleridge was a metaphysician and religious thinker as well as a poet, and his acceptance of a religious solution to the ultimate questions of existence often enters into his work as a force inimical to the working of imagination. In *The Eolian Harp*, poetry asserts itself powerfully, though under the baleful eye of a 'Meek Daughter in the Family of Christ' who is strongly inclined to dismiss these 'shapings of the unregenerate mind'. Elsewhere, Coleridge achieves some of his greatest poetry – and the best of it is among the finest poetry we have – in conditions where the censorious reason of his waking mind is in suspension: dream-poems like *Kubla Khan*, trance-states, poems of dark and mysterious forces such as *Christabel*. Coleridge went on to become one of the profoundest theorists of the self-conscious imagination, but as so often, theory does not accord quite directly with poetic practice.

Keats presents a striking antithesis, since he alone among the foremost Romantics was a committed atheist. (Shelley's so-called 'atheism' was a much more equivocal affair, a resistance to certain kinds of thinking rather than any dogmatic conclusion about religious realities.) Rather than setting out to conquer the domain of 'Mystery' for the human imagination, like Blake, Keats limited the sphere of imagination to the humanistic and to natural reality. By doing so he placed what is perhaps an intolerable burden on the finite self, which in his vision faces the world alone. Often he is oppressed by the sense of gloom, of powerlessness, by the wish for death. He wrote in his *Fall of Hyperion*, an initiation-poem based on his earlier and unfinished epic:

> Without stay or prop
> But my own weak mortality, I bore
> The load of this eternal quietude,
> The unchanging gloom, and the three fixed shapes
> Ponderous upon my senses a whole moon.
> For by my burning brain I measured sure
> Her silver seasons shedded on the night
> And ever day by day methought I grew
> More gaunt and ghostly – Oftentimes I prayed
> Intense, that death would take me from the vale

> And all its burthens – Gasping with despair
> Of change, hour after hour I cursed myself . . .

> (*The Fall of Hyperion* Canto I, 388–99)

It is doubtful whether man can survive the imagination (as opposed to the theory) of so negative a universe. Like the original epic *Hyperion*, the later *Fall* was never completed.

Coleridge and Keats stand high among the most imaginative writers; and in tackling the most fundamental questions with their imaginative resources they are visionary poets. If they do not occupy the stage in what follows, it is because complicating factors such as those we have indicated would too often call for extended special consideration. It is part of their greatness as poets that they wrestle with these problems. One special fascination of Coleridge is his intellectual and philosophical brilliance, another his religious insights; Keats' focussing on the finite self in its 'weak mortality' makes him the most human of the Romantics, the least likely to forfeit human interest in pursuit of a 'visionary rhyme'. But an attempt to trace a line of approach, a broadly conceived 'high argument', through the visionary poets has led me to concentrate attention on a trajectory leading from Milton through to Yeats – together with one or two analogies and influences from elsewhere.

What I mean by the Christian spirit, rather than belief, comes most clearly into focus when we examine the role played by love in the thought of these poets. In Shelley, for example, it soon emerges that love is not simply a relationship between persons, or even limited to the human world. It can be directed upon inanimate nature, upon living beings or upon the unfathomable source of life and experience which is Shelley's unknown God. Love is an essential part of human nature, though it exists in many forms. 'Hence in solitude', wrote Shelley in the essay *On Love*, 'or in that deserted state when we are surrounded by human beings, and yet they sympathise not with us, we love the flowers, the grass, and the waters, and the sky . . . There is eloquence in the tongueless wind, and a melody in the flowing brooks and the rustling of the reeds beside them, which by their inconceivable relation to something within the soul, awaken the spirit to a dance of breathless rapture.' Love is our ability to give ourselves up to another being. It does not seek to possess – and in this respect it is the opposite of the Luciferic and Ahrimanic aspirations, both of which aim at grasping ultimate knowledge or power for the self.

Understood in this wide but profound sense, love is the foundation of all knowledge. Luciferic and Ahrimanic may be the two modes through which we assimilate experience to our self, to what we already know or already are. But this process depends upon our having previously given ourselves in some measure to the phenomena, allowing them to reveal themselves in their uniqueness. Even the most rigorously 'scientific' knowledge has its roots in this primal love for the manifestations of truth. And in the arts, love is the power by which we discover our possible response to the beauty of things – even things which in ordinary life we would not have noticed, or would have found repellent. We uncover their 'inconceivable relation to something within the soul'. 'Wouldst thou think', says the Earth-Spirit in *Prometheus Unbound*:

> that toads, and snakes, and efts,
> Could e'er be beautiful? yet so they were,
> And that with little change of shape or hue.

For in the regenerate universe Shelley imagines there, man has learnt to look within himself and find the springs of a love which will give a place in his heart even to the humblest and ugliest of creatures.

We cannot therefore adequately represent Shelley's imagination, or that of other visionaries, simply in terms of a tension between Luciferic and Ahrimanic. There is another dimension: an axis of love joining man at his highest moments to cosmic reality. Critics who have treated Shelley as a mind torn between scepticism and idealism, realism and fantasy, have failed to grasp the core of his thinking. The powers which struggle on the axis of conscious wisdom are related to man as a knower, his attention turned to the universe around him. Shelley's doctrine of love, on the other hand, treats of man in his essential being. (See Figure 1). Yet the role of the contending powers is crucial, since love itself and the nature of man are susceptible of being warped, distorted out of recognition, if inner equilibrium is lost.

Love can never be brought under the control of the conscious self, however. For it is openness itself: it is the possibility of new discovery, of growth, of self-transcendence. Consciousness can only hold itself in readiness for the epiphany of such a power, not

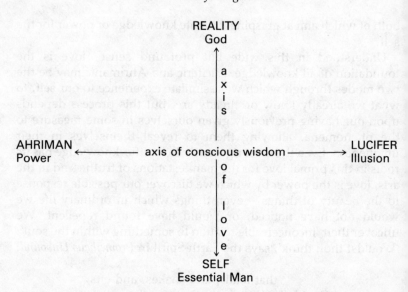

Figure 1. Imaginative Consciousness. The Shelleyan Mythic Polarities.

compel it to appear. Goethe likewise, in the *Final Scene* of *Faust*, acknowledges the existence of that force. He adds to the conscious striving of Faust, which makes him capable of redemption, the descending grace of love imaged in the falling rose-petals scattered by the heavenly host. No more than Shelley was Goethe ever able to assent to Christian belief: yet he noted in a conversation with Eckermann that his imagination of Faust's redemption by eternal love ('von oben die ihm zu Hilfe kommende ewige Liebe') accords completely with our religious conception. As Alan Cottrell notes, we do not need to decide whether this is 'Goethean' or 'Christian'. It is Goethean in so far as it arises purely from Goethe's imaginative vision; it is Christian, not in expressing a belief, but in its essential structure and values. It has a parallel in the concept of love found in that 'atheist', yet at times profoundly Christian, poet Shelley. And like Shelley, Goethe distinguished love from the powers of conscious wisdom which rule man's life. 'Love does not rule – but it forms, and that is more' (*Das Märchen*).

The *Final Scene* is an attempt to penetrate in imagination the world beyond the normal limits of consciousness altogether: the world beyond death. Shelley too undertakes that experiment in *Adonais*, one of his most brilliantly successful longer poems. It is written out of his sense of the imagination's power and in his love for John Keats, for whom it is an elegy and a defiant celebration in the face of hostile criticism. Shelley had written in *Prometheus Unbound* of the 'happy Dead, whom beams of brightest verse / Are clouds to hide, not colours to portray'. His exploration of the uttermost frontier of consciousness, the final cessation of death, is demanding and difficult to fathom. It engages all the forces we have described: indeed, it is in *Adonais* that their workings achieve Shelley's most perfect fusion of energy with the formative stresses, the actual morphology of the poem.

'I weep for Adonais – he is dead'. The admirable hardness and pathos of the first line does not disguise the fact that Shelley is writing in a conventional elegiac mode. He is expressing a personal grief, but also tackling matters that concern collective values: religious, poetic and moral traditions. Beginning from the fact of death, the first movement within the poem, consisting of some hundred-and-fifty lines, is an attempt to rise 'vertically' through several empowering analogies toward some consoling intuition or metaphor. The result is dazzling poetry, and there are occasions when Shelley momentarily claims success. Yet his satisfaction soon passes, and he acknowledges, as Richard Cronin says, the evasive character of his metaphors; they succeed only through inconsistency. The Luciferic movement toward transcendence is only possible when certain aspects of experience are ignored or denied – and here actual experience is at its most unpalatable, the imagination of physical death and corruption, pale limbs and icy lips. The metaphors by which Shelley tries to escape the consequences of awareness become ever more extravagant, 'conceited'. Cronin rightly sees in this section of the poem further evidence of Shelley's mastery of seventeenth-century techniques, employed in the man-nered poetry of the followers of Petrarch and Calderon, imitated in England by Donne and the so-called Metaphysical poets. The dead Keats' dreams and images are summoned to enact fantastic rituals of love and death, attempting to assert though their symbolic ingenuity the power of the imagination to assimilate even the final horror of individual death. But Luciferic extravagance only ends by making the inconsistency between truth and fantasy blatantly clear: Luciferic aspiration toward a transcendent consolation shat-ters and leaves a sense of an inimical outer nature. As in the second stanza of the *Ode to the West Wind*, here again the renewal of outer nature with the returning spring will not suffice:

Ah, woe is me! Winter is come and gone,
But grief returns with the revolving year . . .

(*Adonais*, XVIII)

Man cannot be reborn like the impersonal multitudes of natural things. Hence for man the vision of cyclic nature becomes an Ahrimanic doom.

The Luciferic consolations, though sanctified by religion and by a certain strain of poetry, showing that they correspond to actual though partial tendencies of feeling and mind, prove inadequate to Shelley's determination to preserve wholeness, the integrity of the self. A daemonic cycle is completed; but the poem is by no means over.

A countermovement begins, calling in question the heartless vision of cyclicity in its turn. New protagonists appear: Adonais' fellow-poets, including Byron (the 'Pilgrim of Eternity') and others recognizable as Tom Moore, Leigh Hunt and Shelley himself. They exemplify a depth of experience and introspection which, even if as in Shelley's case the effects are ambivalently disturbing, exposes the hollowness, the egotism and vindictiveness of the mundane world – exemplified now in the reviewer and his kind, who hunted Keats to his death according to the myth adopted by Shelley. The world of the critic, the natural man, reveals a drab and painful reality more dehumanizing than the uncertainties of the world beyond death, the desire for which is so deeply grounded in man's spirit. However impossible it may be to follow the dead soul beyond the painted veil, the critic's natural reality is equally accepted only at the cost of denying parts of essential experience. Shelley will not renounce the profundity of experience suggested by poetry – above all by the poetry of Keats. What is certain is that Keats attained to some condition which the literal-minded man would be the last to fathom, has gone where he could not follow.

In the final complex movement of the poem, therefore, Shelley investigates a third way: a transcendence of the phenomenal world that is not linear, like the metaphorical projections explored earlier, but one that consists in a deepening of experience itself. Already through his poetry Keats has achieved a new kind of life, even of immortality. He has transformed our perception of things, revealing the loveliness of nature through hitherto unapprehended relations. In this sense he has become part of our experience of the world:

He is made one with Nature: there is heard
His voice in all her music, from the moan
Of thunder, to the song of night's sweet bird;
He is a presence to be felt and known
In darkness and in light, from herb and stone,
Spreading itself where'er that Power may move
Which has withdrawn his being to its own;
Which wields the world with never-wearied love,
Sustains it from beneath, and kindles it above.

He is a portion of the loveliness
Which once he made more lovely . . .

(*Adonais* XLII–XLIII)

What Shelley presents is not just the 'notion that the individual's life after death consists in being subsumed in an impersonal life-force' (Cronin), but the idea that the greatest poetry, when it is honest to the contradictory aspects of our experience, moves toward the apprehension of a fuller reality, inadequately revealed through our everyday consciousness. It can be understood as the formative power of the 'one Spirit' behind the multiplicity of nature, whose 'plastic stress':

Sweeps through the dull dense world, compelling there,
All new successions to the forms they wear;
Torturing th' unwilling dross that checks its flight
To its own likeness, as each mass may bear;
And bursting in its beauty and its might
From trees and beasts and men into the Heaven's light.

(*Adonais* XLIII)

Shelley suggests that what we know as death may be the falling away of the blinkers of space and time, birth and death alike, the shattering of the many-coloured dome which stains Eternity, and so the perfecting of a vision already partly embodied in the intensity of poetic awareness. Adonais, the essential Keats, has not died but in his vision has already transcended death. He has awoken from the 'dream of life'.

In the light of such a possibility, Shelley presses on in his own quest to the limits of the imaginable, to a death–rebirth, an expansion of consciousness, which explicitly glances back to his masterpiece the *Ode to the West Wind* ('The breath whose might I have invoked in song'): his 'spirit's bark' is driven:

> Far from the shore, far from the trembling throng
> Whose sails were never to the tempest given;
> The massy earth and sphered skies are riven!
> I am borne darkly, fearfully, afar;
> Whilst, burning through the inmost veil of Heaven,
> The soul of Adonais, like a star,
> Beacons from the abode where the Eternal are.

(*Adonais*, LV)

Part I
Neglected Visionary

2

Milton's Inner Journey

Why should we honour those that die upon the field of battle; man
may show as reckless a courage in entering into the abyss of himself.

– Yeats

What is it in Milton's poetry that arouses such hostility? A review
of the 'public image' of the poet would probably reveal that the
causes lie more in our presuppositions than in our response to his
verse. From our schooldays we have an impression of *Paradise Lost*
as an epitome of tedium: a Bible story retold in terms of the *Oxford
Classical Dictionary*. We believe that it has a strong moral purpose,
and we know (I almost shudder to say it) that he was a Puritan.
The case is complete.

What he actually wrote is a highly personal, even intimate
document. It contains that movingly personal poetry on his own
blindness, on his sense of loss and isolation, and need for grace to
continue writing the work. It was also compelling poetry which
rose out of unfathomed depths. Much of it came to him in dreams:
it was by no means just another inert literary convention when he
attributed the results of his pen not to himself but rather to the
presence of an inspiring power, his Muse or:

> Celestial Patroness, who deigns
> Her nightly visitation unimplor'd,
> And dictates to me slumbering, or inspires
> Easie my unpremeditated Verse.

Such spontaneity certainly contrasts strongly with the image of the
laboriously edifying moralist! Of course, Milton brought to the
vision – of Paradise and its infinitely painful loss, already sharply
and ironically juxtaposed in the title – his full, conscious powers.
Yet in the end it is the forces of mystery, dream and vision which
leave a lasting impression. Perhaps even to a disturbing extent, the
poem remains with us as a memorial of an encounter with the
depths of the mind.

Now it is perfectly true that Milton tells us a story which is recognizably the story of Adam and Eve in the first chapters of Genesis (though he refers to a great many other stories, 'myths' as well). And it is true that he blatantly employs literary forms and devices from the classical epic as practised by Homer and Vergil. For example, he begins *Paradise Lost*, as the classicists say, *in medias res*: that is, he does not begin at the chronological beginning of his story (which for Milton's story would be the beginning of every-thing), but in the midst of events, with Satan already fallen and cast into Hell. Yet the outcome of all this is not a Hellenized Bible-epic-*cum*-morality-play. I want to suggest rather that Milton uses this, and other devices, to conform the given material of his subject to a deeper pattern of his own. By disrupting the straight-forward narrative of Adam's fall which occupies a few hundred words in Genesis, Milton is enabled to make a detour through inner and outer worlds, a visionary universe. He can rearrange the images and symbols of the story to outline an initiatory voyage into the chaos and abysses of his imagination as well as the brightly apprehended paradise within the mind. In fact, having once fractured the narrative line of the tale, he allows his detour to embrace everything.

Milton's language, like his narrative, diverges from the clear and straightforward, and becomes complex, compressed. Rather than follow conventional usage or aim for a classical simplicity and naturalness, Milton shapes a language which always seems labouring to mean more than can be made explicit, suggesting hidden depths of meaning latent in every utterance. Dr Johnson, an admirer of the classical style and its 'public' surface, found Milton's speech a 'Babylonish dialect'. It would be nearer the truth perhaps to say that Milton – the first major poet in English to put so much weight on his personal experience, his own spiritual authority – needed to fashion such a tongue when he moved away from the clear, daylight world into the complex inner depths. Like Rembrandt's painting, Milton's poetry creates a universe of sharp contrasts, lights and shadows; sound, musicality, is as important as literal meaning; irrational forces play through the whirlpools, the streams and confluences of the celebrated rhetorical para-graphs whose meaning emerges in the governing energy, the powerful currents which sustain the long units of verse. Exotic names create their own resonance and air of mystery. Such a language had to be evolved by Milton, as the Romantic poets who followed him had likewise to form their own language. Up to the time of Shakespeare, and even a little beyond, poets still identified with public language in a way that did not throw their individual perceptions into relief; but from the seventeenth century, a deepening of individual consciousness can be traced which finds expression in the personal standpoint, the idiosyncratic use of words, the attempt to convey the private significance which public utterance tends to play down. This change in consciousness has many deeper layers of significance, some of which we shall try to fathom in understanding Milton. Milton was the first English genius to realize the huge possibilities inherent in a personal, evocative, disjointed language of poetry: with it he saw the potential for conquering the domains of religious and philosophic truth for the imagination. His impulse is the origin of the whole broad movement surveyed in this book, informing the great Romantic generation a century or so after his time; nay more, is still the impulse, as I should say, behind the most significant poetry of today.

Where did that impulse originate? The question cannot easily be answered. Vast processes of the evolution of consciousness and language, historical shifts of perspective, and the special circumstances of England during the spiritual ferment of the Civil War, not to mention Milton's own wrestling with his assertive ego can all be invoked in explanation. But the situation in which a man finds himself is never more than opportunity: to make use of it, he needs insight into the new possibilities his circumstances afford, awareness of the further reach of development that unfolds for those who can see it. The possibility of a radical step forward in consciousness at Milton's time was foreseen by various thinkers and expressed among various groups, movements, societies and sects. Though Milton retained a distance from any sectarianism in his poetry, his name like that of Blake has been linked with several of these groups, which were often of an esoteric or Gnostic nature. Certain of Milton's central insights, the historian Christopher Hill has pointed out, can be seen crystallizing among the so-called 'Ranters' – a sort of Gnostic group who worshipped God as the 'Fulnesse' or 'Immensity', regarding themselves and all other beings as his 'Fellow creatures' sustained by the one Life.* They

---

*A good account of the Ranters can be found in Norman Cohn, *The Pursuit of the Millennium* (which includes some Ranter texts). See Appendix 3.

tried to describe their sense of the divine Life within but, lacking
Milton's extraordinary linguistic power, no doubt often justified
the 'ranting' reputation which gave them their popular name. Yet
they offered the most radical account of the potential conscious-
ness available to the man who would grasp his own freedom.
Indeed, they took their freedom to the lengths of an absolute
liberation from the bonds of custom and the Law. Milton too was
fascinated by this freedom – though, as we shall see, it is not clear
that he fully trusted man to possess it or saw at all consistently the
spiritual foundations on which it must be based.

We know that Milton was deeply influenced by other, more
Christian and more intellectual movements, notably by the
Rosicrucians, as represented by (for example) the notable thinker
Robert Fludd. The mysterious Order called by the name of the
'Rose Cross' had become, in the seventeenth century, the centre of
all sorts of speculations, but also of a learned, esoteric and
Christian vision of life, which such thinkers as Fludd, nowadays
recognized as one of the pioneers of modern concepts in the
theoretical and applied sciences, sought to embody.* Milton had
certainly studied Fludd and other such writers, and it may have
been through him that he came to know something too of the
Christianized *cabala*, a mystical system that had originated in
Jewish and Gnostic circles of late Antiquity. At any rate, ideas from
Rosicrucian and cabalistic thought can undoubtedly be found in
the framework of Milton's poetic universe, as in the marvellous
hymn to the primal divine Light which begins Book III:

> Hail holy Light, offspring of Heav'n first-born,
> Or of th' Eternal Coeternal beam . . .

Here we are concerned not with the created light of conventional
Christian theology, but a mysterious 'effluence' of uncreated spirit
– which, since 'God is Light', is itself virtually divine; a 'pure
Ethereal stream, / Whose Fountain who shall tell?'

Hermetic ideas from the pagan esotericism of ancient Alexandria,
which had also been shaped by Gnostic influences, were also
studied by Milton. His archetypal image of the thinker in the lonely

---

*See Joscelyn Godwin, *Robert Fludd* (London, 1979) for a basic acount of Fludd and
his ideas, with many valuable illustrations. For some remarks on Milton and the
Rosicrucians, see Frances Yates, *The Rosicrucian Enlightenment* (St. Albans, 1975)
pp. 217ff.

tower, pondering Plato and Hermes, was to surface again and again in Romantic poetry until Yeats employed it as the very emblem of modern consciousness. Thus Milton in *Il Penseroso*:

> Or let my Lamp at midnight hour
> Be seen in som high lonely Towr,
> Where I may oft outwatch the *Bear*,
> With thrice great *Hermes*, or unsphear
> The spirit of *Plato* to unfold
> What Worlds, or what vast Regions hold
> Th' immortal mind that hath forsook
> Her mansion in this fleshly nook:
> And of those *Daemons* that are found
> In fire, air, flood, or under ground,
> Whose power hath a true consent
> With Planet or with Element.

Such ideas took on a new life in the seventeenth century, the great age of cosmology and alchemy; and Milton strove to blend them with what he knew of the scientific world-view that was slowly emerging at the same time. The 'new cosmology' cast doubt on the wisdom of Hermes, considered as astronomy. Yet in some respects the dynamic universe of forces and bodies in motion was itself the discovery of thinkers extending occult and esoteric thought. And certainly Milton's imagination continued to look for inner support to the ideas of the old 'poetic theology'.

Drawing on these and similar sources, and using them to articulate his own imaginative experience and inner struggles, Milton wrote *Paradise Lost*. He wrote it at the height of his powers, after a life which had been spent trying to reach his fellow men by more outward, direct means: political campaigning and pamphleteering directed at radical reform in education, religion, law, and at basic attitudes toward sex and divorce. In *Paradise Lost* he turned from outer to inner struggles, and depicted with unsurpassed imaginative energy an inner journey, a descent into one's own soul and a vision of paradise.

We can follow his journey. Instead of treating the poem as 'biblical epic', we can put the story in brackets (so to speak). We can follow the poem as a sequence of images, imaginative states linked by inner rather than external or narrative necessity. Blake pioneered this form of interpretation: he even sketched his own map of 'Milton's track' through the visionary universe among the 'Zoas', through the mental 'States' of Satan and Adam. He made of Milton's journey a journey of his own, re-imagined in strikingly Blakean terms. Nevertheless, his principle holds good. And, against Frank Kermode's suggestion that the structure of *Paradise Lost* might derive from the order of the Jesuits' spiritual exercises, I shall propose that we should understand it as a 'Rosicrucian' progression through levels of vision. Milton's imagination takes us not into 'other worlds', but into new ways of seeing; deeper apprehensions of the truth of this world. The landscape will appear to alter and be transformed around us, but in reality it is we ourselves who change. Hence we must begin by confronting ourselves. And this brings us immediately face to face with the protagonist of the first books of the poem – Satan.

If Milton were a mere moralizer, Satan would be a warning horror. Some critics have maintained he should be just that. In reality, however, it is essential to Milton's grand imagining of the journey that we recognize a great deal of ourselves in the fallen consciousness which is Satan. We must sympathize, even identify with Satan; for he is the consciousness in the poem which is most like ours. Unlike the angels or unfallen Adam and Eve, he has the faults, the selfishness, and the aspirations which mark us out as human beings in the world of imperfection and suffering. Some critics have thought Milton so successful here that he overbalanced the poem and made Satan its hero; that in turn is an exaggeration. But Satan (whatever he may be to the theologian) is certainly in imaginative terms a depiction of consciousness torn by contradictions, delusions, touched by a pride more noble as well as more destructive than any pride we know in the human world, a heroic fortitude we can and must admire as well as pity in its desperate hopelessness. Satan is drawn on a larger scale than the human, but for that very reason includes and subsumes in his consciousness all our human complexities and moral confusions. To find the truth of imagination, we must first confront ourselves in our fallen nature, our imperfections, the tangled knot of the self. Paradise will not be truth but an unreal dream unless we begin here in what Yeats called 'the foul rag-and-bone shop of the heart'.

The situation of the fallen Angels in Book I, then, is all too like the situation in which we find ourselves, so that we share the sickening sense of their 'fall' into the depths. Like them we have 'rebelled' – we have asserted our identity, our self, and we cannot go back. We cannot but agree with Mammon in Book II when he contemplates the possibility, if God should allow it:

> Suppose he should relent
> And publish Grace to all, on promise made
> Of new Subjection; with what eyes could we
> Stand in his presence humble, and receive
> Strict Laws impos'd, to celebrate his Throne
> With warbl'd Hymns, and to his Godhead sing
> Forc't Halleluiahs ...

> *(Paradise Lost* II, 237–43)

(That would make us not Christians but followers of Blake's 'Creeping Jesus' or Antichrist.) Though, unlike the damned Angels depicted by Milton, we long to find a way to come once more to God, it must be a way forward not a way back.

Like us, too, the fallen Angels awaken from their stupefying fall to discover an alien world. The theologian's hell may be a metaphysical concept, some 'absolute' state of negation beyond this life; but the dreadful landscape Milton paints is again familiar from human experience. It is indeed the necessary correlative of the consciousness so deeply imagined in the figure of Milton's Satan: a world of alienation, outwardness, death, yet haunted by the suppressed fears of the soul, a world in which man is forever a stranger. Milton depicts in a superb passage the Ahrimanic universe which, when we strip off our customary evasions and face it in its naked intensity, is the counterpart of our conscious separateness:

> Thus roving on
> In confus'd march forlorn, th' adventrous Bands
> With shuddring horror pale, and eyes agast
> Viewd first thir lamentable lot, and found
> No rest: through many a dark and d夜 drearie Vale
> They passd, and many a Region dolorous,
> Ore many a Frozen, many a Fierie Alp,
> Rocks, Caves, Lakes, Fens, Bogs, Dens, and shades of death,
> A Universe of death, which God by curse
> Created evil, for evil only good,
> Where all life dies, death lives, and nature breeds,

Perverse, all monstrous, all prodigious things,
Abominable, inutterable, and worse
Than Fables yet have feignd, or fear conceiv'd,
Gorgons and *Hydras*, and *Chimeras* dire.

(*Paradise Lost* II, 614–28)

However changed in their fall from grace, Satan and his Angels remember vividly their heavenly origin and find themselves agonized strangers in this alien world (Book I, 242ff). Both in awareness of the irreversible step they have taken by seizing their own identity, and in nostalgia for a transcendent reality still strongly felt in the soul, they experience the human condition, and we are at once sympathetic and appalled at the paralysis which afflicts them, trapping them eternally where we as men still hope constantly to be free.

Yet such horrifying outward conditions are in some strange way possible, even desirable for them to accept. They allow Satan's hosts to be what they are; to shirk the still greater horror of confronting their inner corruption and the exertion of spiritual energy needed for that hardest of all efforts, the effort of self-transformation. In the Ahrimanic universe of our twentieth-century science and technology we see this still all too clearly. Many people in modern civilization find themselves more willing to live with outer fear and meaninglessness than to break the taboo of self-confrontation. A fear yet more intense hides man's own nature. A 'happy blindness', the barrier of the unconscious makes possible man's life, renders tolerable his day-to-day existence by diverting his attention outward and away from the '*Gorgons* and *Hydras*, and *Chimeras* dire' and those worse monsters of our thought. The fallen Angels, like many a modern man, are trapped between constricting fears outside and within, and are inclined to an uneasy, restless acceptance of their fate.

There is more of spiritual aspiration, however, in the deeper figure of Satan himself, the central consciousness of the early parts of the poem. Here the full paradox of Milton's imagination strikes us. We see that his Satan includes the spark of Promethean fire, the nobility of man's self-assertion, along with man's failings. He has no trace of half-hearted acceptance; he will risk his whole being, he will fathom the whole depth of his condition first. Therefore he rejects the limitations imposed by fear on his conscious mind. He refuses to become homelessly at home in the alien world. Milton's myth-making power responds to the challenge of self-exploration here with one of its profoundest achievements, which we shall examine in some detail: a journey to the threshold of the unconscious depths. He shows that long before Freud, a poet could handle themes of repression, and the making conscious of the unconscious, with imaginative assurance and truth. Indeed, it can be argued that he achieves a wider resonance in his treatment of the theme than is possible within the framework of modern psychology.

The journey must begin by facing the fact of alienation. There must be no compromise, not even the shadowy caverns and dolorous peaks of a cursed world, but pure loneliness. Satan must 'tempt with wandring feet / The dark unbottomd infinite Abyss', the 'void', the 'abortive gulf'. He must find the courage needed 'to accept / Alone the dreadful voyage' (Book II, 425ff). Blake's visionary heroines, starting with Thel, Shelley's Asia in *Prometheus Unbound*, Goethe's Faust on his way (or rather no way) to seek the Mothers, must likewise begin here and refuse any premature solution, anything short of the required metamorphosis, the transformation of the self.

Satan sets out once more toward the remembered regions of light, then, but is almost immediately confronted with the threshold Powers. There is a threefold Gate, impenetrable, burning 'impal'd with circling fire, / Yet unconsum'd'; and guarding it two figures:

> The one seemd Woman to the waist, and fair,
> But ended foul in many a scaly fold
> Voluminous and vast, a Serpent armd
> With mortal sting: about her middle round
> A cry of Hell Hounds never ceasing barkd
> With wide *Cerberean* mouths full loud, and rung
> A hideous Peal; yet, when they list, would creep,
> If aught disturbed thir noise, into her womb,
> And kennel there, yet there still barkd and howld
> Within unseen.
>
> (*Paradise Lost* II, 650–9)

Who is this hideous shape? As she shortly explains, she is the content of Satan's unconscious mind, and he must recognize her as such if he is to cross the threshold. She reminds Satan how once:

> when at th' Assembly, and in sight
> Of all the Seraphim with thee combin'd
> In bold conspiracy against Heav'ns King,
> All on a sudden miserable pain
> Surpris'd thee, dim thine eyes, and dizzie swumm
> In darkness . . .

(Paradise Lost II, 749–54)

In that momentary lapse of consciousness she was formed, and sprang from Satan's head, like him in shape and countenance, at which all the Angels recoiled and called her 'Sin'. With her Satan has since engaged in a narcissistic, self-regarding sort of love, selfishly desiring himself –

> who full oft
> Thy self in me thy perfet image viewing
> Becam'st enamourd, and such joy thou tookst
> With me in secret, that my womb conceiv'd
> A growing burden.

(Paradise Lost II, 763–7)

Thus unknowingly Satan has begotten an unacknowledged child on his own image, on himself as the object of his selfish desire. And now he confronts her in amazement at the threshold of the void, at the outset of his lonely voyage, barring his way.

She is one aspect of Satan's 'double', his *Doppelgänger*. The other is the shadow of all self-worship or self-love: the fear of one's own extinction, death. 'Death' is the child he has begotten, the secret fear attending on his narcissim:

> The other shape,
> If shape it might be calld that shape had none
> Distinguishable in member, joint or limb,
> Or substance might be calld that shaddow seemd,
> For each seemd either; black it stood as Night,
> Fierce as ten Furies, terrible as Hell,

And shook a dreadful Dart; what seemd his head
That likeness of a Kingly Crown had on ...

(*Paradise Lost* II, 666–73)

And the two aspects of his unconscious, his hidden corruption,
have bred together in turn, each aspect aiding and yet violating the
other. The abortive offspring of these horrors are the dogs creeping
in and out of their mother's womb – powerful images of frustrated
creativity, distorted and suppressed at the threshold of birth, and
so thrust back in 'perpetual agonie and pain'.

Into the hands of the Double have been committed the keys of
the threshold, 'These Gates for ever shut, which none can pass /
Without my op'ning'. The 'Fantasm' of death guards the way. Yet
Satan, by acknowledging his own progeny, is able to persuade the
powers to open the Gates, producing a psychic shock like thunder
or the bursting out of flame from a furnace:

Before thir eyes in sudden view appear
The secrets of the hoarie Deep, a dark
Illimitable Ocean without bound,
Without dimension, where length, bredth, and highth
And time and place are lost ...

(*Paradise Lost* II, 890–4)

They gaze out into the world, or rather the vacuity beyond the
threshold.

What seems at first a boundless darkness and loneliness
gradually reveals the presence of vast energies: a world of
primordial flux. What was hidden in the penumbra of conscious-
ness, like the scene outside the windows of a brightly lit room, and
seemed mere emptiness, Non-Entity, takes shape as a chaos of
conflicting forces, a 'wilde Abyss, / The Womb of nature and
perhaps her Grave'.

Satan now launches upon his journey, undeterred, abandoning
even the ground beneath his feet:

At last his Sail-broad Vanns
He spreads for flight, and in the surging smoke
Uplifted spurns the ground, thence many a League

> As in a cloudy Chair ascending rides
> Audacious, but that seat soon failing, meets
> A vast vacuitie: all unawares
> Fluttering his pennons vain plumb down he drops
> Ten thousand fadom deep . . .

> > > > > (*Paradise Lost* ii, 927–34)

He is battered as if by storm and fire, by elemental forces that threaten to overwhelm consciousness:

> a universal hubbub wilde
> Of stunning sounds and voices all confus'd
> Borne through the hollow dark assaults his ear
> With loudest vehemence . . .

> > > > > (*Paradise Lost* ii, 951–4)

Yet Milton possesses the imaginative strength to grapple with even these tremendous powers, and the chaos slowly clears. Light begins to gleam in the distance; Heaven itself becomes visible; and out of the confusion emerges the primal, unfallen world, shining like a star. The first stage of the initiatory voyage is over.

I call it a voyage of initiation. Nor is this to import notions foreign to Milton's own understanding of his work. For in the invocation to Book iii, the point in the poem at which we have now arrived, the poet makes his claim explicit. On the basis of the imaginative achievement presented in Books i and ii, he ranks himself with Orpheus, the Thracian bard and shamanist who descended into Hell and returned to see the light of day, albeit without rescuing his lost soul, his beloved Eurydice. Milton's mission has indeed been more successful, as he says while contemplating the newly dawned light and the primordial earth, 'Won from the void and formless infinite':

> Thee I revisit now with bolder wing,
> Escap't the *Stygian* Pool, though long detain'd
> In that obscure sojourn, while in my flight
> Through utter and through middle darkness borne
> With other notes than to th' *Orphean* Lyre
> I sung of *Chaos* and *Eternal Night*,

> Taught by the heav'nly Muse to venture down
> The dark descent, and up to reascend,
> Though hard and rare: thee I revisit safe,
> And feel thy sovran vital Lamp.

> (*Paradise Lost* III, 13–22)

Milton presents himself as one who has been down into the realm of the shades and returned to life, an initiate, an Orphic bard who in the power of the Christian muse has been able to achieve all, and more than the pagan seer.

He does not mean that he has literally died, of course, any more than the 'holy Light' he now sees is literal brightness. Milton's physical eyes are 'quencht' (he was completely blind by the time he wrote *Paradise Lost*) but this only draws more attention to the inner light of vision irradiating the mind. And it is by such illumination that Milton claims the authority to speak of 'things invisible to mortal sight' in a poetry of the supersensible.

A further level of vision thus begins to unfold in the poem. The chaos of psychic energies unleashed at the crossing of the threshold has been harmonized, brought into order and beauty by the light of consciousness. The primal world is restored. Properly speaking, it belongs already to a reality hidden from normal vision. If Milton expounds it in imaginations, pictures drawn from sense, it is because of the peculiar character of this world, which is from one point of view the very nature of things which the senses strive to reveal to us, yet to which we and our senses always prove inadequate. Here then it is the image-forming power, the shaping spirit, prior to perception, which is important rather than the specific imagery – strikingly beautiful though many of the pictures may be. Milton draws too on his intuition that spiritual and material need not be opposing truths, for:

> what if Earth
> Be but the shaddow of Heav'n, and things therein
> Each to other like, more than on Earth is thought?

> (*Paradise Lost* V, 574–6)

The question is answered implicitly by the perspective upon Paradise which unfolds before us now: from cosmic distances in

Book III, in closer detail in Book IV; then in Books V–VIII, through the discourses of the archangel Raphael, we gain more insight into the paradisal scheme of things, again on the universal scale. But above all, Milton has succeeded in breaking out of the world of alienation. Paradise is his awakening sense of relatedness, wholeness, fulfilment.

It was Satan's appalling boast that he neither feared nor valued any created thing. In Paradise, contrarily, everything material bears spiritual significance, and man is an integral part of his world. In this respect Milton recovers the old power of creating 'myths' of cosmic significance, and the narrative of *Paradise Lost* can be compared to the myths of ancient cultures. Raphael (who seems to be 'anticipating', as it were, much Hermetic and alchemical thinking) explains that all things are made from the *prima materia*, the substantial unity of being which proceeds, it appears, directly from God:

> O *Adam*, one Almightie is, from whom
> All things proceed, and up to him return,
> If not deprav'd from good, created all
> Such to perfection, one first matter all,
> Indu'd with various forms, various degrees
> Of substance, and in things that live, of life;
> But more refin'd, more spiritous and pure,
> As nearer to him plac't or nearer tending
> Each in thir several active Sphears assignd,
> Till body up to spirit work . . .

> (*Paradise Lost* V, 469–78)

Such easy, gradual transformation of body into spirit had been mentioned before by Raphael, and declared to be no wonder –

>   if by fire
> Of sooty coal th'Empiric Alchimist
> Can turn, or holds it possible to turn
> Mettals of drossiest Ore to perfet Gold
> As from the Mine.

> (*Paradise Lost* V, 439–43)

Yet Raphael takes up a more 'natural' analogy in the present speech, invoking a figure of 'organic' process which was to exert a great fascination on his Romantic successors:

> So from the root
> Springs lighter the green stalk, from thence the leaves
> More aerie, last the bright consummat flowre
> Spirits odorous breathes: flowrs and thir fruit
> Mans nourishment, by gradual scale sublim'd
> To vital Spirits aspire, to animal,
> To intellectual . . .

(*Paradise Lost* v, 479–85)

Hence man and nature appear in constant process of transition to a higher state. Whatever the theoretical background of Raphael's rather esoteric philosophy, it enables Milton to imagine a Paradise where the sensory is constantly turning into the spiritual. Nothing is separate or closed in upon itself; all is conjured out of the protean 'first matter' and grows into higher forms of participation. (Other traditional models are mentioned too – such as the meteorological process where 'of Elements / The grosser feeds the purer', and even, commencing the whole angelic discussion, the model of human digestion: see for the whole passage, Book v, 404ff.)

Hence man may look forward to a kind of evolutionary prospect. Raphael surmises that the

> time may come when men
> With Angels may participate, and find
> No inconvenient Diet, nor too light Fare:
> And from these corporal nutriments perhaps
> Your bodies may at last turn all to Spirit,
> Improv'd by tract of time, and wingd ascend
> Ethereal, as wee, or may at choice
> Here or in Heav'nly Paradises dwell.

(*Paradise Lost* v, 493–500)

For a similar process is happening all around Adam and Eve. It would be mistaken to suppose, however, that their leisure is occupied by contemplations of the theoretical future. Paradise is

essentially fulfilment, and its essence is present actuality indeed, a
fullness of presence denied in our ordinary, 'fallen' world.

More than anything else, Paradise is desire fulfilled just as the
outsider-consciousness of Hell is desire frustrated. The governing
metaphor is that of Adam and Eve 'Imparadis't in one anothers
arms' (Book IV, 506), as they appear surrounded by the gambolling
beasts of the earth:

> the lovliest pair
> That ever since in loves imbraces met.

Paradise is the half-remembered state of sexual totality we spend
our lives and relationships striving to re-achieve. Milton's initia-
tory journey, and confrontation with his own unconscious imagi-
nation, has enabled him to picture this primal sexuality with
extraordinary power. Nature itself overflows in Paradise with a
sexual exuberance, making it:

> A Wilderness of sweets; for Nature here
> Wantond as in her prime, and playd at will
> Her Virgin Fancies, pouring forth more sweet,
> Wilde above rule or art; enormous bliss.

> (*Paradise Lost* V, 294–7)

Paradise is an inner state, and also a mode of perception, a higher
vision; it is Blake's world of 'Beulah', 'Where Sexes wander in
dreams of bliss among the Emanations', and corresponds to the
desire-world or world of images described by earlier visionaries.
All knowledge in Milton's Paradise is close to sexual knowledge.
Adam's discourses to Eve are intermixed with grateful 'digres-
sions', solving 'high dispute / With conjugal Caresses'. And there
are hints that Milton may have intuited a kind of cosmic–sexual
polarity when he reflected on the possibility of other worlds:

> and other Suns perhaps
> With thir attendant Moons thou wilt descrie
> Communicating Male and Femal Light,
> Which two great Sexes animate the World.

> (*Paradise Lost* VIII, 148–51)

The whole phenomenal world is visible only through the combination of active luminosity ('male' light) and passive ('female') reflectivity, and Milton seems to propose that the polarity may be part of a still deeper one. Man's apprehension in Paradise, at any rate, is marked by that peculiar openness and sensitivity we have when we see the world in the company of our beloved, just as his ordinary perception has an intensity known to most adults only in sexual experience.

On the level of the story, Milton's imagined Paradise is a lost world at the beginning of history. But on the level of the 'inner journey', Paradise is a vision obtained through the working-out of those inner struggles at the threshold of the Abyss, the initiatory encounter with the content of the unconscious psyche. The themes flow out of that encounter directly. Satan saw the product of his narcissistic love, turned back upon itself, in the figure of Sin, his own female likeness. Narcissism is projected in Milton's imagination of Eve, too (Book IV, 449–69), who sees her own image in the 'watry gleam' on her first awakening; and, as she says, 'there I had fixt / Mine eyes till now, and pin'd with vain desire' – had it not been for the mysterious voice, a warning from the invisible heights or depths, 'What there thou seest fair Creature is thy self'. Paradise is affirmed in Milton's imagination through the conducting of the energies of love to their original channels, linking man to his world. The 'love-dimension' of the imagination is opened up, as the self-obsession hidden below the apparent objectivity of the onlooker-consciousness is overcome. A balance is obtained in the warning voice of self-recognition, and love is directed first to Adam and through him to God and to the divinely revealed creation.

It is in the light of that redirected force within the psyche, indeed, that the world appears as Paradise. With deep insight, Milton further describes how even contact with the other, with the 'manly grace' of Adam, is not sufficient to turn desire of itself from self-regard. Eve almost returns to the softer beauty of her own reflected image. Her own passion must be integrated into something greater, a wisdom beyond her own desires, and so incorporated into a larger design, before it can reach its true fulfilment. Adam recalls her, with the profound paradox of human relations expressed in the terms of the biblical myth: that in loving him she will find her own 'Substantial Life', as each of us must discover our own deepest selves not in isolation but in the giving of ourselves to another, to others or to the world itself around us and from which we come into being. Such is the 'necessary narcissism', the self-discovery which is also self-transcendence, which makes Milton's vision of Paradise. Through it, man approaches the state he imagines for his Angels, whose perception is the exact opposite of the onlooker's world-view. They do not stand, detached and alien, but give themselves entirely to the being of the perceived, or to the content of the thought, or the feeling:

> All Heart they live, all Head, all Eye, all Ear,
> All Intellect, all Sense . . .

> (*Paradise Lost* VI, 350–1)

They live in constant transformation, free from the rigidities of the selfhood.

Milton grasps the truth which has slowly come to be understood by much modern thought: inner changes also give us new visions of the world, new ways of seeing. The confrontation at the threshold leads to the imaginative liberation of Paradise: not only self-knowledge but also new insight into the world around, the ability to enter deeply into the world through a redirected power of love.

If Milton were D. H. Lawrence, Paradise would be the furthest reach of imagination, and man's sexual integration would be seen as his ultimate fulfilment. But Milton aspires much higher in his poetic 'flight'. Like Blake, he is convinced that the roots of man's being lie deeper than the sexual, just as much as they lie beyond the separateness of his ordinary conscious mind. One part of the confrontation at the threshold has been worked through. There remains, however, the dreadful shadow: death, or the terror of death.

Milton commences Book IX with an abrupt modulation. The opening 'No more . . .' prepares us for the shift in tone: 'I now must change / Those Notes to Tragic'. Rudolf Steiner, describing the stages of initiation-experience, characterizes the vision of the world of images, the first stage, as extraordinarily blissful. It 'is accompanied by an intense feeling of happiness; the flooding of the entire image-world by such an inward, wonderfully pleasurable feeling is man's first higher experience'. We might compare it with Milton's imagination of Paradise. But Steiner further describes stages of deeper awakening, leading in a fuller sense to the knowledge of a spiritual world. We have the feeling of standing 'on the shore of existence' and behold – or rather, 'hear' in a way somehow analogous to music – a reality beyond that of images, which are expunged from our consciousness. With this achievement of an 'empty' consciousness, moreover, 'what I have characterized as an inwardly experienced and all-embracing, cosmic feeling of happiness gives way to an equally all-embracing pain. We feel that the world is founded upon cosmic suffering.'*

At this point in *Paradise Lost*, therefore, we may again see a new level of vision beginning to unfold. It is an expression now of cosmic suffering, or (if I may borrow a phrase from T. S. Eliot) of 'tragic clairvoyance'. What on the level of plot is rendered in the loss of Paradise enables Milton, on the level of the inner journey, to attain new depths of human insight, a new perspective or dimension of poetic insight.

If man did not delve more profoundly within himself than the vision of Paradise, he would become (and perhaps remain) a blissful innocent: open to the wonders of nature, but living in a sort of second infancy. The 'tragic' turn of events in Books IX and X of *Paradise Lost* gives rise to a poetry more sombre than that of the preceding parts, but also more adult. The terrible emotions which stir in the hearts of the wrangling Adam and Eve (Book IX, 1067ff) are painful, but at the same time give them, for us, the mature depth of character which otherwise we can find in the poem only in the figure of Satan. Our 'first Parents' lose Paradise; but they also grow in stature. Indeed, Adam himself will shortly assimilate his own case to that of the fallen Archangel ('To *Satan* only like both crime and doom'), and if he shares something of Satan's tortured inner complexity, he is also touched by some of his heroic greatness and radical aspirations. Milton begins here to draw some of his threads together, and achieves a poetry that is more strikingly 'modern' than much of Romanticism, and speaks to us more directly nowadays than many more recent poets.

Adam finally emerges, especially in the great soliloquies of Book X, as a consciousness able to confront the imperfections and contradictions, the savage ironies of the human condition as well as its paradisal simplicities. Above all, he wrestles with the fact of death. Indeed, Sin and Death, revealed to imagination as the powers of the threshold, normally suppressed because we have

*Rudolf Steiner, *The Evolution of Consciousness* (London, 1966) pp. 29, 31.

not the strength to wrestle with and transform them, now mytho-
logically 'bridge over' the great divide. Man must face a world in
which corruption and finitude have a part. He must face his own
transience, and more than that: the irony of his death hanging over
him even while he is granted life. Even when he has accepted
death, Adam is appalled by this grim prospect:

> Be it so, for I submit, his doom is fair,
> That dust I am, and shall to dust return:
> O welcom hour whenever! why delayes
> His hand to execute what his Decree
> Fixd on this day? why do I overlive,
> Why am I mockt with death, and lengthend out
> To deathless pain? how gladly would I meet
> Mortalitie my sentence, and be Earth
> Insensible, how glad would lay me down
> As in my Mothers lap! there I should rest
> And sleep secure; his dreadful voice no more
> Would Thunder in my ears, no fear of worse
> To mee and to my offspring would torment me
> With cruel expectation.

(*Paradise Lost* x, 769–82)

Yet such is the very condition of human self-consciousness. The
animals may live without awareness that they will one day die, but
man cannot escape that knowledge. Accordingly, he must find the
strength to live with it – or suppress it once more, retreat into the
Hell of surface-consciousness, the fear and loneliness which the
inner journey aspires to transcend.

Adam finds the sources of that strength within him, just as he
finds the strength for reconciliation with Eve. No doubt most of us
remember the 'paradise' stage of a love-relationship; and most of
us know that the period following it brings many difficulties as
well as unalloyed delights, but that the survival of the relationship
represents not a loss but a deepening of adult love. These patterns
of life underlie the deepening of the poetry in Books IX and X, and
Milton sees further into the human heart than in the parts which
preceded, paradisal though they were. He comes to grips with the
greatest problems of the human condition: not only those of love
and the fear of death, but the moral riddle of man's responsibility

in a world he can only imperfectly control. It is a moral delusion to suppose, after all, that we can be responsible for our own acts and not impinge on the freedom of others. Such responsibility, simply for ourselves, most people could cheerfully accept. The difficulty of life consists in the fact that (unless one is a total recluse of self-sufficient means) the ripples of action spread outward from each of us to affect other moral beings. Even the best intentions have to be actualized in an imperfect world, and may well produce evil as well as good – indeed must always produce some mixture of the two. This is the problem which brings Shelley to the verge of despair in *The Triumph of Life*: the problem of 'why God made irreconcilable / Good and the means of good'. So it is for Adam, too. He cannot console himself that his act has condemned himself alone, nor is death just his individual end:

> Ay me, that fear
> Comes thundering back with dreadful revolution
> On my defenceless head; both Death and I
> Am found Eternal, and incorporate both,
> Nor I on my part single, in mee all
> Posteritie stands curst: Fair Patrimonie
> That I must leave ye, Sons; O were I able
> To waste it all my self, and leave ye none!
> So disinherited how would ye bless
> Mee now your Curse!

(Paradise Lost x, 813–22)

The moral effects of our deeds follow to infinity, and yet we must take responsibility as finite beings subject to death and change. There is a great temptation here to shift the blame onto God, to retreat from difficult moral awareness. But this retreat too Adam withstands, and survives however precariously against the back-drop of the hopelessness and powerlessness he feels as he confronts the world. He survives, that is, as a human 'ego', intensely self-aware and bearing the existential burdens that are the conditions of man's self-awareness.

Oddly, then, we can say that Adam successfully resists tempta-tions, though on the level of the story it is his fall into temptation which is described as the catastrophe of the 'Fall' for man and the world! Milton grows in poetic stature and in profundity, entering upon that third level of vision in the 'tragic' part of his poem. Yet once more the poem comes up against barriers of knowledge. In the final analysis the human consciousness represented by Adam wins survival only at so great a cost that he lives in a kind of moral paralysis.

He can bear the loss of paradisal delights with Eve; he can resist the reduction of life to absurdity by the fear of death, and face the infinity of the consequences of his act – 'That burden heavier than the Earth to bear, / Than all the World much heavier'. But his energy is thereby exhausted. He has nothing left over. He has won the strength to be, but has no reserves of creativity, no power to project his future or to shape a positive meaning for his existence.

Now the 'Fall', resulting in the human condition we live in, is a teaching common to Judaism and Christianity. (It has analogies in other religions, too, though sometimes having a rather different interpretation.) Both Judaism and Christianity foster a certain self-consciousness, attribute to man a certain right of autonomy and moral freedom – differing in this respect from the cosmic religions of the Far East, for which the individual ego is an 'illusion', an obstacle on the path. Both Judaism and Christianity acknowledge the burdens with which Milton's Adam has to come to terms; and both are implicitly aware of the paralysis, as I have called it, which besets the conscious self in bearing them.

For both of them supply that future projection, or super-added power needed to give positive significance to life, beyond mere existential strength. At the same time, there is a profound difference between them. Judaism accords man the power to move forward by offering him a hope: and articulates that hope through the doctrine of God's 'covenant' with man, through the ideal of 'righteousness', and in the expectation of the future Messiah. If man's consciousness does not possess the power of conferring meaning on life, then, now and actually, yet for Judaism human life moves on through history toward a revelation of meaning, and so transcends the paralysis of the conscious self in its mere self-assertion.

Christianity, on the other hand, introduces a radically different perspective. For it grasps that expected revelation of meaning in the Mystery of Golgotha, in an event of human history which has already taken place! One way of interpreting this is to say that for Christianity man's conscious self does indeed possess, historically and actually, the power of creativity, the energy to project a positive future. Small wonder that the catastrophe which originated man's 'fallen' condition, and far more importantly opened the way to this conferring of meaning, should be for many Christian thinkers the 'fortunate Fall' (*felix culpa*)! Seen on the level of the history of human consciousness, Christianity marked an immense step forward, in that self-consciousness was for the first time endowed with the energy to create its own significance, to be radically free.

Milton is not unaware of the Christian consciousness. Indeed he embarks, in the final two Books of *Paradise Lost*, on a further stage of vision, a fourth and still higher perspective releasing the poem into forward movement once more. Such a level of vision should reveal the very essence of man in his freedom and his inherent divinity – if so we may call his participation in the nature of Being in the world and history. It should lead beyond even the purities of Eden, and tragic necessity, toward that 'paradise within thee, happier farr', man's harmony with his own inmost self.

Yet it is the most disappointing part of the whole poem. Michael's revelation of Christ in prophetic vision to Adam on the mount has little of the human urgency we know from Books IX and X, nor the angelic harmony of Raphael's discourses in Paradise; Books XI and XII of Milton's epic are perhaps the least remembered and least re-read.

Why is it that Milton fails to realize this fourth level of vision in his poem? The question must be seen in connection with other imperfections in Milton's poem.

For it must be said that, despite his genius, the poet's achievement in *Paradise Lost* is decidedly uneven. The difficulties and lapses of style have been harped upon by so many hostile critics over the years that I do not think it worth rehearsing them again. The significant ones (other than minor contradictions, that is, or inadequacies in the execution of scenes in Heaven, apparent failures in God's omniscience, etc.) are those suggesting a certain ambivalence or unresolved tension in Milton's consciousness. The Romantics first drew attention to these, and many more recent critics have detected a contradiction between the surface level and the 'deep' meaning of the work. A similar result emerges from our temporary dissociation of the narrative level from the level of the 'inner journey' undergone by the poet. If we now look again at the poem in its unity, we cannot but remark that the narrative Milton developed in order to articulate his imagination of the 'journey' is strikingly inadequate at several points to his purpose – or better said, to the energies of his imagination.

It is a little odd that he can fulfil his theme of aspiration in the opening books, the descent into the underworld and confrontation at the threshold, only through the figure of Satan, for example. It seems that the aspiration to burst out of the world of 'outness', of alienation, though affirmed as Orphic and regenerative by his imagination, was regarded in many aspects by Milton's more superficial, narrative-making mind as 'demonic'. To the extent that Milton's imagination actually realizes itself through this aspiration, Blake was certainly right in declaring Milton to have been 'a true Poet and of the Devil's party without knowing it'; we shall make further analyses to a broadly similar effect in the next chapter. Here we need only mention the important analogue of the Faust-theme: Faust's aspiration to deeper knowledge likewise appears first in literature under the guise of a 'Satanic' pursuit.

Marlowe, in his *Doctor Faustus*, still felt that the human self could not bear the burdens and vastly increased potentialities of the consciousness he grasped at. The soul of such an aspirer, he suggests, would disintegrate and be torn apart by the forces of egotism and sensuality. Only later, in the evolution of the tradition, culminating in Goethe's mammoth *Faust*, does it become clear that Faust's longing is the central theme of modern consciousness. The deeper meaning of the Faust-legend is the possibility of man's unfolding an inner strength, a self-awareness that is able to hold these powers in its reins, to advance to new levels of knowledge and imagination through inner striving.

Milton's imagination, then, accepts the Faustian aspiration with which Satan is imbued in Books I and II, though his reasoning and doubting mind misgives. But a consequence of the disparity is that Milton does not manage to unite himself fully with his theme. The stages of the inner journey unfold, but in the imagery of the poem they fall apart into several *personae*: Satan; the 'imparadis't' Adam and Eve; fallen man; then Michael (as the bearer of the visionary, forward-looking faculty which Adam does not possess for himself). Milton cannot hold all these together as aspects of a unified imaginative self. Hence in Blake's profounder treatment of the elder poet's work, not the famous aphorisms from the *Marriage of Heaven and Hell* but in his *Milton, A Poem,* it turns out to be the case that Milton's 'journey' must be undertaken again. Despite Milton's conclusive enthronement in his own version of 'heaven' by the time the Blakean treatment begins, he realizes that he has not succeeded in transforming, in bringing with him, essential aspects of his being; his 'Emanation', as Blake calls those aspects, still lies 'scatter'd thro' the deep / In torment'. He must descend again into 'Eternal Death' to redeem his lost self.

Blake saw clearly enough that Milton's problem lay in the relationship of his conscious mind to the energies of imagination. But his solution in *Milton, A Poem* is a quintessentially Blakean one, based upon the Gnostic vision which we shall characterize later in this book. He disposed of the problem, and united the severed aspects of Milton's soul; but he did not retain that important self-consciousness, the maturity of intense self-knowledge achieved by Milton's fallen Adam. Blake's is another route, less concerned with man's consciousness but reaching his deeper mind through dream and vision, the mystery of symbols. He freed the self from the paralysis investing Milton's Adam, it is true; but he also sacrificed something in Milton's imagination which is of unique interest to modern man.

Milton's failure to achieve the final, 'apocalyptic' movement of *Paradise Lost* may be related, then, to a lack of integration between the elements of his mind. Unlike Blake, or Shelley, he does not come to the point of proclaiming his apocalypse, or transfiguration of the world in visionary imagination. It is a telling moment at which he wishes to insert himself into the poem directly, and so to possess an apocalyptic voice, and yet can only announce his inability to do so:

> O for that warning voice, which he who saw
> Th' *Apocalyps*, heard cry in Heaven aloud . . .

> (*Paradise Lost* IV, 1–2)

We may put Milton's 'lack of integration' another way. He did not achieve that kind of balance of forces which constitutes fully the 'truth of imagination'. The structure of consciousness he tried to project imaginatively was not quite attained. And yet, by some magic or miracle of the imagination itself, he does achieve it: in the last, haunting paragraphs of the poem we do suddenly hear the music of that ultimate vision in the quiet mixture, the inner complexity of suffering and hope and love as our first parents are ushered out of Paradise.

How could all these forms of the imagination be more thoroughly unified? How could the apocalypse be achieved? These were questions which the Romantics took up. But their visionary awakening can hardly be understood at all without a knowledge of their great forerunner and guide in the exploring of inner worlds, John Milton.

3

Milton's Christianity and the Birth of the Ego

Reading Milton's *Paradise Lost* in the way we have attempted to describe can be a profoundly imaginative experience: a descent into the inner depths and a process of self-renewal undertaken by the poet in his own person, but a journey that can be echoed in every individual. Milton is our guide on an astonishing spiritual journey, a hierophant who can conduct us on our perilous descent into the underworld:

> Taught by the heav'nly Muse to venture down
> The dark descent, and up to reascend,
> Though hard and rare ...

His 'heav'nly Muse' – we may gloss her, to begin with at least, as the imagination itself, the source of inspiration within him – has shown him also the vision of Paradise, and even the realms of 'Eternal wisdom', compensating his outward blindness with the apprehension of 'things invisible to mortal sight':

> Up led by thee
> Into the Heav'n of Heav'ns I have presum'd,
> An Earthlie Guest, and drawn Empyreal Air.

Like the initiates, the seers and prophets of old, Milton has been in Hell and Heaven, and claims the authority of the inspired bard. He is not retelling stories known from the Bible and concerned with the prehistoric past, but powerfully recreating his own spiritual experience. When he addresses his creative faculty with the famous words, 'fit audience find, though few', it is scarcely any exaggeration to say that Milton is envisaging the foundation of a band of *illuminati*, an esoteric readership of those who have seen and understood – who have shared in his inner struggles and won through to his own profundity of vision.

Yet it is at the moments when he comes closest to proclaiming his authority as seer and hierophant, in those characteristic personal 'asides' which interrupt the narrative of *Paradise Lost*, that Milton is most attacked by doubts and uncertainties. He has aspired to ascend into Heaven in the power of his conscious imagination. But he also disturbingly recalls those legends of others who aspired and were cast down for their pride and importunity. He has become a modern Orpheus (the 'Thracian Bard'), an initiator in the Mysteries. But there intrudes upon his reflections

> the barbarous dissonance
> Of *Bacchus* and his revellers, the Race
> Of that wilde Rout that tore the *Thracian* Bard
> In *Rhodope*, where Woods and Rocks had Eares
> To rapture, till the savage clamor drownd
> Both Harp and Voice; nor could the Muse defend
> Her Son. So fail not thou, who thee implores:
> For thou art Heav'nlie, shee an empty dream.
>
> (*Paradise Lost* VII, 32–9)

Of course, he can conclude, his Christian imagination has a grasp on the truth which was not available to the Thracian Orpheus and the pagan 'dream'. Nevertheless, a note of uncertainty has been sounded, and the address to the creative power swings suddenly away from the authoritative to an 'imploring' call for defence against the barbarous and dissonant world.

It seems as though Milton cannot feel total confidence in the vision he himself has expressed in such potent imagery and language. There remains a lurking fear that the 'truth of imagination' may turn out to be 'an empty dream'. Put slightly differently: Milton cannot quite believe in the power of man – the ego, the human individuality – to fulfil the high role his imagination has shaped for him in the highest flights of his visionary poem. He does not wholly believe that man's ego can take upon itself such enormous responsibility as goes with such aspiration. The temptations to selfish pride and monstrous egotism, a part of him feels, would be too great. Whoever attempted it might well be cast down by an offended Deity, or be torn to pieces by the psychic forces he had unleashed, as in the Orphic legend.

Milton may be compared here with the attitude of Marlowe in his portrayal of *Doctor Faustus*: Marlowe's hero likewise aspired to an imaginative glory, to knowledge and power beyond the normal bounds of humanity, and in the end he cannot control the cosmic forces or use them for his final good. He is destroyed at the end of the play by the energies he tried to manipulate for his selfish pleasures, swept out of the reach of the divine into that state of inner estrangement (emphatically not a place, but a psychic condition) called Hell. At the same time, however, Marlowe is stirred in his psychic depths to imaginative sympathy with his character's Faustian aspirations. That is why he wrote the play, and why it has so great an imaginative impact, why it does not strike us for an instant as a piece of moralizing.

In Milton's case we must say that imaginative aspiration was still closer to the poet's inmost heart, for it is a theme he developed not for a fictional character, but for himself as a poet. Yet he too still fears the destructive psychic consequences of following in the path his imagination has blazoned for him. He feels contradictory emotions when he brings most clearly before himself the Faustian role into which he finds himself stepping. Before we go any further, it may be worth noting that in expressing his real doubts, Milton is only being honest. And honesty is no mean virtue in an area where nothing is easier than to sweep under the carpet actual complexities and anomalies of man's nature, to set oneself up as a prophet or a hierophant. And this Milton will not do, because of his commitment to the 'truth' of poetry.

Nevertheless, there is certainly a lurking contradiction in Milton's poetic vision – not just an intellectual contradiction, but a real, a 'lived' contradiction. And on one level it corresponds to the conflict between Milton's own immensely creative imagination and the image of man which Milton inherited from traditional, mediaeval Christianity. Despite the inner power he feels, Milton cannot yet free himself from the limitations imposed on him by his acceptance of the older Christian view of man's creaturely weakness, inherited in turn from the Old Testament. For centuries, man had been seen as prone to sinfulness, essentially dependent and unable to determine his own being: he could attain to 'salvation' only through obeying the dictates of Society, embodying justice and sovereignty, or above all the special society of the Church, the guardian of revealed truth. But in the awakening consciousness of the Renaissance and Reformation, in the arts and in religion, in spirits such as Shakespeare, Marlowe and Milton himself, we see something new breaking in. A new sense of man's intrinsic value and power, his uniqueness and moral capacity for self-determination expresses itself in imaginative figures like Faustus, and even more profoundly in the poetry of *Paradise Lost*, though it is still struggling to free and define itself.

In fact, the sense of infinite potentiality which man started to feel and embody in imagination was something qualitatively unprecedented, new in the whole history of man's evolving consciousness. For although in the ancient world it had been possible to have the kind of intense imaginative experiences that lead to inner transformation – 'initiatory' experiences like those offered in the Mysteries, with their great cosmic symbols and daunting ordeals – these had not been undertaken with the kind of self-consciousness we find in Milton's time. Imaginative intensity had been achieved at the expense of the conscious self, by dimming self-awareness to a dream-like level, or in altered states (ecstasy, trance). The soul emerged from the experience 'reborn', transfigured: but the initiates described the process in terms of cosmic myth, in impersonal images that echoed from the primordial past, not as the discovery of individual freedom. Milton attains to the power of the mythical in his great imagination of *Paradise Lost*, but there it is equally clear that the loss of Paradise was also man's finding of himself, the discovery of his individual capacity of right and wrong – and that Milton feels in his heart of hearts that much was gained.

In the cosmic imaginations, the myths and ritual enactments of the ancient world, vivid pictures blotted out ordinary self-awareness. And with self-awareness went also the usual consciousness we have of the 'objective' world, the universe of things spread out around us in space and time. The greater reality of the myth asserted a timeless time and created its own space: the primal happenings of creation could be caught again in the telling of the story, or re-actualized in the procedures of ritual. Milton resists that fading out of self-consciousness, and holds of the modern sense of self. He wishes to attain to the supreme imagining which includes his own self, not that denies it. But following the insights of Rudolf Steiner, we may begin to understand the anomalies and contradictions of Milton's vision if we take further the realization that self-consciousness is bound up with our relationship to the objective world, the universe of things.

It was one of the most important insights of Rudolf Steiner's

Geisteswissenschaft that consciousness depends on a certain tension, a dynamic equilibrium, between those psychic tendencies which bring about our submission to external reality, making us passive receivers of impressions from without, and those which draw us into ourselves, into self-absorption, which if given sufficient rein may become a mystical turning of the gaze within. If either of these elemental tendencies grows too strong, it will threaten to disrupt our normal consciousness of self and world. The first will become an Ahrimanic subjection of man to external forces, an enslavement of his spirit and the reduction of man to an automaton. The second will become a Luciferic absorption, where all boundaries blur, and man has the nebulous illusion that he himself has become everything, and his ego, his self, nothing. But in the rhythmic balance of these powers that makes up man's rich life of perception and thought, impression and contemplation, lies the play of consciousness.

If, therefore, Milton seems to have foundered upon inner contradictions between imaginative urge and his actual estimate of man's nature, one might well suspect – even if we did not possess Steiner's critical thoughts on the subject – that it is because he has failed to find a proper equilibrium between these polar energies within the greater world his imagination has opened up. For it is on the establishing of such equilibrium that the preservation of the conscious self in extended conditions of vision depends.

Now it is just along these lines that the Romantic poet–critics of the late eighteenth and nineteenth centuries were beginning to think when they tried to account for the shortcomings which they too experienced in Milton's poetry. For indeed, from one point of view the Romantic movement can best be seen as the attempt by a generation of brilliant poets to rewrite *Paradise Lost* and to give its themes their true value. Above all, Blake and Shelley tried to effect a reorientation in English poetry while taking up Milton's challenge and promise; and the same is true in different ways of Wordsworth and Keats. Blake and Shelley have also left us their explicit comments on the Miltonic original, and it will be interesting to consider these along with the remarks of Rudolf Steiner.

The Romantics saw Milton's problem in their own terms, and from the standpoint of their own poetic aims. In effect they draw attention to what prevents Milton from yet being, in his age, a Romantic poet. One aspect on which they seized, as especially revealing, was Milton's choice of Satan to be the central character (the Hero, according to Shelley) at least of the earlier part of his poem. And in truth it surely is significant, in view of what we have said about the ambiguities in Milton's attitude to the role for the self shaped by this imagination, that he chose to write about the figure who in the Bible story aspired to the status of divinity, and was cast down by God. Milton chose the figure of Lucifer from the myth, as we have seen, to embody his imagination of man's fallen self. What the Romantics noticed was that Milton seemed to have too much poetic sympathy with Satan and his heavenward aspirations, and so involved the reader in disturbing and tangled reflections on the moral issues which interfered with the deeper experience of the poem.

Like Blake, the philosopher William Godwin and others among his contemporaries, Shelley found Milton's Devil in considerable likelihood of stealing the interest of the poem from Milton's God and Messiah. Satan possesses courage, majesty, 'firm and patient opposition to omnipotent force', Shelley wrote, but there are also those 'taints of ambition, envy, revenge, and a desire for personal aggrandisement, which, in the Hero of *Paradise Lost*, interfere' – so Shelley claims – 'with the interest.' He accused Milton of blurring rather than clarifying the moral issues:

> The character of Satan engenders in the mind a pernicious casuistry which leads us to weigh his faults with his wrongs, and to excuse the former because the latter exceed all measure. In the minds of those who consider that magnificient fiction with a religious feeling it engenders something worse . . .

Blake's views were even more clear-cut. Having little time for the deliberating, conscious ego, Blake thought that a real poet would value the intense imaginative energies represented in Milton's Satan. He took Milton's choice of Satan to feature centrally in the poem to prove that, 'without knowing it', Milton was precisely such a Blakean 'true poet'; and that his attempt to present the values of consciousness in the poem was the mistake which introduced the inner contradictions. Critics ever since Shelley and Blake have debated whether Milton could really have been of the Devil's party without knowing it; but their energies have been, I think, largely misplaced, since they did not see that a significant change has come about between the time of Milton and the time of Shelley. That change sees the completion of a shift in the prevailing sense of the self.

Both Blake and Shelley are thoroughly on the side of the imagination, and both detect that Milton was not entirely able to be so, despite the tremendous imaginative vitality he demonstrated in his poetry. Blake thinks it would be best to give full rein to the Luciferic aspiration of Satan, because in essence, as we shall discover, Blake thinks that any weapon is justifiable to fight against the Ahrimanic, against the vision of man's alienation. Shelley is more subtle and internally complex: he wishes, at the same time as fighting against alienation and for man's imaginative life, to resist the moral dangers, the diabolical 'casuistry' which may corrupt the soul. He wishes to retain his conscious, discriminating self amidst the intensities of the imagination in its projection of man's hopes, fears and secret dreams. He therefore wants to set Milton right by correcting what seems to him unclear and unbalanced in Milton's own attempt.

These and similar thoughts on consciousness and the imagination were taken further by Rudolf Steiner, in a course of lectures on the themes of apocalypse: particularly on those we associate with the great imagination of Michael warring against the dragon in the Book of Revelation. He adds a further dimension to the discussion by pointing out that there is one place already in the history of consciousness where we find the type of balance between spiritual powers, the kind of imaginative self-consciousness that Milton is struggling for: in early Christianity itself. We find it later, too, in various 'esoteric' forms of Christianity with which Milton might conceivably have been in touch. Christianity became many different things in the course of its centuries-long development. Besides the Christianity which leaned heavily on the Old Testament, with its doctrine of man as utterly dependent in his creaturely weakness on the goodness of God, there had from the beginning been a strain in Christianity which stressed that through Christ, through God becoming man, man had transcended this abject state. In Clement of Alexandria, Athanasius, Irenaeus and other pioneers of early theology, we find it stated that:

Christ became as we are, in order that we may become as he is.

They spoke of the 'divinization' of man which the coming of Christ had rendered possible. And some of them, notably Clement of Alexandria, understood a good deal about the balance of forces that must be attained in the human soul if man is to go forward in

the Christian spirit without succumbing to the huge additional
dangers and responsibilities that attend such an undertaking. He
spoke of the perilous course between the 'devil of sheer power'
and the 'devil of subtle deceit', and the way through which had
been shown by the incarnation of the Word.

Closer to Milton's own time, the Rosicrucians who mysteriously
addressed the world in a series of pamphlets outlining new ways
in religion and science in the early seventeenth century, developed
the concept of the spiritual as a balance between contrary cosmic
forces. Using a terminology derived from alchemy, like Jacob
Boehme and other Christian mystics and theosophers, they saw
what was called the *mercurius* as the principle of freedom, as the
middle essence between the dissipating, expansive power called
sulphur and the contracting, densifying tendency they called *sal*.
By these names they did not at all designate the common
substances mercury, sulphur and salt, but purely dynamic poten-
cies, existing in all nature and in the human soul. If man was to
achieve the 'Great Work' of inner transformation which was the
real goal of mysticism and alchemy, he had to establish a 'mercu-
rial' equilibrium, and resist the one-sided tendencies toward
Luciferic expansion or Ahrimanic contraction. It seems quite likely
that Milton had studied and sympathized with some of the
Rosicrucians, notably the encyclopaedic writer Robert Fludd who
did so much to establish Rosicrucian ideas in England, and from
them derived some of the esoteric elements in his imaginings of
Heaven and Hell.

It was this 'esoteric' strain in Christianity which Steiner saw as
alone fully compatible with the spiritual demands of modern self-
consciousness. Indeed, no imagination of the divine or of the
Christ can satisfy modern consciousness, he stressed, unless it
achieves this enabling balance of opposing psychic forces and
establishes a 'third way' between the Luciferic and Ahrimanic
polarities. In his lectures Steiner repeatedly emphasized that it was
impossible to find a genuine concept of free self-consciousness, i.e.
the full realization of man's moral capabilities, within the frame-
work of an imaginative duality. A triadic structure was necessary,
so that a real equilibrium could be established, involving opposing
powers and a course of inner balance.

Employing our own terminology, we may say we have to deal
with three main factors in the nature of things: namely the

Luciferic, representing one end of the balance; the Ahrimanic, representing the other; and the state of equilibrium which stands for the Christ-impulse.

To be fully human in the modern sense, as a self-conscious being, man must orientate himself harmoniously toward all these psychic co-ordinates – something that was achieved in different ways, Steiner says, in the great myths and religions, but which is often inadequately conceived in the imaginative works of modern times. He criticizes the lack of clarity, for example in *Faust*, in the representation of Goethe's daemon Mephistopheles.

Then he turns specifically to Milton. (We need not here concern ourselves with his additional strictures on *Der Messias*, by 'the German Milton', Klopstock.) Steiner takes Milton to task on one of the very same points as Blake. 'Milton', wrote Blake, 'wrote in fetters when he wrote of Angels & God'. And that is the essence of Steiner's charge: the inadequate imagination of the Divine conveyed by Milton's poem. Blake detected intuitively that this had to do with an 'inversion' of values in *Paradise Lost*, and it led him as we have seen to his theory that Milton was 'of the Devil's party without knowing it'. Steiner's analysis is a little more complex, though it too depends on something like an 'inversion', or recognition of a distorted alignment of values. The inadequacy springs, he suggests, from failure to meet the requirements of the modern consciousness, the ego which has developed in the course of man's evolution, which looks to the Divine for the source of its free moral activity. This is incompatible with the cruder dualism which has infected the moral perspective of the epic:

In respect of those beings which are to be regarded, in relation to ourselves, as divine – we only have the right sense of and feeling for them in so far as we conceive them to effect an equilibrium between the Luciferic and Ahrimanic principles. We can never have the right feeling of the Divine unless we enter into this threefold structure. In Milton's *Paradise Lost*, however . . . there is no real grasp of a triadic constellation in the world, but instead there is the conflict between the supposed Good and the supposed Evil, Heaven and Hell. The misleading duality is imported into man's spiritual evolution, the illusory contrast of Heaven and Hell rooted in the popular consciousness . . . It is of no avail that Milton and Klopstock designate their heavenly

beings 'divine'; they would only be so for man if they were
conceived within the threefold structure of things; then it would
be possible to describe the conflict of Good and Evil. But with the
assumption of a duality, one constituent receives the attributes
of the Good and a name drawn from the Divine, and the other
stands for the Diabolical, the anti-Divine.

The significance of this is nothing less than the deposition of
the Divine from consciousness, and the usurping of the name of
the Divine by the Luciferic principle. Thus we have in reality a
conflict between Lucifer and Ahriman. However, Ahriman is
endowed with Luciferic attributes, and the realm of Lucifer with
the attributes of the Divine.

You see how far-reaching are the consequences which such
reflections reveal. People believe that in the contrasts depicted in
Milton's *Paradise Lost* . . . they are contemplating the Divine and
Diabolical, whereas in reality they have to do with Luciferic and
Ahrimanic. No awareness of the genuinely Divine is present: the
Luciferic is gifted with divine names.

The Miltonic pattern, continues Steiner, echoes a widespread
pattern of popular religious feeling in the modern age. These
patterns actively prevent a real imagination of the spiritual, i.e. of
the essentially free moral being of man, of Christ. Nevertheless, he
rejects the solution of straightforward inversion (and thus implicit-
ly Blake's positive cult of energy, the so-called 'diabolism' of the
Marriage of Heaven and Hell).

We need not join with those who issue anathemas against heretics,
and declare Milton's *Paradise Lost* and Klopstock's *Der Messias*
productions of the devil. We may continue to enjoy their beauty
and grandeur; but we must realize that such works, the flowers
of popular modern civilization, do not speak of Christ at all . . .

Paradise Lost describes the expulsion of man from Lucifer's
realm into the realm of Ahriman. It renders man's longing, not for
the Divine world, but for the Paradise which he has lost – i.e. his
longing for the realm of Lucifer. You may regard Milton's *Paradise
Lost* and Klopstock's *Der Messias* as beautiful descriptions of
human desire for the realm of Lucifer . . . for that is what they are.*

Die Sendung Michaels (Dornach, 1962); translated as *The Mission of the Archangel
Michael* (New York, 1961) pp. 8–15.

Steiner's argument is incisive and illuminating – and perhaps a fraction too forthright for the special purposes of literary criticism.

It does not seem fully to take into acount the poetic unevenness of *Paradise Lost*, the wonderful authenticity, for instance, of the first theophany, before God and his Angels slip into their Luciferically ambivalent roles:

> Now had th' Almighty Father from above
> From the pure Empyrean where he sits
> High Thron'd above all highth, bent down his eye,
> His own works and their works at once to view:
> About him all the Sanctities of Heaven
> Stood thick as Starrs, and from his sight receiv'd
> Beatitude past utterance; on his right
> The radiant image of his Glory sat
> His onely Son . . .

> > > > (*Paradise Lost* III, 56–64)

Nor does Steiner quite seem to account for the dramatic complexity of the character of Satan. Nevertheless, his criticism seems to me to go further than any other in revealing the underlying structures of imagination in Milton's poem. We can represent these symbolically as polarities in space, adapting our original diagram designed to show the balance between Luciferic and Ahrimanic. (See Figure 2.) First of all we may show the vertical polarity of Heaven and Hell, Lucifer and Ahriman, as the groundwork of Milton's moral action. And we may reduce Hell to its first principle, the Ahrimanic darkness of potential matter, '*Darkness* and *Eternal Night*', where Milton enthroned his Demogorgon – anticipating Shelley in *Prometheus Unbound*, and again probably utilizing the Rosicrucian cosmology of Robert Fludd.

But for Satan we may extend Steiner's remark that Luciferic and Ahrimanic attributes are here not clearly distinguished. The imaginative fascination of Milton's Satan arises from the fact that, as in man himself, there is a mingling of the different powers. The Ahrimanic world, the 'Universe of death' which is the object of Satanic consciousness, as we saw in the preceding chapter, marks him out as fundamentally an Ahrimanic being, in accordance with Steiner's suggestion. Yet, expanding on Steiner's further remark that 'Ahriman is endowed with Luciferic attributes' in the blurred

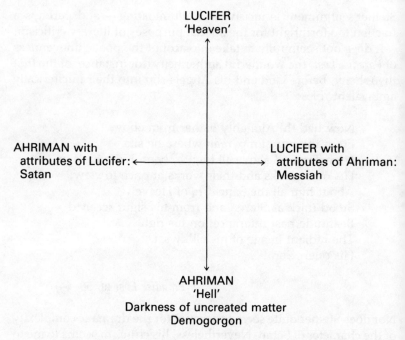

Figure 2. The Structure of Imagination in *Paradise Lost*.

vision of the poem, we may add that Satan is really the type of a
consciousness that is torn or warped between the destructive
opposites. He has aspired Luciferically beyond the limits of the
actual, desiring to lay hold on divinity for his own selfish
purposes, and has suffered the inevitable backlash from the actual,
the Ahrimanic, which is the fate of all such unbalanced aspirers.
Hence arises his 'human' pathos, prefiguring the guilty heroes and
inner torment of Byronic and other Romantic writers. Hence too
comes his peculiar magnificence, his blend of Luciferic pride and
the horrific scars he has suffered in his struggle against the real
nature of things. Here he is in his Ahrimanic Hell with the other
fallen Angels:

> he above the rest
> In shape and gesture proudly eminent
> Stood like a Towr: his form had yet not lost
> All her Original brightness, nor appear'd

Less than Arch-Angel ruind, and th' excess
Of Glory obscur'd: As when the Sun new ris'n
Looks through the Horizontal misty Air
Shorn of his Beams, or from behind the Moon
In dim Eclipse disastrous twilight sheds
On half the Nations, and with fear of change
Perplexes Monarchs. Darkend so, yet shon
Above them all th' Arch-Angel: but his face
Deep scars of Thunder had intrencht, and care
Sat on his faded cheek, but under Brows
Of dauntless courage, and considerat Pride
Waiting revenge: cruel his eye, but cast
Signes of remorse and passion to behold
The fellows of his crime, the followers rather
(Far other once beheld in bliss) condemnd
For ever now to have thir lot in pain,
Millions of spirits for his fault amerc't
Of Heav'n, and from Eternal Splendors flung
For his revolt, yet faithful how they stood,
Thir Glory witherd. As when Heavens Fire
Hath scath'd the Forrest Oaks or Mountain Pines,
With singed top thir stately growth though bare
Stands on the blasted Heath.

(*Paradise Lost* I, 589–615)

The whole point about Satan is that the Luciferic and Ahrimanic pull destructively together in his nature, and he does not possess the centre, the source of equilibrium, the ego, corresponding to the Christ-principle, to hold them in true balance. Ahriman is endowed with Luciferic attributes to form a kind of shadow-self which is in a state of constant dissolution. In this way Milton has created a fine and deeply imaginative image of the fallen self suited to the complexities of modern consciousness. All of us have to contend with the inner forces which keep Satan in a permanent inner Hell of self-dissolution – a Hell we suffer too in so far as we do not fully realize in our consciousness the psychic balance of free self-knowledge, the expression of the spiritual ego within. Milton's shadow-self or Satan is a definitive imagination for our age, even though we must admit that Milton did not see clearly into the constellation of forces that lay behind it.

The failure to see clearly into the constellation of forces which affect man's existence has more serious consequences in the presentation of Milton's Messiah in the poem. In Book VI of *Paradise Lost* we have recounted to us the 'War in Heaven' that led to the primaeval events of the Fall of the Angels. There is immense carnage and destruction ('Warr seemd a civil Game / To this uproar'). The Messiah is finally sent in by God, but in a way which has struck many critics as morally compromising. It seems inappropriate, undecorous for a supreme God to foresee and permit all this vandalism for the express purpose of letting his Son make a grand entry to sort it out. The theatricality and the over-explicit theme of the 'glory' that resounds to the Messiah's name from this somewhat 'staged' exploit points to a triumph of the Luciferic tendency in Milton's imagining at this point. In fact, when he arrives on the scene, the Messiah exhibits a purely Luciferic character that has no relation to the actualities of the situation that the poem has established. In his presence the carnage simply melts away, is neatly harmonized out of existence. Milton intends a brilliant 'magical' effect: and such on one level it is. But its implied imaginative message in the passage seems to be that for those with God's Messiah on their side the struggles and efforts toward self-knowledge in the inner life can be allowed to just melt away; likewise the pain and suffering going on all around will simply disappear when one hears the harmonies of the angelic choirs: the essence of the Luciferic gospel! We soon learn, however, the true nature of the Messiah, when he resorts to cruder violence against the rebel Angels, showing the real source of outward protection needed to make room for this harmonious Heaven. The Messiah and his God can afford to dream harmoniously and to be worshipped by their adoring multitudes, it seems, because they possess the ultimate weapon, Ahrimanic omnipotence. Milton's Messiah, in these least successful imaginations of the Divine, emerges as a strict counterpart to Satan: in this case a Lucifer endowed with the power of Ahriman – thus forming a sort of illusory image of a false higher self, projected beyond the necessary struggles of the inner life. Here again, the basic flaw in the vision was shrewdly detected by Blake, who asserted that in the Bible 'Milton's Messiah is call'd Satan' – i.e. the Luciferic tempter of Judaic tradition.

Thus Milton's horizontal axis (corresponding to conscious wisdom) is occupied by a morally disintegrating consciousness, torn by illusory longings for a higher state and mocked by false images of transcendence. That, after all, is the theme of *Paradise Lost*: the Fall and its consequences.

The imaginative polarities of Milton's world further determine the nature of action along the vertical axis – the axis of love which inevitably concerns the relation between man and 'God'. This axis too has been drawn into the Lucifer–Ahriman opposition, the 'naturalistic' dimension of 'conscious' wisdom. As Steiner points out, it does not represent the relation between the Divine and the free spirit of man. The pattern which emerges in the story of Adam, occupying basically Books III–IV and IX–X, bears out his contention. The story begins in Paradise and unselfconscious fulfilment, but since Adam has not been granted by his creator the full resources of a moral consciousness, able to know good and evil and determine his own destiny, it is ultimately inevitable that he will succumb to temptation. This is strenuously denied by God and the Angels, of course, who claim that they made man fit to stand, yet free to fall: but no amount of sophistry can get around the obvious truth that if, like Milton's God, you do not prepare a person to withstand an onslaught that you know will come, you cannot really be surprised when he is taken by surprise and succumbs. The import of Milton's story of man therefore amounts to a purely naturalistic, rather than a religious vision, since it does not involve all the co-ordinates of man's self-consciousness. According to the pattern actually presented, consciousness, beginning in Luciferic innocence and spontaneity, comes to a confrontation with the inevitable negation of itself, death.* And in all this, it must be admitted, there is nothing of an essentially Christian nature: the axis of love is usurped by the daemonic powers.

Only in the last lines of the whole poem, with their tone of mingled sadness and hope, does Milton enter the genuinely Christian sphere. For the first time in the whole poem Milton evokes a human awareness which is not deluded with a false sense of security, nor inwardly divided by unreal and incompatible hopes, nor despairing in the vision of death. Adam and Eve accept the justice and the reality of their state, and admit into their hearts both a genuine sorrow for the loss of innocence and a forward-looking hope and determination. There is true self-consciousness

---

*Milton took the results of his vision seriously: in his theological writings he affirms the heresy that the soul dies with the body in 'total death' – though he expects both to be raised at the Last Day.

and at the same time true love between them. It is one of the most moving scenes in all literature, and one of the most Christian, as they go out into the fallen world:

>   for now too nigh
> Th'Archangel stood, and from the other Hill
> To thir fixt Station, all in bright array
> The Cherubim descended; on the ground
> Gliding meteorous, as Ev'ning Mist
> Ris'n from a River o'er the marish glides,
> And gathers ground fast at the Labourers heel
> Homeward returning. High in Front advanc't,
> The brandisht Sword of God before them blaz'd
> Fierce as a Comet; which with torrid heat,
> And vapour as the *Libyan Air* adust,
> Began to parch that temperat Clime; whereat
> In either hand the hastning Angel caught
> Our lingring Parents, and to th'Eastern Gate
> Led them direct, and down the Cliff as fast
> To the subjected Plain; then disappear'd.
> They looking back, all th'Eastern side beheld
> Of Paradise, so late thir happie seat,
> Wav'd over by that flaming Brand, the Gate
> With dreadful Faces throngd and fierie Arms:
> Some natural tears they dropd, but wip'd them soon;
> The World was all before them, where to choose
> Thir place of rest, and Providence thir guide:
> They hand in hand with wandring steps and slow,
> Through *Eden* took their solitarie way.

>   (*Paradise Lost* XII, 625–49)

It is noteworthy in view of Steiner's analysis that these lines have frequently been criticized: a 'Christian', it has been said, would have ended on a note of pure hope. That would have meant yielding finally to the Luciferic impulse. Instead, Milton captures for the first time in his great epic the true tone of Christian spirit, and is able to present an imagination of a balanced yet inwardly complex human ego. Man in these concluding moments is at last shown as able to bear the inherent contraditions of his existence, and find in them a source of freedom and reconciliation.

Milton's Christianity stands at a point of transition in the history of consciousness. On the one hand there are many features in it which held back his deeper understanding of the ego, and the imaginative demands made by the free spirit. He was tainted by the popular 'dualistic' Christianity which saw existence in black and white terms, God and the Devil, Heaven and Hell. Yet at the same time, Milton comes before us as the first great poet who wishes to place himself into the imaginative world, experienced in unparalleled intensity, with his full capacities of self-awareness. He is a visionary who begins to reveal the potentialities of that other, 'esoteric' strain in Christianity, which understood the essential 'divinity' of man that had been achieved through Christ: man's ability to take upon himself the responsibilities, the burden and the creative energies that had hitherto belonged to the gods alone, or to the creator God at the beginning of time.

If he did not succeed in fully articulating that vision or in diagnosing the ultimate play of psychic powers that shaped his imagination of man and God, his 'adventrous Song' was to be taken up by the next generation of visionary poets, a century or more later: the Romantics.

Part II
Devil's Companions – Romantic Mythologies

4

Blake, Initiation, and
The Book of Thel

Few poets have been so wholeheartedly on the side of imagination as William Blake. Not only a poet but also a painter of considerable merit and, if we are to believe what his friends had to say, a composer of melodies for his own lyrics, he tried to live as fully as was possible the imaginative life.

He sought intense experiences, scaling the heights and depths, insisting that the superiority of imagination over nature lay in its increased clarity, sharper particularity and greater resonance of feeling. His poetry is full of 'howling despair', dumb horrors and heart-bursting joys. The Wordsworthian man who simply looked around him and registered what was there seemed to him grossly impoverished by comparison with the artist who absorbed his sensual and emotional perceptions, transformed them inwardly and raised them to a new level of purity. Blake seems never, if we except an early life-drawing probably of his brother, to have worked from an external model, but to have tried to render the effect he felt in the depths of the soul. The human body, when he represents it, becomes a pattern of inner tensions – 'Energy' is one of Blake's watchwords – rather than something which is intended to 'look like' the body seen from without. In Blake's later work we sometimes have images suggestive of the internal structure of the body and its organs, the sort of images that appear in dreams that reflect the inner life of the organism. He never ceased to scorn what he called the 'blotting and blurring' art which used patches or colour to evoke the 'indefinite' appearance of bodies under conditions of natural light, and he insisted upon strong outline which, as he put it, 'organiz'd' the forms of perception and made them appear as manifestations of a controlling energy, held or bounded by the defining limit: the 'black line of the Almighty'. It is this imaginative ability of Blake *par exellence*, to put himself inside things and forms, which gives them when he is successful their extraordinary power. When he falls back on his acquired drawing technique, he can be lamentably inept. Indeed the contrast between Blake's formal accomplishments in art and the force of his imaginative power when it operates raises problems in evaluating him as an artist. The impact of his uncanny imaginative penetration into the underlying 'Energy' of outer forms is mystical and clairvoyant, and only secondarily aesthetic. Fewer problems are created by his poems, where Blake fashions a powerful language to communicate his visions, and handles it with considerable assurance.

In his poetry too, Blake is totally committed to imaginative intensity. His work therefore appears as a first complete incarnation of the Romantic impulse. In fact it remains perhaps the most complete embodiment of a long life's work that never seriously wavered in its primary imaginative commitment. Most of the other Romantics died young, or died as poets before they died as men; but Blake's Energy seemed ever self-renewing and consumed away as dross all outward disappointments and obstacles, of which there were many in Blake's materially difficult, spiritually triumphant life.

Perhaps his strength came from a bold act of self-identification, which is extended to include all men although they do not all realize it. At any rate in modern times, man tends to identify himself with his individual characteristics, his personal wishes and feelings, together with the centre of consciousness, the Ego, which relates all these to itself. For most people, imagination is regarded as one activity of such a self-existent 'selfhood', a 'state of mind' in which we are sometimes engaged. Blake will have none of this. He identifies essential humanity with the imagination. What he feels as ultimately real within him is not his personality but his power of imaginative penetration into inner truth:

The Imagination is not a State: it is the Human Existence itself.

This is, of course, a paradox. Blake is saying that what most deeply constitutes 'me', the essential man, is not what makes me a separate individual, but that capacity which enables me to enter into the experiences, sufferings and joys, of others. In the last analysis, as Blake knew from his own visions, it enables us to enter into the inner nature of everything in the universe. It should be stressed that for Blake this was not theory. Looking into his own being, the most real element in it presented itself to him as the

imagination: his selfhood seemed superficial, an 'Incrustation' over
the boundless, immortal Energy he felt beneath, so shadowy upon
examination that he often described it as a 'Spectre'. It is merely the
hardened remnants of our earlier acts of imagination, and is swept
away by our subsequent acts. Hence for Blake, in our true nature
we are all one another, and our individual essence is our power of
sharing. He sees our collective imagination and gives to it a name
borrowed from British mythology, recalling the fact that in earlier
times the sense of human individuality was far less developed and,
like Blake, ancient man identified himself readily with an imagina-
tive wholeness: the Giant Albion. To begin with he is the British
People, but through him we find our participation in all mankind.
Beyond that, we discover in imagination our unity with the source
of all Energy and all Form:

Man is All Imagination. God is Man & exists in us & we in him,

as Blake put it in an annotation to Berkeley. Elsewhere, imagina-
tion is 'the Divine Humanity', the 'Divine Body of the Lord Jesus',
an archetypal man who has realized his imaginative community
with the whole cosmos and with God. Blake seeks ultimate
intensities, and follows his imagination through until it becomes a
profound mystical vision. In formulating his ideas with the clarity
found in his later writings, Blake seems to have been aided by his
studies of Paracelsus, the mystic and physician who, long before
psychoanalysis, had emphasized the influence of imagination in
illness and recovery, and who had also seen imagination as the
Holy Spirit manifest in man, the Comforter promised by Christ.

Blake sought to strip away from the intensity of imaginative
experience all that was inessential, that belonged to the selfhood,
the 'selfish centre'. In a celebrated passage from *The Marriage of
Heaven and Hell*, he attempts to shock us out of our usual
preconceptions, overturn our prejudices and make us look afresh,
seeing with new eyes. For, he says:

If the doors of perception were cleansed every thing would
appear to man as it is, infinite.

He likens the effect of the cleansing to corrosives such as those he
himself used in his printing, 'melting apparent surfaces away, and
displaying the infinite which was hid'.

This attempt to burn away all that appears 'finite & corrupt', i.e. no longer imaginative, in our perception also determines the form of Blake's poetry, which has certainly caused great problems to many of his readers. For he rejects many of the techniques used by other poets for ordering their material in space and time – even the most fundamental devices such as narrative, since for Blake linear time like that of the biographer or historian belongs to the realm of the illusory selfhood. Imagination cuts across centuries and enters into human situations of the distant past as easily as it jumps over spaces. Clock-time is 'spectral', the mere shadow of creativity which establishes its own rhythms and sequences. Blake sought rather for a form which expressed intensity, Energy, and allowed him to deepen his original impression by repetition, rather than moving on from it in time (narrative poetry) or space (contemplative, e.g. landscape poetry). In short, Blake tended to bring everything he wrote about into the form of lyric. Here, although the lyric poem may have several verses, there is not usually any movement, but rather the attempt to capture or express in depth a single aspect of experience.

When once we realize Blake's commitment to the lyric mode, we also begin to see that the contrast assumed by many critics between the poet of *Songs of Innocence and Experience*, who wrote some of the finest short poems in the English language, and the visionary enthusiast who wrote the vast and unintelligible epics such as *The Four Zoas*, is simply not there. We can follow Blake's development from the short *Songs*, through the shorter 'prophetic books', *Europe, America, Urizen*, etc., to the vast achievements of *The Four Zoas* and *Milton, A Poem*; and what is remarkable is precisely its continuity. Only when he came to compose his immense *Jerusalem* did Blake attempt a rather different ordering, and even then he preserves much of his established technique. Once Blake had discovered the sort of themes he wished to use, and the type of poem he wished to write, he simply went on working at them and reworking at them. He composed larger and larger lyrics – but he never experienced any change of ambitions which drew him to the epic mode.

Many of the features which perplex us when we read the longer prophecies as 'epics' arise because they are not really epics at all. In *The Four Zoas*, for instance, we are puzzled when we hear about the same events over and again, in ways which never quite agree. We begin to understand when we grasp that the movement of the poem is not a forward one of narrative events, but a deepening, intensifying one. It is, in fact, best seen as a huge lyric. We can even trace passages of it back through various stages of their growth to poems which are well-known as short lyrics in Blake's earlier collections. One such case concerns the famous 'Introduction' to the *Songs of Experience*:

> Hear the voice of the Bard!
> Who Present, Past, & Future, sees;
> Whose ears have heard
> The Holy Word
> That walk'd among the ancient trees,
>
> Calling the lapsed Soul,
> And weeping in the evening dew;
> That might controll
> The starry pole,
> And fallen, fallen light renew!
>
> 'O Earth, O Earth, return!
> Arise from out the dewy grass;
> Night is worn,
> And the morn
> Rises from the slumberous mass.
>
> Turn away no more;
> Why wilt thou turn away?
> The starry floor,
> The wat'ry shore,
> Is giv'n thee till the break of day!

The lyrical power of this short poem is extraordinarily concentrated, so that it seems to sum up an infinite depth of experience. It expresses a cry of the soul against the fallen world, a pain and a longing which we all sometimes feel although we have not normally the power of bringing it into awareness with Blake's clairvoyant capacity of imagination.

The poetic 'moment' gathers everything together; we enter some mythological world which is not clearly defined but in which events of unfathomable importance have taken place (the fall of the 'light', some hinted disruption of the 'starry pole') and in which some new dawning is earnestly anticipated and desired. But the important thing is that we do not ask to be told the whole story. Its essence is collected into the 'moment' of the poem, making us believe that the Bard whose voice we hear calling us to awaken can see in a glance present, past, future and eternity. In later, longer poems Blake does tell us the story of his mythological world – at least to some extent: yet he constantly disrupts the narrative, or shatters it into different facets as in *The Four Zoas*, so as to insist that narrative is not the real centre of interest. In order to communicate with his readers, Blake must express himself sequentially, as if he is talking about a series of events, but in reality the poem fuses everything into a 'moment' in exactly the same way as the shortest of the *Songs*. We miss Blake's point if we think of his narrative as primary: it unfolds a significance which finally denies the sequential time from which Blake wishes to redeem us.

We have seen that Milton in *Paradise Lost* already used narrative to carry forward the interest of his poem, while at a deeper level he fashioned a set of images that reflect an inner transformation. Blake's poetic technique, however, is far more radical than Milton's. One can read *Paradise Lost* for its narrative without being disturbed by deeper elements of the poetry. In Blake, narrative keeps fizzling out, repeating itself, contradicting itself. Thereby it demonstrates its own inadequacy, and forces us to look for underlying elements of coherence at profounder psychic levels, in the images and symbols which exist in an 'Eternal Now' in the soul.

In the later Blake, images and symbols have a life of their own, independent of any particular poem. They become Beings, visionary Friends and companions of the imagination; Blake saw them in the world around him with his inner eye. They were not hallucinations which he mistook for physical presences. He knew very well that they were in his imagination, but that only made them more real. The essence of man was imagination: they were as real therefore as his physical contemporaries, nay more real, because they were free from the delusions of selfhood which kept men 'shut up' within themselves as though they lived in dark caverns. The Four Zoas and other Beings existed in Blake and in all mankind; they existed too in nature when this was experienced imaginatively, and not just passively as a realm of 'objects' somewhere 'out there' around us. By the time he came to write *Night the Ninth* of *The Four Zoas*, the 'moment' which he had captured in the 'Introduction' to *Songs of Experience* had become part of a larger, more comprehensive 'moment' of apocalypse, or revelation. It had also become associated with some of Blake's visionary Beings:

Invisible Luvah in bright clouds hover'd over Vala's head,
And thus their ancient golden age renew'd; for Luvah spoke
With voice mild from his golden Cloud upon the breath of
                                                    morning:

'Come forth, O Vala, from the grass & from the Silent dew,
Rise from the dews of death, for the Eternal Man is Risen.'

She rises among flowers & looks toward the Eastern clearness
She walks yea runs, her feet are wing'd, on the tops of the
                                                    bending grass,
Her garments rejoice in the vocal wind & her hair glistens with
                                                    dew.

She answer'd thus: 'Whose voice is this, in the voice of the
                                                    nourishing air,
In the spirit of the morning, awaking the Soul from its grassy
                                                    bed?
Where dost thou dwell? for it is thee I seek, & but for thee
I must have slept Eternally, nor have felt the dew of thy
                                                    morning.
Look how the opening dawn advances with vocal harmony!
Look how the beams foreshew the rising of some glorious
                                                    power!
The sun is thine, he goeth forth in his majestic brightness.
O thou creating voice that callest! & who shall answer thee?'

'Where dost thou flee, O fair one? where doth thou seek thy
                                                    happy place?'

'To yonder brightness, there I haste, for sure I came from
                                                    thence
Or I must have slept eternally, nor have felt the dew of
                                                    morning.'

'Eternally thou must have slept, nor have felt the morning
                                                    dew,
But for yon nourishing sun; 'tis that by which thou art arisen.

The birds adore the sun; the beasts rise up & play in his
                                                        beams,
And every flower & every leaf rejoices in his light.
Then, O thou fair one, sit thee down, for thou art as the grass,
Thou risest in the dew of morning & at night art folded up.'

                              (*The Four Zoas*, Night the Ninth, 385–409)

The style here is looser, more relaxed than in the 'Introduction',
though the effect is still lyrical. By this means Blake can integrate
the 'moment' into the larger 'moment' of *Night the Ninth* (his
apocalypse). Further, the 'revelation' of *Night the Ninth* is itself not
something added to the narrative, but the truth of which we have
been in search throughout the poem, which now breaks upon us
with the force of ultimate vision. It is the moment which subsumes
all other moments. We have not really gone a journey, but woken
up to where we are.

                        *   *   *

Blake's characteristic mode of poetry can be appreciated in one of
the earliest of the 'prophetic books', namely *The Book of Thel*. It is
one of the books in which he first discovered certain essential
aspects of himself as a writer, i.e. of his own imaginative being.
Although it appears to narrate four episodes involving a female
called Thel and other entities such as a Cloud, a Clod of Clay, etc.,
it is best understood as a sequence of intensifications, deepening
our experience of the poem 'lyrically', and seeking to awaken in
the reader a parallel process of self-discovery.

The symbolism of *Thel* has been the subject of several learned
interpretations by eminent Blake-scholars and critics. I do not
propose to enter into controversy with any of them – but whether
or not Thel should be understood, for example, as an unborn soul
descending into birth, or as a young girl on the verge of sexual
experience, it will be well to ask first what feelings she evokes in us
as we read, or what experiences find embodiment in the poem. As
readers, none of us are unborn souls, nor many of us inexperi-
enced young girls. Yet the poem expresses a series of inner states
in which we are immediately involved – and to these, of course,
the images of the 'virgin' or the 'pre-natal soul' may turn out to be
highly relevant as these states in purer or more intense form. For

the moment, however, *Thel* engages us in its aspect as source and generative spring of a psychic pattern whose elaboration and expansion occupied much of our poet's career.

The world in which the poem's questioning heroine wanders is a pastoral one, recalling a long tradition in English poetry. On the title-page Thel herself is depicted with a shepherd's crook, and we hear of her angelic-sounding sisters, the 'daughters of Mne Seraphim', leading round their 'sunny flocks'. The first line in this way introduces the suggestion of circularity that runs through the whole book, dominated by the pastoral-natural world in its seasonal coming-to-be and passing-away. Again on the title-page this is beautifully implied in the great curve of the tree, rising, arching and then directing our gaze down to meet the newly springing flowers.

In the centre, before Thel's chaste eyes, is a representation of this great generative process – the sexual embrace of a veiled maiden and a dynamically flying youth, possibly the Cloud and the virgin 'fair-eyed dew' of the text. Replying to a question from Thel, the Cloud explains his participation in the universal cycle, and the 'love' and 'peace and raptures holy' which are his lot:

> Unseen descending, weigh my light wings upon balmy
> > flowers,
> And court the fair-eyed dew to take me to her shining tent:
> The weeping virgin, trembling kneels before the risen sun,
> Till we arise link'd in a golden band and never part,
> But walk united, bearing food to all our tender flowers.

> (*Thel* 3, 12–16)

In a splendid image this melting of the dew into sunlit golden vapour becomes in Blake's mind a fount from

> the golden springs
> Where Luvah doth renew his horses.

> (*Thel* 3, 7–8)

Blake's spirit of love and desire here makes his first appearance, with his 'horses of passion'. *Thel's* pastoral garden, then, is a garden of love: the endless cycle of sexual union, birth and decay.

Borrowing a phrase from Parmenides, we may say that this is nature seen as the 'lovely grove of Aphrodite', much-honoured goddess of generation.

The body of the poem contains further questions from Thel addressed to a 'Lilly of the valley', the Cloud, and 'matron Clay' with her childlike Worm, who in turn inform our heroine that they have no fears whatever in relation to their transient separate existence, because they belong to the vast organism of the world as a whole. Individually, the Lilly is so humble and weak that she cannot even support a butterfly:

> Yet I am visited from heaven, and he that smiles on all
> Walks in the valley and each morn over me spreads his
>   hand . . .
>
>   (*Thel* 1, 19–20)

The Clod of Clay modestly describes herself as 'the meanest thing':

> My bosom of itself is cold, and of itself is dark;
> But he, that loves the lowly, pours his oil upon my head,
> And kisses me, and binds his nuptial bands around my breast.
>
>   (*Thel* 4, 12 – 5, 2)

In both cases – explicitly in the second – there are strongly sexual overtones. The poetry is full of the moist 'honey of generation': an overflowing, exuberant sexuality in which earth is caressed by heaven and receives the kisses of an amorous sun. This innocent fecundity may be imaged in the playful children shown at the end of the poem riding on a snake.

But in this world there is no place for separate existence. The Lilly is cropped by the browsing lamb, the Cloud fades, life decays into clay; at the same time a new flower springs, the dew flies up in golden vapour, the clay itself fosters the worms. And all is happiness so long as the participants in the cycle are content to remain unselfconscious, innocent, not demanding an identity.

In all their beautiful vitality, abundance and transitoriness we see the 'rainbow gardens' of luxuriant nature. Finding herself present in nature, Thel too likens herself to the brilliant but momentary 'wat'ry bow', to a 'parting cloud', to an impermanent 'reflection in a glass', all of which fade away just as she will. But unlike her sisters, still leading their flocks in the innocent circles of an angelic paradise, Thel has become detached: she is in exactly the condition diagnosed by Goethe, seeing all the 'regular reappearances of external things' revolving before her eyes but taking no part in them, leaning passively on her crook beholding the eternal nuptials but not sharing in their joys.* Thus she becomes aware of herself as separate from nature, as an individual consciousness looking out at the world and at herself in it. The danger of that 'greatest evil' accordingly steals upon her, and she loses the sense of purpose in shouldering the burden of existence.

Blake describes her withdrawal from seraphic participation in a significant phrase: 'she in paleness sought the secret air' (1,2). This anticipates a passage in a later poem where man is pictured refusing to give himself to the full possibilities of experience, closing himself up as in a cave. Ironically, he may

> himself pass out what time he please; but he will not,
> For stolen joys are sweet & bread eaten in secret pleasant.

> (*Europe* plate iii, 5–6)

Thel has also sought this 'secrecy', a private awareness, a self-consciousness. She therefore finds herself a conscious being looking out on the unreflective process of the universe. She sees it *ab extra*, but at the same time she herself is subject to the inevitable course of generation and decay. Like the creatures of Spring she has been born and will soon die. For her alone, however, this has grown to be a burden. Unlike all the other characters she cannot submit herself joyfully to the all-fulfilling cycle, since consciously she is no more a part of it. She remonstrates with the Lilly that whereas by her flowers the lambs are pastured, honey is distilled and perfumes wafted on the air:

> Thel is like a faint cloud kindled at the rising sun:
> I vanish from my pearly throne, and who shall find my place?

> (*Thel* 2, 11–12)

---

*Cf. Goethe, *Truth and Poetry from my Life*, XIII: 'All gratification in life is founded on the regular reappearance of external things. The alternation of day and night, of the seasons, of flower and fruit, and everything else that confronts us at regular intervals so that we may, and should, enjoy it: these are the very springs of our daily life. The more openly we avow these pleasures, the happier we are. But if these phenomena revolve severally before us and we take no part in them, proving unreceptive to these precious gifts – then the greatest evil, the most dire sickness breaks out in us, and we look upon life as a repulsive burden.'

The Cloud's moisture feeds the flowers and makes them grow; but Thel's existence has no such purpose or value:

> And all shall say, 'Without a use this shining woman liv'd,
> 'Or did she only live to be at death the food of worms?'

> (*Thel* 3, 22–3)

Everything, it seems, has its place and function in the world-order. Thel alone can discover no place into which she can fit, or use for her being alive. The Cloud's hard-pressed suggestion that feeding worms is glorious use enough scarcely amounts to a comfort. She has separated herself and now stands outside the on-going revolutions, outside all physical life in the intensity of her consciousness.

To experience the full nature of this isolation in consciousness is potentially terrifying. Hence there is a powerful temptation to turn aside from the recognition of it and attempt to remain, despite one's separateness, a part of the cycle. Blake traces the results of this solution in the beings with whom the heroine holds conversation. There appears to be a hierarchy reaching from the total or perfect participation of Thel's sisters, the 'daughters of Mne Seraphim', who seem to revolve somewhere above the world of the poem – through the Lilly and the Cloud, who have a marginal sense of individual dissolution and reappearance – to matron Clay, who, as her nature would suggest, knows what it is to die or cease to be. But the Clay will not face her awareness, insisting most strongly that she like everything belongs to the great whole, even though she can appeal to nothing in her experience (in contrast to the Lilly and Cloud) to explain how she does so:

> But how this is, sweet maid, I know not, and I cannot know;
> I ponder, and I cannot ponder; yet I live and love.

> (*Thel* 5, 5–6)

She is content simply to accept the cycle of life and death, receiving whatever it brings with a trust in something she does not claim to understand. Death may seem meaningless from our earthly vantage-point, but we must just have faith in the mysterious ways of him 'that loves the lowly'. This seductive religious alternative to confronting our situation in all its urgency even momentarily convinces Thel – until in an excess of zeal matron Clay shows her too well what her world is really like.

Blake, then, is exploring in *Thel* the nature of self-consciousness, or existence isolated from immediate participation in the enfolding world-process. As a conscious being, man is separate from nature, while paradoxically still constituting one element in its cycle as a natural creature subject to growth and dissolution. To escape awareness of the full intensity of isolation the soul is tempted – like matron Clay when she comes to realize her predicament – to fall into the purely passive role of acceptance and remain in the natural cycle as before.

Blake was no doubt thinking of orthodox Christian 'faith' and its trust in a metaphysical 'beyond' comprising a benignant universal consciousness, a providential God. Some such acceptance of the world as objective, material and 'out there' generally characterizes our modern secular and scientific kind of awareness – our working relation to the world. Historically, however, we see this response to conscious experience first receiving clear articulation in the last great philosophy of Antiquity – Stoicism. It is among the Stoics, as Owen Barfield points out, that the modern distinction of 'objective' and 'subjective' is first given philosophical expression. It was in this form that it strongly affected subsequent Christianity. Thus, according to Cicero the Stoic thinker Chrysippus observed that:

Just as a shield-case is made for the sake of a shield, and a sheath for the sake of a sword, so everything else except the world-as-a-whole, was created for the sake of some other thing; thus the corn and fruits produced by the earth were created for the sake of animals, and animals for the sake of man: for example, the horse for riding, the ox for ploughing, the dog for hunting and keeping guard; man himself however came into existence for the purpose of contemplating and imitating the world; he is by no means perfect, but he is a very small fragment of that which is perfect.

This could virtually be Blake's Clod of Clay given a philosophical voice: nature is conceived as a cosmos, i.e. as a self-contained and continuously self-renewing whole, in which nothing 'lives unto itself' but exists for the sake of the other parts.

This is true even of man, who has reached the stage of conscious life. Yet, as the climax of the scale of creation, man does not directly serve the needs of anything higher than himself, but exists to devote himself in contemplation to understanding the cosmic order and 'imitating' it in his moral actions. His understanding of it is still imperfect, but he can consciously frame his deeds to harmonize with the order he sees exemplified in these orbitings of the heavenly bodies above his head. His actions are sustained by the faith that, even though the fact of his consciousness seems to deny it, he does somehow ultimately belong to the order of nature, and all that happens is necessarily, though mysteriously, for the best. Thus the cosmic order is revered by Stoicism as the wisest and most perfect of beings, and in its aspect as a consciousness it is God. As a little part of its perfection, therefore, human consciousness must and ought to resign itself to whatever fate may bring. (We still speak colloquially of 'stoicism' with similar connotations.) In this way man's consciousness of isolation from the world is mitigated and his metaphysical discomfort assuaged.

But Blake will have nothing to do with such a solution, either in the pragmatic form of our ordinary consciousness, or as a pious surrender – at least he would not by the time he came to write the fourth and climactic section of the *Book of Thel*. Thel accepts the invitation to enter fully into a state of consciousness alienated from physical life and nature. That alien universe now appears before her with horrifying immediacy. Goethe warned that in this state life becomes repulsive and we feel ourselves in the grip of deathly forces: Thel now beholds the 'couches of the dead', and the 'fibrous roots' with their 'restless twists' of human hearts – a 'land of sorrows', of 'clouds' and dark, oppressive valleys where she pauses to listen to 'the voices of the ground' (*Thel* 6, 4–8). The world seems totally external and inimical to life. The delights of the world revolve before her but she takes no part in their joys. Earlier, Thel had shown herself liable to a mild morbidity:

> Ah! gentle may I lay me down, and gentle rest my head,
> And gentle sleep the sleep of death, and gentle hear the voice
> Of him that walketh in the garden in the evening time.

(Thel 1, 12–14)

This is now intensified to the point of nightmare. She recognizes as the essence of her state the death-in-life of imprisonment in the

1. William Blake, *Satan, Sin and Death*, from the illustrations to Milton's *Paradise Lost*. Watercolour (Huntington Library, San Marino, California).

3. William Blake, title-page to *The Book of Thel* (Copy O). Relief etching (The Lessing J. Rosenwald Collection, Library of Congress, Washington, DC).

4. Rudolf Steiner — Arild Rosenkrantz, painting in the small cupola of the First Goetheanum (detail).

outer course of nature and the sense-world. From her own grave-plot she hears her own spectral voice crying out against the power of the senses:

> Why cannot the Ear be closed to its own destruction?
> Or the glist'ning Eye to the poison of a smile?
> Why are Eyelids stor'd with arrows ready drawn,
> Where a thousand fighting men in ambush lie?
> Or an Eye of gifts & graces show'ring fruits & coined gold?
> Why a Tongue impress'd with honey from every wind?
> Why an Ear, a whirlpool fierce to draw creations in?
> Why a Nostril wide inhaling terror, trembling, & affright?
> Why a tender curb upon the youthful burning boy?
> Why a little curtain of flesh on the bed of our desire?

All these images depend for their force on our realizing that this gloomy world is the same that we saw represented earlier as the lovely grove of Aphrodite. It is not another 'place', but the world seen from a new spiritual perspective.

Thel's soul shrinks back from this vision. The significance of her motion has been variously interpreted, and many critics have reproached her for not entering fearlessly into earthly generation. Certainly we may gather from Blake's subsequent poems that her attempt to regain the happy and innocent state of her sisters cannot directly succeed: for when Thel appropriated a separate awareness for herself, the pastoral cycles in which they selflessly express themselves hardened for her into an external system or cosmos in which she is a subordinate part. The way forward now can only lie in recognizing unflinchingly the deathly nature of the state of being she has entered. Nevertheless, it is undeniably true, as John Beer has pointed out, that we naturally sympathize with Thel here – and that is equally important. Starting back in horror from the recognition of the alienated, divided condition of worldly consciousness, the soul defines itself, to begin with, as essentially other than the world as it appears to our ordinary self. It fashions an image of itself as a pure, unified and innocent nature whose real being is not to be found within empirical experience at all. In Blake's later poems the image receives a variety of names – Oothoon, in *Visions of the Daughters of Albion*, Ololon in *Milton, A Poem*, and finally Jerusalem in the enormous poem depicting man's spiritual life which bears her name.

The *Book of Thel* thus establishes a pattern of imagination which is to remain central to much of Blake's visionary work. His meditative technique of overlaying leads to a progressive 'lyrical' deepening of our experience, so that we come finally to examine our situation with unprecedented and vivid awareness. The world which we take so much for granted in our practical, day-to-day working attitude of mind can then take on a nightmarish 'otherness'; the full extent of man's alienation as a conscious being oppresses us, causing a crisis and the turning of the imagination in upon itself.

This is the pattern of an initiation. We can detect traces of it in many of the religious practices of traditional peoples, who still practise puberty initiation-rites, for example – as well as in the rituals belonging to the great world-religions. In the case of the tribal youths who have to be initiated into adult life, and therefore into the meaning of human existence as spiritually understood, the end of childhood security is marked by a period of exile: they are sent out into the bush or wilderness, and often have to face harrowing ordeals. Everything is done so as to make them recognize the potential hostility, the alienness of the world known to uninitiated consciousness, a vision from which they have hitherto been protected by maternal solicitude. They must now assume the full burdens of life, and in the crisis they suffer must draw on inner resources and strengths they did not know they possessed. They return to the life of their tribe on a new level, and are initiated more fully into its spiritual teaching. Similar stages are found in the Mysteries of the great civilizations in Antiquity: a phase of 'homelessness' and wandering marks the beginning of the career of numerous holy men and heroes, and survives as an imaginative theme in sagas and legends through to later ages.*

Traces of initiation-practices can certainly be found among several groups down to modern times. In the seventeenth century, with its phenomenal religious vitality, many groups of a quasi-esoteric or Gnostic nature sprang up. There were fringe-groups

---

*Cf. Rudolf Steiner's description of the state: 'This intensity of consciousness, of "standing outside all physical life", is not produced until initiation ... A moment comes when a man confronts his physical body, whose hands he can move during waking life, with whose feet he can walk, whose knees he can bend, whose eyelids he can open and shut, and so on, but now he feels as though his whole physical body were petrified, as though it were impossible to move the eyelids, the legs, the hands, etc. A moment comes when he knows that there are eyes in his physical body, but they are of no use for seeing.' – *Mysteries of the East and of Christianity* (London, 1972) pp. 17–18.

among the radical Protestants such as the Ranters, who may have been successors of the mediaeval Manichaeans and Brethren of the Free Spirit; Blake certainly seems to have known something of them and their teaching. Or on a higher intellectual level, there were Rosicrucians searching for an esoteric key to the understanding of nature's secrets and the nature of the soul; critics such as Kathleen Raine have shown that Blake knew a good deal of their symbolism and mystical writings. Yet all the evidence we have concerning Blake's life and his cast of mind speaks against our looking for the origin of the initiatory pattern in his poetry in the ritual procedures of an esoteric group.

Blake was fascinated by the symbols and mystical teachings of seers such as Swedenborg, the great 'theosopher' Jacob Boehme, Hermetic and alchemical doctrines: but he was interested in them because they seemed to correspond to, or confirm, his own imaginative convictions. When he felt that they had betrayed their living imagination and erred by systematizing or distorting or moralizing what they saw, he was always sharply critical. He placed much more reliance on Milton and Shakespeare – although in their case too he was often prepared to practise his vocation as 'a corrector of other people's visions'. Boehme he accused of having turned the spiritual significance of things upside-down, presenting the fiery Energy whose nature is 'Eternal Delight' as a threatening force of 'divine Wrath'; Swedenborg he satirized mercilessly in the *Marriage of Heaven and Hell*, thereby underlining the importance of Swedenborg in his own mind while at the same time making it clear that he could not submit without protest to Swedenborg's interpretation of what he had seen 'in the company of Angels'. With the fanatical seers of his own day, such as the eccentric Richard Brothers, Blake took an even stronger line. What he trusted was the truth of his imagination, and only then did he look to the teachings of others, where he found a good deal that was helpful – though much more that had to be criticized.

It is highly unlikely, therefore, that Blake would have submitted to the authority of any religious or esoteric group to the extent of being initiated. We should rather consider that the initiatory pattern is extremely widespread, and has continued from archaic times to the present, although certainly with some changes and developments. It must correspond on a deep level to elements of the human psyche which can be released under certain circumstances, and under certain psychological conditions which are reproduced with remarkable similarity over many different parts of the world. We are therefore justified in looking for something in Blake's personal life-experience which might have triggered the manifestation of an archaic pattern: an event with a structure that can be regarded as of initiatory significance. In this context we should also mention that 'spontaneous initiation' is by no means unknown among shamans and other adepts of the archaic modern societies.

One common misconception about Blake's life is the notion that from his childhood onwards the poet had a constant stream of visionary experiences. This is not the case. It is true that as a small child he had had a number of strange visions, anecdotes of which have been retailed by all his biographers: he saw an angel in a tree on Peckham Rye, and saw God looking in at the window, terrifying him. But after his childhood days, there was a long period during which Blake struggled with down-to-earth difficulties, training as an engraver and trying to support himself in the competitive London world of trade. In the curious satire he wrote in early manhood, *An Island in the Moon*, there is little trace of the visionary confidence we find in the 'prophetic books'. Rather there is a biting sense of cynicism, hollowness, still recalling the eighteenth-century rationalists and their scathing reduction of man's spiritual pretensions. Blake seems at this time to have been essentially lonely, and perhaps felt intellectually lost.

One positive feature in his life, however, was his strong affection for his brother Robert. It was the latter's death in 1787 that seems to have been the turning-point in Blake's inner development. The two had been constant companions, fellow-explorers of life and art, though Robert had none of William's gifts. Nearly twenty years after he died, Blake could still recall him with fresh affection; the immediate effect must have been indescribable grief. Blake sat by his brother's bed for the last fortnight of his illness, hardly sleeping. It was then, we may presume, that he underwent the ordeal of alienation and death-like abstraction from the world. At the end of his vigil he collapsed into a death-like sleep of three days' and nights' duration.

Such a three-day sleep was of central importance in the events of many ancient as well as modern 'primitive' initiations. Evidently it corresponds to deep psychic rhythms. Mircea Eliade admits that we still understand little of the deeper dimensions of initiatory practices, but this rhythm of renewal from the unconscious depths perhaps provides a key to certain of their mysteries.* From prehistoric times three days appears as the time of transition from the world of the living to the homeland of the dead, or of the post-mortem awakening of the soul. In Christianity it was given a new meaning in the resurrection 'after three days' of the crucified Christ. Among the Gnostics, adepts were known to have 'died' and on the third day returned to life.

Blake's experience was certainly the beginning of a new stage in his inner life. When he came round from apparent unconsciousness, he described a vision he had seen: his brother's spirit had leapt up from the body and disappeared through the ceiling of the room, 'clapping its hands for joy'. Blake's converse with the visionary world, disrupted since his infancy, was reopened and was to continue until his death.

That gesture of joy in the liberated spirit meets us again in the innocent humanity of the children in *Songs of Innocence*, the collection of lyrics Blake completed in 1789 to embody his new vision. In the *Book of Thel*, dated to the same year, he also made a first attempt to embody the imaginative pattern which he felt at the root of his new-found imaginative powers: the initiatory pattern we have tried to outline. For Blake saw that the beauty of the 'innocence', the eternal essence of the child who continues to exist in everyone, must be set against the darker elements of vision, of man's loneliness and estrangement, if he was to tell the whole truth. Indeed, he probably continued to work on *Thel* up to the time when he added to *Innocence* the sombre *Songs of Experience* (1794). Through the developments of the pattern in his 'prophetic books', Blake showed that he had raised a personal confrontation with the death-world into an initiatory ordeal; he had descended into the underworld and been reborn.

* * *

Blake forms a striking contrast to Milton, despite the fact that he is a visionary poet in the same line, and one who regarded Milton as his greatest predecessor.

Milton had sought to find a balance between the dynamic forces of the soul that would place in the centre of vision the free self, the Ego. Yet he fell short of a wholly Christian resolution of the

*Mircea Eliade, *Rites and Symbols of Initiation* (New York, 1965) p. 104.

energies he had awakened, and was finally unable to find an adequate role for the imagination which was nevertheless so strong in all he wrote, so that beneath the surface of *Paradise Lost* there are strange cross-currents, dangerous eddies of the soul. Blake on the other hand is so strongly on the side of imagination that he can find no place at all for the virtues of self-consciousness.

The nature of consciousness is experienced in *Thel* as separation; and the world of the conscious self is a death-world, a Satanic inferno from which the artist is saved by recognizing its negativity. Yet it was also the world that was 'real' to his contemporaries, the world that was being explored by science and reduced to physical laws of attraction. In his longer poems Blake calls it Ulro, and its presiding God is Urizen, the Zoa of Reason in the fourfold vision of man he gradually developed. But how and why did this world come into being? Why should it ever have come into existence to mar the life, beauty and innocence of the imagination? Had it been made by the same God who created the energetic spirit of man? In Blake's experience the two levels seemed rather to be radically distinct. Juxtaposing them in *Songs of Inocence and Experience*, Blake raised more questions than he found answers. The only immediate answer seemed to be that the two worlds simply were not related; an ontological gap yawned between them, mythically supposed the result of some primordial disaster. In the books he wrote after 1794 Blake moved rapidly towards a Gnostic dualism of spirit and matter.

It was because Blake was so determined to preserve the primordial unity of the imagination that he was prepared to hand over the external realm, the world of objective consciousness, to Ahriman. He achieves his initiatory awakening by casting off the limits of the conscious self and its correlative rational and perceptible universe. The 'demonization' to which he subjects them means in effect that Blake admits the impenetrability of the scientific cosmos to the power of imagination. The God of the world explored by science is not the God who dwells in the flaming fire of the creative Energies, but a brooding Demiurge, Urizen (whose name perhaps hints at a pun with 'reason').

The situation in which Blake found himself was quite different from that of the initiates in ancient times, or of archaic societies. After a period of alienation, the ancient adept was given a new relationship to nature and saw it henceforth as the manifestation of spiritual forces, the gods or the ancestors; after his insight into human estrangement, the spiritual gap was closed upon a new and deeper wholeness of experience. But then, the extent of the gap was not so huge and yawning as it had become by the late eighteenth century. By Blake's day, the progress of science had meant that, for their special purposes of comprehending and controlling nature, philosophers had created a picture of the world as a vast mechanism: sheer surface with no 'inside', a collection of particles orbiting about in space, ruled by 'laws' which no human or other will could cause to swerve.

Recent studies of the 'Newtonian revolution' have allowed us to respond more fully to the religious significance of Blake's 'anti-cosmism' as we may call it. They have shown that the Latitudinarians, a party of churchmen within the Church of England, took up the Newtonian world-picture and emphasized those very features of repetitive motion, necessity, lifelessness which Blake found so horrifying. They believed that by showing the mindless and ultimately meaningless dependence of nature on these laws, they could point to a meaning which had to be introduced from above, from the God outside nature and outside human experience (except through his special revelation). Even Newton himself may have thought that he was defending the Christian idea of 'the creation'. Blake defied such a remote God. For it was argued that God, having set the whole in motion, declined any further intervention. The scope of man's sense of estrangement was intensified by the emergence of this scientific world-picture to a degree unprecedented in the history of human consciousness. It is hardly surprising therefore that the imagination could at first respond to it only by demonization, by the vision of what Blake calls the Ulro. Total reintegration no longer seemed possible.

Such an attitude to the natural world fits awkwardly together with Blake's professed Christianity. And in fact, we are forced to conclude that Blake's attitude is less genuinely Christian than Gnostic, i.e. it corresponds to a dualistic strain of thought, compounded from many of the same elements which were taken into Christianity but with a different essential structure. Gnostic religion flourished in the first centuries of the Christian era and arrived at its own understanding of Christ – as did Blake; it certainly influenced the early Christians directly too. But it was older, and sprang from an oriental milieu with roots in Iranian spirituality and Babylonian star-wisdom, and it existed also in an Egyptian transposition associated with the name of the sage

Hermes Trismegistus (Hermes standing for the Egyptian divine scribe, Thoth). Recently there have been considerable discoveries of Gnostic writings, preserved for centuries in the dry sands of Egypt near Nag Hammadi. The ancient Gnostics had their successors in mediaeval times, although it is very unclear how far Gnostic doctrines were handed down or whether Gnostic ideas have tended to emerge anew under similar conditions out of potential patterns on a deeper level of the psyche. At the heart of Gnosis is the initiatory experience. In the case of ancient Gnosticism, it seems to have sharpened into a dualistic form in response to the Judaic world-view, the shock of contact between the oriental mind for which nature was a 'Fulness' of divine powers and the specifically biblical idea that the world is a finished 'creation', not in itself divine or sacred (to suppose otherwise being 'idolatry'). Judaic experience of the world had then recently joined forces with the Greek scientific Enlightenment pioneered by the Stoics, thus constituting a powerful new picture of the world.

Blake certainly knew something of historial Gnosticism, as I have shown elsewhere, since he mentioned it to his friend Crabb Robinson. He could have known something too from his Unitarian and theological friends. But the real roots of it are, it is clear, personal, to be found in his own experience. Consider in his poetry how the complex and unstable categories, notably 'Innocence' (where the Christ, or ideal of human perfection, merges with Luciferic nostalgia for an unregainable state) and 'Experience' (a world created by a deluded divinity, a monstrous mixture of Ahriman and God) already point the way towards the radical Gnostic mythology of his subsequent 'prophetic books'.

A study of Blake's later mythology suggests a spiritual configuration which cannot be expressed in terms of our 'cross' of psychic forces. For the Gnostic, inner stability is achieved not through balance, but through the root-separation of the Ahrimanic tendency and a powerful fusion of the other forces into a Fulness (*Pleroma*) of spiritual attraction. In achieving autonomy in this way, however, the Ahrimanic principle inevitably usurps some of the attributes of God as traditionally conceived. Hence is generated the figure of the Gnostic Demiurge – or in Blake, that central character of many myths, Urizen, the God–Devil, the Satanic Creator. Yet the only real candidate for identification with God is obviously the Pleroma itself, which the Gnostic Basilides regarded explicitly as 'consubstantial' with God. For Blake, too, God was not separate from the imagination. But the dualism of Innocence and Experience was only accentuated in this way, so that Blake found himself troubled by the deepest and most disturbing intuition of Gnostic thought: a divided Godhead.

In the Gnostic world-view, therefore, Ahriman is not membered into the psychic totality; and the world of conscious experience (the cosmos), rather than reflecting an interplay of cognitive powers, appears a hell of material imprisonment – Blake's Ulro. The sense of being trapped in that cosmos results from the inability of the psyche to relate the Ahrimanic pole to any of the other forces. Instead, even the Divine must suffer division.

The outcome of the collocation of forces in the Pleroma is clearly seen in Blake's visionary teaching. The positive aspect of God is to be found in man; 'Thou art a man, God is no more', and every man in his essential being is Jesus, as Blake told a somewhat startled Crabb Robinson. Christ ('human perfection') merges in ultimate identity with God, making anything like the process of the Incarnation theologically redundant. But not only is the Jesus Christ in every man identical with God – God and Christ are terms interchangeable with imagination, and the imagination is not a capacity of human mind but the actual identity of man. Blake thus reproduces the Gnostic pattern of the Divine Anthropos, or primal God–Man, who is also identical with the faculty of visionary *gnosis*. In this highly Gnostic fashion, Blake attains a total commitment to the validity of imagination, identified with 'being' itself, free from the Ahrimanic doubts with which a more self-conscious poet such as Shelley had to contend. Or, to put it another way, he managed in his God–Man (Christ) to subsume in addition the figure of Lucifer: for him, the power which tends to diminish our self-consciousness and raise us imaginatively above the level of the object-world is simply a part of the spiritual whole. Only by the demand for self-consciousness is the Luciferic brought into contra-diction with the other powers. In his painting *The Fall of Man* (Victoria and Albert Museum), which shows the expulsion from Paradise and is unparalleled in treatment throughout Western art, Blake images the Gnostic myth that it was Christ who played the Luciferic role, entered the serpent and led Adam and Eve out of a delusive Urizenic garden of material delights.

The Gnostic mythology permits a certain *rapprochement* between a humanism and the religious mind, though it is totally different from the incarnational and historical humanism which has arisen on the basis of Christianity and its secular derivatives. The Gnostic reaches a conviction of the divinity of man and the truth of imagination – but at enormous cost to the integrity of the self and its experience, denying the significance of consciousness itself (a 'counterfeit spirit' in man according to the Gnostics, a 'Spectre' or Satanic 'Watch-fiend' according to Blake) and making all moral deliberation worthless since it only obscures the authentic impulse from the depths. Nevertheless, it is a price that many visionaries have been willing to pay.

5

The Devil for a Companion – Goethe and Shelley

With surprising affability, the Lord in Goethe's audacious *Prologue in Heaven* to the great poetic drama of *Faust*, receives Mephistopheles before the celestial throne. Evidently at ease, the visiting Devil explains that he has often found occasion to call on 'the old fellow' up above, and speaks appreciatively of God's magnanimity in allowing him free access to realms where he hardly belongs: he has always been treated, he says, very civilly. For his part, the Lord accounts for his indulgence thus:

> The active spirit of man soon sleeps, and soon
> He seeks unbroken quiet; therefore I
> Have given him the Devil for a companion,
> Who may provoke him to some sort of work,
> And must create forever.

These short lines take us – as we might expect of remarks from the Lord – without more ado into the profundities of Goethe's poetic vision. And their significance, I shall try to suggest, is even more readily appreciable today than when Goethe wrote them over a century-and-a-half ago.

But that brings us to another Prologue full of irony.

* * *

Literary fashions are fickle and transient affairs. So the evidence is clear: the English aversion to Goethe is no mere fashion, but an enduring temperamental fact. It is not even that English culture has turned against one of the greatest figures in world literature, for such Goethe is acknowledged to be; it has never seriously come to terms with him at all.

The trend was established early: the most promising ambassadors of German Romanticism in England were oddly unsympathetic.

Coleridge, looking back on the time he was offered a hundred pounds by his publisher for a rendering of Goethe, recollected prudishly: 'I debated with myself whether it became my moral character to render into English – and so far, certainly lend my countenance to language – much of which I thought vulgar, licentious, and blasphemous. I need not tell you that I never put pen to paper as a translator of *Faust*.' Charles Lamb called the *First Part* of *Faust* (the only part published in Goethe's lifetime) a 'disagreeable canting tale of seduction'; the reviewer William Taylor wrote in 1810 that 'the absurdities of this piece are so numerous, the obscenities are so frequent, the profaneness is so gross, and the beauties are so exclusively adapted for German relish, that we cannot conscientiously recommend its importation, and still less the translation of it, to our English students of German literature.' One of Goethe's earliest English translators, John Anster, omitted the *Prologue in Heaven*, explaining that it 'contains a great deal that is written in a light and irreverent tone, and possesses, we think, very little merit of any kind.' Wordsworth summed up the English response: 'I have tried to read Goethe. I never could succeed.'

The irony of this earthly, English prologue to an understanding of Goethe is that, whereas the great names in the encounter of English with German Romanticism averted their eyes in holy dread from the outrages on taste they saw perpetrated in *Faust*, our best poetic versions of Goethe come from the pen of their younger contemporary who scarcely knew enough German to read him – Percy Bysshe Shelley. It was Shelley who boldly translated the scandalous *Prologue* and the infamous *Walpurgisnacht* revelry which all the earlier translators had left out. It was Shelley who interpreted *Faust* extempore, possibly along with passages from Goethe's autobiography, for the benefit of the admiring Byron, and so indirectly furnished the inspiration for Byron's Faustian drama of *Manfred*. Byron was of the opinion that Mephistopheles ranked as 'one of the finest and most sublime specimens of human conception.' (Goethe, of course, felt rather the same way about Byron himself, who formed the historical original of Euphorion in the labyrinthine *Second Part* of *Faust*.) It was Shelley who mediated Goethe's influence on English literature, and in the process he acquired a Faustian nickname. When he read to Byron the verses where Mephistopheles refers nonchalantly to 'my aunt, the renowned snake' ('meine Muhme, die berühmte Schlange'), Byron pulled him up with the comment, 'Then you are her nephew'; and Shelley was henceforth known to his friends as 'the Snake'.

Certainly it seemed to Wordsworth and the English reviewers, bishops, censors and other worthies that Byron had, in some sense or other, taken the Devil for his companion. And perhaps they saw in the radical Shelley, self-exiled in Italy, the Devil himself. That, however, would be an oversimplification.

THE AHRIMANIC PHILOSOPHY

There is a delightful passage in *Nightmare Abbey*, a satirical novel by Shelley's close friend Peacock. Shelley is reflected in the character of Scythrop, and there are plans to find him a suitable wife (evidently no easy matter), one suggestion being the daughter of the mystical Manichaean millenarian Mr Toobad. Peacock takes the opportunity to poke a little fun at Romantic solemnities on both sides of the channel:

> A match between Scythrop and Mr. Toobad's daughter would be a very desirable occurrence. She was finishing her education in a German convent, but Mr. Toobad described her as being fully impressed with the truth of his Ahrimanic philosophy, and being altogether as gloomy and antithalian a young lady as Mr. Glowry himself could desire for the future mistress of Nightmare Abbey.

Peacock himself planned an epic poem to be called *Ahrimanes*, and it is also he who assures us that *Faust* was among the half-dozen books which most influenced Shelley's mind.

All these allusions, in combination, suggest that behind the humour lies a serious tale of Shelley's encounter with the 'Ahrimanic philosophy', and that the story of Faust may have been to him something more than just a cautionary tale.

Mr Toobad was based upon another prominent member of the Shelley–Peacock circle: the occultist John Frank Newton. It is almost certainly he who introduced Shelley and his friends to the 'Ahrimanic philosophy'. He was a student of Indian, Iranian and other antiquities, a keen advocate (like Shelley) of vegetarianism, and the author of a work on the Hindu zodiac. Peacock made him into Mr 'Toobad' because of his firmly held conviction that his age, with its rationalism and materialism, was under the rule of the spirit of denial – the spirit generally called in occultism 'Ahriman', following the mythology of ancient Iran with its twin daemons of Darkness and Light. That dualism had influenced Christianity itself, especially that form of Christianity, later declared heretical, which is called Manichaeism. Newton saw the Ahrimanic spirit represented wherever men took the material world for the whole of reality, resulting in a denial of the creative human spirit. If the objective world 'out there' was the ultimate truth, human mind could be nothing but its inessential reflector, a passive mirror. And where would be man's freedom if his mind could do no more than acknowledge the unalterable laws of outward Necessity, the end-less chain of causes and effects in a universe of strict natural law?

Yet that was the world-picture the eighteenth-century rationalist and empiricist philosophers had painted. Man, as seen by Locke or Hume, was inwardly a blank screen waiting to be illuminated by the light of external nature, his mind a *tabula rasa*. And such, too, was the view of man adhered to by the youthful Shelley. Under the influence of eighteenth-century philosophy he even planned to write novels exhibiting a strict cause-and-effect psychology! He rejected any sort of revealed religion, writing the famous student pamphlet *The Necessity of Atheism* for which he was expelled from Oxford. In his juvenile propaganda-poem *Queen Mab* he cheerfully hailed the

> Spirit of Nature! all-sufficing power,
> Necessity! Thou mother of the world!

He was soon to find, however, that the materialist world-view in its significance for the whole being of man proved something less than all-sufficing. He explored its findings with growing poetic sensibility in his earliest mature poems; and he discovered that a philosophy of external perception and the submission of mind to an abstract Necessity, though it appealed to the intellect, left him deeply unfulfilled. Some profound and essential part of his humanity remained unacknowledged, unplaced, and made itself felt first of all in a sickening sense of hollowness.

Shelley's first great poem, *Alastor or The Spirit of Solitude* deals with this theme. It describes a search for truth, in a youth who is led by the highest ideals 'to the contemplation of the universe', as a Preface explains. 'The magnificence and beauty of the external world sinks profoundly into the frame of his conceptions, and affords to their modifications a variety not to be exhausted . . . But the period arrives when these objects cease to suffice.' The youth is driven to restless and interminable wandering, and is finally destroyed by his quest. And such must be the fate, Shelley intimates, of all those who would follow him. They inevitably 'perish through the intensity and passion of their search . . . when the vacancy of their spirit suddenly makes itself felt'.

Pursuing in external nature an ultimate yet humanly satisfying reality, Shelley's young hero attains an intensity of experience which transcends the physical world. But he finds beyond it only the Ahrimanic vacancy – like the 'black and watery depth' that lies behind a pastoral mountain scene reflected on the surface of a lake.

Alastor is a dark vision for so young a poet. But the darkness was only intensified still further by Shelley's visit to the Alps in 1816, when he stood in meditation before the huge ice-and-rock mass of Mont Blanc. In the scene then spread before him he saw an epitome of the 'everlasting universe of things', all the objects which are presented to man's senses and endlessly flow through his mind. *Mont Blanc* like *Alastor* moves toward an apprehension of the Ahrimanic void behind the sense-world, an apprehension that comes to us when, as Shelley wrote elsewhere, 'we find within our thoughts the chasm of an insufficient void'. That yawning vacuity is all we can experience of the Power which inhabits Mont Blanc.

> Some say that gleams of a remoter world
> Visit the soul in sleep, – that death is slumber,
> And that its shapes the busy thoughts outnumber
> Of those who wake and live. – I look on high;
> Has some unknown omnipotence unfurled
> The veil of life and death? or do I lie
> In dream, and does the mightier world of sleep
> Spread far around and inaccessibly
> Its circles? For the very spirit fails,
> Driven like a homeless cloud from steep to steep
> That vanishes among the viewless gales!
> Far, far above, piercing the infinite sky,
> Mont Blanc appears, – still, snowy, and serene –

Man flies in dread from the vicinity of its creeping glaciers, its desert of ice peopled only by storms, savage birds of prey and wolves, its hideously scarred and riven formations of rock. In human terms it is pure alienation – 'solitude' and 'vacancy': the darkness of a moonless night, snow falling unseen, winds howling unheard, the distant 'voiceless' lightning's vast energy innocently expended. It is truly a vision to teach 'awful doubt', a terror of the void confronting the human spirit when it stands before the natural forces of creation and destruction.

Nor was all this just literary reflection. A long letter Shelley wrote back to his friends in London reveals that *Mont Blanc* is surprisingly close to being a record of spontaneous feeling. 'The verge of the glacier', he wrote for instance,

> presents the most vivid image of desolation that it is possible to conceive. No one dares to approach it ... there is something inexpressibly dreadful in the aspect of a few branchless trunks which nearest to the ice-rifts still stand in the uprooted soil. The meadows perish overwhelmed with sand and stones.

The ineluctable Power in the glacier, destructive on a scale no human mind can conceive, already signals the presence of the evil daemon, the spirit of negation proclaimed by his friends Peacock and John Frank Newton:

> Do you who assert the supremacy of Ahriman imagine him throned among those desolating snows, among the palaces of death and frost sculptured in this their terrible magnificence by the unsparing hand of necessity, and that he casts around him as the first essays of his final usurpation avalanches, torrents, rocks and thunders ... and above all, those deadly glaciers at once the proofs and symbols of his reign?

Whatever his friends may have pictured, that is certainly the vision embodied in Shelley's poem.

I shall quote some further passages from the letter, begun on 22 July 1816 and continued over several days, because it throws considerable light on the quality of experience (as opposed to the elaboration of thought) underlying the poem and is extremely revealing of Shelley's sense of spiritual forces in nature. *Mont Blanc* is not obviously an 'occasional' poem; yet the letter from Chamonix demonstrates the remarkable extent to which it actually records Shelley's immediate feelings on a unique occasion. Even as he stood before the mountains and glaciers, and wandered amongst them, he apparently felt them as embodying the 'daemonic' powers. In the essay *On Life*, Shelley refers to his own idiosyncratic use of the word 'signs' in cases where we would ordinarily see nothing 'signified' at all. He expands the term to cover many everyday experiences. Indeed:

> In this latter sense, almost all familiar objects are signs, standing, not for themselves, but for others, in their capacity of suggesting one thought which shall lead to a train of thoughts.

That is exactly what we see happening in the marvellous first section of *Mont Blanc*. What is suggestive about the letter is its hint that much of Shelley's spontaneous perception was shot through with this type of symbolic resonance – unreflectively, not only in retrospect. He saw even common things and objects as the focus of far-ranging associations; not as inert and fixed, but floating in a whirlpool of mental processes, spiritual energies.

Shelley writes of his arrival in Chamonix, during which they moved windingly along: 'still following the valley, or now rather the vast ravine which is the couch and the creation of the terrible Arve . . .' As for the mountain itself:

> Mont Blanc was before us but was covered with cloud, and its base furrowed with dreadful gaps was seen alone. Pinnacles of snow intolerably bright, part of the chain connected with Mont Blanc shone thro' the clouds at intervals on high ... The immensity of these aerial summits excited, when they suddenly burst upon the sight, a sentiment of extatic wonder, not unallied to madness ...

The inaccessibility of the summit, from its base caught sight of through cloud-gaps, is already strongly suggested. In the poem this becomes a sign of the unapproachable, alien Power which inhabits the sheer rock. The unbearable glare of the peaks suggests their inhuman and destructive power and their ability to disturb the mind to its depths. The scene felt to Shelley a direct expression of his own mind:

> the snowy pyramids which shot into the bright blue sky seemed to overhang our path – the ravine, clothed with gigantic pines

and black with its depths below ... was close to our footsteps.
All was as much our own as if we had been the creators of such
impressions in the minds of others, as now occupied our own.
Nature was the poet whose harmony held our spirits more
breathless than that of the divinest.

Here we have the origins of the sublime first section of the poem.
Many further details of the poem, too, have their origin in Shelley's
impressions: the 'unsculptured image' beneath the veil of the
waterfall was a rock 'precisely resembling some colossal Egyptian
statue of a female deity' which can still be seen near Magland; the
mountains were so high and sharp 'that they seem to pierce the
sky' (an image transferred rather inappropriately in the poem to
the bold, blunt outline of Mont Blanc itself); the chasms were deep
and blue like the sky; Shelley has heard with some horror that
there are troops of wolves among these desert mountains.

The glaciers terrify him – we quoted the passage earlier – and
directly anticipate the vision of utter disintegration in the fourth
section of *Mont Blanc*, the grinding of life in the grip of Power
which signals the presence of Ahriman. Moreover, in the letter he
turns to consider human suffering face to face, where in the poem
he relies upon his imaginative impact on the reader:

Add to this the degradation of the human species, who in these
regions are half-deformed or idiotic, and all of whom are
deprived of anything that can excite interest and admiration.
This is a part of the subject more mournful, and less sublime: –
but such as neither the poet nor the philosopher should disdain.

The letter from Chamonix demonstrates how closely the poet, the
philosopher and the man in Shelley were interwoven, and forms a
valuable supplement and counterweight on the side of sponta-
neous reaction to the reading of *Mont Blanc* against the background
of Shelley's sceptical thought.

Mont Blanc and *Alastor* demonstrate the young Shelley's determi-
nation to penetrate the veil of appearances, and to face even the
dark powers he senses beyond. With what sense of inner recogni-
tion, therefore, must he have read the first scenes of the *First Part*
of *Faust*! By the time he came to do so, he had advanced far on his
remarkable path of spiritual development. Yet it must have been
hard for him not to have seen, in the discontented Faust, some

reflection of his own youthful strivings. Faust too had sunk himself
in the intellectual learning of his time, mastered the intricacies of
its philosophy, and found in his thoughts what Shelley called 'the
chasm of an insufficient void'. For what does it prove, all his
hard-won intellectual achievement?

> The impossibility of knowledge!
> It is this that burns away my heart;
> Of course I am cleverer than the quacks,
> Than master and doctor, than clerk and priest.
> I suffer no scruple or doubt in the least.
> I have no qualms about devil or burning.
> Which is just why all joy is torn from me.
> I cannot presume I c⸱⸱⸱' open my mind
> To pro⸱⸱⸱lytize and im⸱⸱⸱⸱ mankind.

So Faust lamen⸱⸱, and the wish expressed in the last line – 'die
Menschen zu bessern und zu bekehren' – must have been
especially poignant, since it was Shelley's own painfully abandoned
dream before he had to retreat from England to Italy in 1818,
leaving behind the active struggle for social reform.

Also akin to Shelley is Faust's longing to see into the great laws
which knit the universe into a whole, the unifying cosmic power
which 'governs thought, and to the infinite dome / Of heaven is as
a law'. Faust too is transported 'as in a trance sublime and strange'
when he contemplates the sign of the Macrocosm, the great world:

> Lo, single things inwoven, made to blend,
> To work in oneness with the whole, and live
> Members of one another, while ascend
> Celestial powers, who ever take and give
> Vessels of gold on heaven's living stair.
> Their pinions fragrant with the bliss they bear,
> Pervading all, that heaven and earth agree,
> Transfixing all the world with harmony.

The vision surpasses in splendour even Shelley's celebration of
nature in its harmony and diversity. Faust feels himself, to begin
with, a part within the living whole and rejuvenating joy flickers to
life in his veins. But when, like Shelley before the panorama of
Mont Blanc, he desires to go beyond the visible creation to an

underlying reality, the precarious dream collapses. 'A magnificent pageant!' he exclaims – and then suddenly it seems to him an insubstantial image, only a mirage ('Welch Schauspiel! Aber ach! ein Schauspiel nur!'). He senses behind the veil of phenomenal nature the void of unreality:

> A show, that mocks my touch or grasp or will.

No more than Shelley is he able to find in the underlying emptiness an answer to the longings of the heart. He turns disconsolately away from the sign of the Macrocosm, invoking instead the Spirit of the Earth.

Faust is determined to see the truth of things face to face – even, he says, if it means his death. Nevertheless, when the Earth-Spirit appears out of an eruption of flame, he is overpowered by the tremendous energy he has unleashed. He averts his gaze in terror, crying out 'Appalling vision!' ('schreckliches Gesicht!'). He had expanded himself inwardly in the attempt to comprehend a reality of cosmic or planetary dimensions, proclaiming himself a man, an image of the Godhead. But the forces of creation and destruction in which the Earth-Spirit manifests itself terrify him as the earthquake-scarred rocks and the glaciers terrified Shelley. He shrinks into himself, and the Spirit dismisses him saying, 'You are like that Spirit which you can grasp, / Not me!' – at which point Faust's pedantic assistant, Wagner, knocks on the door. Faust's painful ironic deflation is complete.

The absurd, dressing-gowned figure of Wagner restores the balance in Faust's estimate of man, bringing him back to the mundane world where he loses for a time the sense of cosmic vertigo produced by the dissolving of his visions. So long as he remains within the world of phenomena, of natural appearances, he is safe. But it is also inherent in man to aspire beyond, as Faust still does in his heart of hearts. He still longs to attain a cosmic dimension of experience. In his terrified shrinking, however, the vacancy of his spirit has (in the Shelleyan phrase) made itself felt. In Shelley this resulted in intimations of death and dark, watery depths; ultimately in the vision of Ahriman enthroned amid the ice-gulfs and avalanches in the mountain's heart of darkness. In Faust there follow thoughts of suicide and – a scene or two later – the entry into the drama of Goethe's own daemon of denial and negation ('der Geist, der stets verneint'), Mephistopheles.

The sombre reflections of *Mont Blanc* represented a crisis in Shelley's development as a visionary poet. He had confronted dark realities, and the way forward was far from obvious. Should he content himself with a poetry of hopelessness, 'the wisdom of a high despair'? Or should he find a heaven in hell's despite and remain doggedly optimistic? Using the mythology brought to life by John Frank Newton and Peacock, he first tried to work out an epic vision of progress by martyrdom, which can still be read (at stupendous length) in his disastrously unsuccessful poem *The Revolt of Islam*. But he was forcing the issue, and the result is at once naive and strident. Anxious to escape the haunting Ahrimanic terror behind outer reality, Shelley took flight for consolation into an unreal fantasy-world. He dreams of an eternal temple of fame where his martyrs for freedom, free from the clogs of mortality, idle away their eternity in self-satisfied glory and the morning star smiles down on them with a perpetual smile. A pretty dream; but Shelley has temporarily lost his grip on the real struggle his sainted heroes have left behind on earth. He himself soon became dissatisfied with it; for, contrary to certain popular views about Shelley, he was of a profoundly realistic nature and well aware of the limitations of his hopeful idealism. Only a profoundly realistic poet could have looked with such honesty into the Ahrimanic gloom. After his move to Italy Shelley struggled toward a fuller and more integrated image of man, able to do justice both to his idealistic longings and his sense of 'sad reality' in a flawed world. *Mont Blanc* ends by posing the question of the significance of the Ahrimanic void to the total workings of imagination, and to that question Shelley soon returned. He chose to remain true to earthly actuality, even if it meant accepting the Devil for a companion.

Since Shelley's day, the rise of science and the invasion of our lives by technology has made us all the more familiar with the 'Ahrimanic' spirit; the enthroning of outer reality as an absolute, a God in God's place. Many are prepared to worship the spirit of Power. Others have begun to take refuge in dreamy idealisms like that which briefly seduced Shelley into unreal visions of epic grandeur.

Goethe and Shelley, however, in their mature poetry, offer us a vision of the world through which we might begin to come to terms with the material, external realm; to enter into the sphere of Ahriman, yet without being destroyed as was Shelley's youthful hero in *Alastor* or as was the Faust of Marlowe and others before Goethe. Milton was struggling toward a consciousness of the Ego that could sustain such a vision; Blake's Gnostic universe posed the problem for the first time in its full depth, showing us a fallen, Ahrimanized world that had to be dissolved in the creative flux of imagination. But it is Goethe and Shelley who first suggest a modern solution to man's dilemma. They offer us, in other words, a vision which is still highly relevant to our present experience. They look forward to the kind of vision of the world Rudolf Steiner gives us, where there is no question of retreat from the outer world into mystical seclusion or a desperate faith in the ideal because all else is lost. 'We see how necessary it is', Steiner stressed,

> that the modern age should come to understand the world more and more, that it should develop a science so as to master the external forces of nature. And the Lord of external science, of what lives in outer nature, is Ahriman. If, however, we would take flight from the Ahrimanic, we would condemn ourselves to dullness and stupidity; it is not a matter of fleeing from the Ahrimanic, but of entering into that sphere of the world where Ahriman rules under the leadership of the Christ-impulse.*

Thus Steiner gives a name to the spiritual power which can lead us through the Ahrimanic void unannihilated. We may recall what happens in Goethe's *Faust* when thoughts of suicide have almost prevailed. Faust is called back to earthly life by a sudden outburst of bells and a joyful chorus:

Christ is arisen!

And if Shelley was never able to acknowledge that name as it was proclaimed in the churches of his time, it was surely in that spirit nonetheless that he chose to stay faithful to the earth and proceeded on his Faustian way.

THE NEW MANICHAEISM

The Poets of Night and Charnel-house beg to be excused because they have just struck up an interesting conversation with a newly arisen

---

*Rudolf Steiner, *Geisteswissenschaftliche Erläuterungen zu Goethes 'Faust'*, I (Dornach, 1967) p. 102.

Vampire, and this might lead to the development of a new genre of poetry. The Herald has to accept the excuse, and he calls on Greek Mythology to fill the gap, which it does, retaining still both character and charm even in the mask of modern times.

– Stage direction in Goethe's *Faust, Second Part*

I have tried to suggest that the scene of Faust in his high-vaulted Gothic chamber must have struck Shelley when he read it as almost a record of his own experience. Already in his youth he had been deeply interested in natural science, above all in electricity which seemed to suggest some occult power behind nature, and used to terrify his younger sisters with sparks and explosions. Even as a child he had been sensitive to fearful presences lurking behind material reality, the potential terror of the Ahrimanic which he had exploited in his early 'Gothic' novels *Zastrozzi* and *St. Irvyne, or The Rosicrucian.* He recalls in a later poem:

> While yet a boy I sought for ghosts, and sped
>   Through many a listening chamber, cave and ruin,
>   And starlight wood, with fearful steps pursuing
> Hopes of high talk with the departed dead ...

(*Hymn to Intellectual Beauty*, v)

As a student at Oxford he practised alchemy and perhaps magic in his quest for the secrets of nature; in his notebooks he sketched what he called 'daemons and other monsters of my thought', strange elementals rising from a lake and leaping from mountain crags. In Wales he fought with (indeed, took a shot at) a horrific daemon, of which his drawing survives to mystify and perplex his biographers as it perplexed and frightened his first wife, Harriet. The strange thing is that Shelley's magical explorations remained so intimately bound up with his materialism. Faust had no qualms about the Devil or burning, and likewise Shelley remained firmly sceptical about the orthodox scheme of Heaven and Hell. Of questions concerning these absolutes of the moral and natural world he says with confidence:

> No voice from some sublimer world hath ever
>   To sage or poet these responses given –

> Therefore the names of Demon, Ghost, and Heaven,
> Remain the records of their vain endeavour.

> (*Hymn to Intellectual Beauty*, III)

Nonetheless, the poetry of 'Night and Charnel-house' remained one of Shelley's major modes, from his youthful novels to what is probably the greatest Gothic play in English, *The Cenci*.

Mont Blanc had ended by posing the question of the significance of the Ahrimanic 'vacancy' for the total workings of the imagination. How is it possible, he asks implicitly, for human imagination to face the Ahrimanic void and not be destroyed? The great step toward resolving that question came when the poet left England and migrated to the sunnier climes of Italy. He had grave crises to contend with: the death of his children and the undermining of his own health. But he rose above them, partly it may be through the writing of the masterpiece which occupied him from 1818 to late the following year, *Prometheus Unbound*. In Italy he was fascinated by the Greek and Roman sculptures. Above all, the climate promised regeneration. *Prometheus* was chiefly written, as he describes in the Preface, while Shelley was perched high up

> upon the mountainous ruins of the Baths of Caracalla, among the flowery glades, and thickets of odoriferous blossoming trees, which are extended in ever winding labyrinths upon its immense platforms and dizzy arches suspended in the air. The bright blue sky of Rome, and the effect of the vigorous awakening spring in that divinest climate, and the new life with which it drenches the spirits even to intoxication, were the inspiration of this drama.

At the same time, he was re-reading classical drama, and the problem at the heart of his poetic development gradually fused with the idea of writing a lyrical tragedy based upon the myth of the Titan who stole fire from the gods for mankind. Here, in fact, was a theme of Faustian aspiration – but set, not in Gothic Germany, but in the fantastic realm of Greek mythology. Gothic gloom gave way to classical phantasmagoria.

*   *   *

Of course, Shelley did not get to know Goethe's *Faust* until 1822, after *Prometheus* was completed and published. And of course, he

knew only the *First Part* of *Faust*, since the *Second Part* with its amaz-
ing *Klassische Phantasmagorie* did not appear until after Goethe's
death in 1831. If it is remarkable, therefore, that the *First Part*
echoes Shelley's development in the years before he knew it, it is
even more remarkable that Shelley's development in the writing of
Prometheus should so oddly prefigure the course Goethe was to
take in his still unwritten *Second Part*. When the *First Part* came into
Shelley's hands, he must have recognized an astonishing anticipa-
tion of his own poetic thought; and if Goethe had ever come upon
Prometheus Unbound, he would have had to see in it an anticipation
of the direction he had gone in his own subsequent writing!

Part of the explanation of this surprising parallelism lies in the
fact that Goethe had responded in much the same way as Shelley
to the Greek antiquities and the exuberant climate of Italy, which
had also led him to completely remodel his style. The young
Goethe had evolved a taut, sinewy style which he himself had
compared to the Gothic architecture of the cathedral in Strasburg.
And he too had entered into some of the darker aspects of life in
his poetry. Indeed, as the *Walpurgisnacht*, the Witches' Kitchen,
and the Auerbach's Cellar scenes of *Faust* show, he had a more
profoundly realistic sense of the grotesque, seamy and brutal side
of human nature than did the more refined Shelley, for all his
proletarian sympathies. Gargoyles, we may remember, are an
important feature of Gothic buildings, and the Brocken scenes in
Faust are their poetic equivalents. The warm, sunlit world of Italy,
however, brought new ideas; Goethe experimented with and duly
mastered the classical style in poetry, even going back to ancient
Greek metres as well as to mythological themes. In the *Second Part*
of *Faust* he transported his hero back into classical Greece and
recreated the spirit of mythology with unrivalled imaginative
virtuosity, so that in Acts I and II we hardly know that this is the
same Faust who featured in the Gothic *First Part*.

The Faust-books on which Goethe drew had already connected
Faust with Helen of Troy, whose phantom he was supposed to
have summoned up by his demonic arts. Goethe spiritualizes the
story, so that Helen becomes the embodiment of Faust's higher
self. When the listless Faust revives at the beginning of the *Second
Part*, with the nature-spirits singing to the accompaniment of
Aeolian harps of the refreshing powers of sleep, the drama is
transposed to a new level, a new plane. Henceforth it is played out
in inner worlds. Helen embodies that harmony of being which

humanity possessed in ancient Greece at its best, a harmony which has since been lost by our more modern civilization and can only be won again from the inner depths of man's being. Faust glimpses her first in the Witches' Kitchen – though Mephistopheles soon manages to divert his attention; then he calls her spirit back in the magic-demonstration he gives for the Emperor – but when he tries to grasp her, the vision collapses and dissolves. So he must journey back to the past, the mythological past that lies hidden deep inside all of us, to find her in reality.

It would be a mistake, however, to conclude that Goethe was advocating a return to something which had once existed in the life of humanity, without respect for the changing conditions of widely separated epochs in man's history. Goethe was well aware that what is done in world-evolution cannot be undone; any attempt to retreat simply leads to manifold illusions. He was no soft-headed 'primitivist' trying to find his way back to a lost Utopia. Like many of the Romantic poets in England and Germany, he enormously admired the classical ideal, but he knew that it had to be given a new form for the modern age. The best from the ancient world had to be married to the highest aspirations of the modern world – and that is what we are shown in the altogether remarkable poetic achievement of Act III: the marriage of Faust and Helen.

In order for that union to be consummated, however, there has first to be a return to the depths: a confronting of outward realities and a transformation from within. There has to be, in short, an initiation.

*   *   *

When Faust attempted, in the scene we have examined from the *First Part* of the drama, to pierce beyond the visible world he felt himself either lost in an unreal void, or overwhelmed by the appalling energy of the Earth-Spirit who surges in the ebb and flow of things, in the storms of life. He shrank back from the terror of the Ahrimanic. His paltry human ego – which moments before he had called the image of God – felt the threat of annihilation which stems from an apprehension of the vastness of the universe, its lack of concern for human hopes and desires.

When we come to the Faust of the *Second Part* of the play, on the other hand, we find that his intimations of Helen (his higher self) have begun to change his whole way of experiencing the world.

We watch him develop toward a higher mode of consciousness, one in which man is able to confront the external universe and overcome the terror of the void; a kind of consciousness which can enter the realm where Ahriman reigns without the threat of destruction.

Hence we see that in much of the *Second Part* it is actually Faust who has the upper hand over Mephistopheles – whereas previously things had gone very much the Devil's way. The shift in the balance emerges clearly in the wonderful scene describing the Descent to the Mothers, the creative sources of being and life. At the outset, Mephistopheles has to admit that he cannot be of much help to Faust in the search for Helen. He can only tell him a little about the way. He is rather unwilling to say anything at all, and only does so at Faust's express command:

> *Mephistopheles*
>   Loth am I now high mystery to unfold:
>   Goddesses dwell, in solitude, sublime,
>   Enthroned beyond the world of place or time;
>   Even to speak of them dismays the bold.
>   These are The Mothers.
> *Faust*
>   Mothers?
> *Mephistopheles*
>   Stand you daunted?
> *Faust*
>   The Mothers! Mothers – sound with wonder haunted.

Far from being daunted, Faust is eager to set forth. 'Where lies the way?', he demands. But Mephistopheles denies that there is any way: the Mothers belong to hidden depths of being 'beyond the world of place or time', and to reach them Faust will have to enter boldly into that realm of experience he shrank from before. Mephistopheles does his best to intimidate Faust with the Ahrimanic sense of vacancy and estrangement that must accompany his quest for ultimate truth:

> *Faust*
>   Where lies the way?
> *Mephistopheles*
>   There *is* none. Way to the Unreachable,
>   Never for treading, to those Unbeseechable,

Never besought! Is your soul then ready?
Not locks or bolts are there, no barrier crude,
But lonely drift, far, lone estrangement's eddy.
What sense have you of waste and solitude?
                    . . .
And if to ocean's end your path should lead,
To look upon enormity of space,
Still would you see that waves to waves succeed,
Ay, though you have a shuddering doom to face,
You'd still see something. For in the green
Of silenced depths are gliding dolphins seen;
Still cloud will stir, and sun and moon and star;
But blank is that eternal void afar;
There eyes avail not, even your step is dumb,
No substance there, when to your rest you come.

Faust will have to brave the sense of loneliness and emptiness which Shelley explored before *Mont Blanc*, or in the solitary wandering youth in *Alastor* ('Hast du Begriff von Öd' und Einsamkeit?'). Even ocean-wanderers like the Ancient Mariner or the Flying Dutchman have the consoling presence of the dolphins, half seen in the soundless depths, and those inalienable companions, sun, moon and stars. But the metaphysical traveller experiences the quintessence of alienation – what Blake called 'the Void Outside of Existence'.

In the scene from the *First Part*, Faust played into Mephistopheles' hands. He was desperately seeking for some ultimate reality beyond or behind the outer physical world. But unable to transcend the limitations of his human organization, his finite resources of mind and sense, he had been left groping helplessly in the void. He could see nothing beyond phenomenal nature but darkness and vacuity; he felt the very ground taken away from beneath his feet. In the 'Mothers' scene, however, he has begun to realize that the true means of attaining to higher vision lies within. A deeper vision of reality can come only through a transformation of man's own being so as to embody that principle he seeks in the form of Helen, his own spiritual self. And with that realization, the Ahrimanic void begins to lose something of its terror.

So Faust replies to Mephistopheles' intimidations in high humour. He is not to be diverted from his quest by this ordeal and asserts confidently:

Well, let us on! We'll plumb your deepest ground,
For in your Nothing may the All be found.

And not waiting for the ground to be snatched from under him,
this time he stamps his foot and sinks resolutely into the earth.
  According to Blake – if we quote him now a little more fully:

There is a Void outside of Existence, which if enter'd into
Englobes itself & becomes a Womb.

Translated into the terms of Faust in Goethe's poetic drama, this
means that if Faust will trust to his own inner strength as the
ground of truth, if he will boldly enter into the void where before
he grasped fearfully about for external support, he would be
reborn to a higher level of existence. Instead of experiencing an
alien, inhuman world-out-there, he would experience a man-
centred universe, given meaning and truth by the light of human
spirit. He would be able to confront the Ahrimanic vacuity with a
degree of equanimity that he has hitherto been denied. And as we
have seen, Faust does dare to take that plunge and turn the world
inside-out. Accordingly he comes into the creative realm of the
Mothers – one of his many apprehensions in the play of the many
sides of the 'Eternal Feminine', the power which in the amazing
final scene will eventually lead him above into the spiritual world.

*   *   *

The scene of the Descent to the Mothers may help us to under-
stand the scene in Shelley's *Prometheus* where the poet once again
tackles the sombre themes of *Mont Blanc*, the two parallel imagina-
tions illuminating each other.
  Already in the stage setting at the beginning of the play,
describing Prometheus bound on a rocky precipice in the Indian
Caucasus, Shelley returns to his dark intuitions. Prometheus is
trapped in the spiritless Ahrimanic world of external perception:

Black, wintry, dead, unmeasured; without herb
Insect, or beast, or shape or sound of life.

(*Prometheus* Act I, 21–2)

The inhospitable mountain landscape recalls the scarred and riven slopes, the icy deserts of Mont Blanc, the presence of vast forces of creation and destruction. It transpires in the course of the drama that Prometheus is able to attain to a higher vision of the world than this; but at the beginning of the play he is still self-divided, estranged from his real or higher self – which here too appears in the guise of a female ideal of harmony and beauty, the sea-nymph Asia. Like the *Second Part* of *Faust*, much of *Prometheus* is taken up with an initiatory process, culminating in the marriage of Asia and Prometheus in the lyrical Act IV. There are, however, certain differences in the way Shelley handles his mythology which we must register before a genuine comparison with Goethe becomes possible. Asia is at first the representative of Prometheus' higher self before his inner awakening; hence it is she who in this version must make the initiatory descent into the void, and it is only then, when she has been transfigured into the Spirit of what Shelley sometimes called Intellectual (i.e. spiritual) Beauty, that she becomes strictly comparable to Goethe's Helen.

The great Descent is made in Act II. It symbolizes another attempt to probe ultimate reality, beyond the reach of the senses and the ordinary mind. But it would be a mistake to divorce it from the events of Act I – if we may term 'events' those changes in Prometheus' attitude and way of seeing that are poetically described there. They certainly lead to events of the greatest significance, not only for the Titan but for the world which rises to a new level of existence in his awakened sight. The inner process of the first Act may be said to consist in the overcoming of the illusions which in Shelley's epic ventures still thwarted the transformation needed for the self to overcome the threat from without. The shackles of Prometheus are Blakean 'mind-forged manacles'. His fixity is the price paid for deeply cherished illusions, cherished because they enable him to project outward on to the world and its supposed 'Tyrant' the responsibility for his condition. The growth of self-knowledge is inhibited because, like all of us, he has a deep and unconscious wish to escape from the responsibility of his own development. The withdrawal of the 'curse' marks a turning-point. Prometheus recognizes that he has effectually cursed or demonized a part of himself.

In a stroke of great dramatic effectiveness, at the moment where Prometheus comes closest to clear self-knowledge, Shelley shows the Luciferic tendency of the mind asserting itself in a last, desperate temptation: to give up the struggle and exchange it for a dream of spiritual–sensual indulgence. A burst of Luciferic glory from above brings in Mercury, the heavenly messenger. He opens to the Titan a prospect of infinite time, and asks whether he really prefers all that he has and must endure:

> *Mercury*
>   If thou might'st dwell among the Gods the while
>   Lapped in voluptuous joy?
> *Prometheus*
>   I would not quit
>   This bleak ravine, these unrepentant pains.
>
>   (Act I, 425–7)

It is this same courage to confront his situation without retreat which is projected and intensified in the imagination of Asia's descent.

That bold adventure in the deeps of matter and mind takes her (with her sister Panthea) into the realm of Demogorgon – a striking outsider to the classical mythology of the rest of the play. His is the name given to the Power which dwells in the unfathomable abyss Shelley had felt behind the mountain rock and glacier, present in visible nature as the implacable force of the volcano's 'meteor-breathing' chasm. Asia and Panthea come into the world of hidden natural forces: vulcanism, electricity and magnetism. Shelley seems to suggest that these powers in external nature have an affinity with the shadow-side of the mind. He was perhaps thinking especially of the recent experiments in 'animal magnetism' of Mesmer and his pupils, which suggested that there were compelling psychic forces that could be exploited by the power of what we now call 'suggestion'. These forces, Mesmer thought, had a reality like that of physical magnetism. To Shelley they were interesting because he saw mind and world as two sides of a 'hidden' reality, and in tracing such powers to their source he felt that he might discover something of the origins of matter as well as spirit.

At any rate, the force which seizes Asia and Panthea, drawing them ever down into the deep, is comparable to such a magnetism of the mind, transporting them 'As steel obeys the spirit of the stone' or, as he also puts it, by 'Demogorgon's mighty law' of

Necessity. They reach the bounds of sense-perceptible shapes, of
all outward appearance, and pass beyond,

> Through the veil and the bar
> Of things which seem and are

to the 'remotest throne', an absolute realm where even the distinc-
tion of seeming and reality ceases. Their vision again takes the
form of 'icy spires' thrust up by keen 'sky-cleaving mountains'; of
cataracts and ravines, 'continuous, vast, / Awful as silence'; the
inevitable rush of the avalanche. To the human heart it is all
'solitude and vacancy', and the 'remotest throne' suggests that of
Ahriman reigning amid the ice-floes. The veil of outer appearances
is rent away, but reveals only the nightmare depths of the
Ahrimanic void – the Cave of Demogorgon.

Demogorgon cannot be pictured. He is 'a tremendous gloom', a
'mighty darkness / Filling the seat of power', about which no
positive assertion can be made, from which no positive answer can
be wrung. No light shines in the abyss, but

> rays of gloom
> Dart round, as light from the meridian sun,
> – Ungazed upon and shapeless; neither limb
> Nor form, nor outline; yet we feel it is
> A living Spirit.
>
> (Act II, sc. iv, 3–17)

Asia puts to Demogorgon her burning questions about the sources
of being ('Who made the living world?'). But his enigmatic replies
tell her nothing she did not know before. All things were made by
God – but when questioned further Demogorgon merely con-
fesses, 'I spoke but as ye speak'; he turns the question back on the
questioner. The abysm, he says, will not 'vomit forth its secrets', 'a
voice / Is wanting, the deep truth is imageless.' Like Faust in the
Gothic chamber in the *First Part* Asia is left groping in the void
when she seeks ultimate answers from the lord of material reality.
No voice from some sublimer world will reveal the foundations of
truth or morality.

This vision might bring despair and 'awful doubt'. But a dif-
ferent response is possible, and the way forward dawns suddenly

upon Asia as she ruminates on Demogorgon's words. She suddenly sees that moral acts can only be grounded in man's own heart and his vision of truth, that reality is not something to be sought beyond man's soul but in his own depths. Only man can free himself from the 'loathsome mask' of self-ignorance, hypocrisy and fear:

> Asia
> So much I asked before, and my heart gave
> The response thou hast given; and of such truths
> Each to itself must be the oracle.

(Act II, sc. iv, 121–3)

Asia's lines stand almost mathematically at the dead centre of the play, and are the pivot of the action. The Ahrimanic absolute becomes, through this all-transforming realization, a cause of grace in its very negativity. The soul has confronted the void and turns back upon itself in an act of regeneration. In his empty non-actuality, Demogorgon becomes a sign of all that man may become, all he may achieve. The void outside of existence becomes the womb of rebirth; the darkness, 'ungazed upon and shapeless', now suggests the prolific waters of creation on which the creative Spirit brooded like a dove.

At the moment of her rebirth, Asia is transfigured and begins her reascent. Light floods the scene; no longer the natural light of the sun (which stands still with astonishment), but spiritual rays burning through the form of Asia and penetrating the outer dark. The spirits of nature hail man's spiritualized consciousness as the

> Lamp of Earth! where'er thou movest
> Its dim shapes are clad with brightness.

(Act II, sc. v, 66–7)

Nature rises to newly awakened life and beauty before the eyes of transformed humanity. The world ceases to be an alien kingdom of material forms in which man feels himself an intruder; henceforth man is bound to it by the bond of love, which pervades all his experience and makes outer reality a reflection of his inner ideals – a love

Which in the winds and on the waves doth move,
Harmonizing this earth with what we feel above.

(Act II, sc. v, 96–7)

The terror of the void has at last been overcome.

According to Rudolf Steiner's descriptions of the process of initiation, every pupil has at a certain stage to confront the power of Ahriman. It is the experience he often describes as the meeting with the 'Greater Guardian of the Threshold'. The Greater Guardian shows him all that he – and his whole experience of the world – have become under the influence of the Ahrimanic tendency. This experience stands in the way of any unprepared and premature vision of the spiritual world. If someone not yet mature were to come to it without sufficient inner strength, says Steiner, 'he would, on approaching the "Greater Guardian of the Threshold", find himself completely overwhelmed – overwhelmed with a feeling that can only be compared with boundless fear and terror'. We have seen that both Shelley and Goethe's Faust came near to such experiences. But they also had intimations of the later, more mature response to the Guardian. For Steiner goes on to describe a stage at which the pupil

has wrestled his way through to a perception of his Higher Self, and now sees clearly what he still has to achieve in order to gain control over his Double, the 'Guardian of the Threshold'. And he has furthermore had the meeting with the 'Greater Guardian of the Threshold' who stands there before him, continually calling upon him to work further at his development. This 'Greater Guardian of the Threshold' now becomes for him the Ideal, the Example that he will do his utmost to follow. Having once come to this resolve, the pupil will be enabled to recognize who it is that is there before him as the 'Greater Guardian of the Threshold'. For this Greater Guardian now changes for the eyes of the pupil into the figure of the Christ . . .

Only in some such way can we understand the finale of Shelley's *Prometheus*, which is a poetically daring effort to depict the regenerate universe of spiritual perception, pervaded by love. The cold, inanimate moon, a little world of death, is told by the Earth that it will feel

from beneath, around, within, above,
Filling thy void annihilation, love
Burst in like light on caves cloven by the thunderball.

(Act IV, 353–5)

Love interpenetrates the 'granite mass' of Earth, too. And from all directions Demogorgon, no longer a void annihilation but a Christ-like symbol of man's ideal, rises from Earth and is showered like night, calling the vast universe together to be united in man.

* * *

I have tried to suggest that Goethe and Shelley are poets of supreme importance for the modern age, perhaps even more relevant to us now than in their own lifetimes. For they are both poets who can help us to come to terms imaginatively with the Ahrimanic sphere – a sphere into which we have nowadays entered still more deeply. They are, in a multitude of ways, forerunners of the approach to knowledge of nature that Rudolf Steiner was to develop in his spiritual science or Anthroposophy.

Above all they saw the futility of fleeing from man's inevitable connection with the earth into impotent idealisms. They accepted the challenge of the Ahrimanic and willingly took the Devil for a companion: but not for a master. If the world of Ahriman threatens to destroy or unbalance the human soul, they taught us, the answer cannot be to flee from the Ahrimanic, but to expand our humanity to ever greater imaginative heights, to convert an abstract and exterior truth into a fully human reality, into the truth of imagination. Milton may touch greater depths in his search for the hidden sources of a new consciousness, and Blake may have more fully entered into a supersensible world of transforming imaginations. But neither was able to make of their visions an instrument of man's freedom already here, in the physical world, whilst pointing beyond into the spiritual. It is in this respect that Shelley and Goethe add to the 'visionary line' of European poetry, by bringing their vision to an unprecedented extent into the challenges and problems of external life. Both also made brilliant efforts to realize the imaginative potential of the sciences of their day, Goethe in his studies of colour and plant-metamorphosis as well as in poetry, Shelley above all in the last Act of *Prometheus*. I have also tried to suggest that this way – as it is tantalizingly outlined by the Lord in the *Prologue in Heaven* – is also a way that can truly be called the Christian way, as Steiner has taught us to understand it. More exactly, they are the poets of a new or Christian Manichaeism, of the struggle between light and darkness as it must be fought by the free ego of man.

I know of no English poet since Shelley who has gone further with this problem of responding imaginatively to the challenge of Ahriman. His words in *A Defence of Poetry* still seem to point to the root of our predicament today:

> We have more moral, political, and historical wisdom than we know how to reduce into practice; we have more scientific and economical knowledge than can be accommodated to the just distribution of the produce which it multiplies. The poetry in these systems of thought is concealed by the accumulation of facts and calculating processes. There is no want of knowledge respecting what is wisest and best in morals, government, and political economy, or at least, what is wiser and better than what men now practice and endure. But we let '*I dare not* wait upon *I would*, like the poor cat i' the adage.' We want the creative faculty to imagine that which we know; we want the generous impulse to act that which we imagine; we want the poetry of life; our calculations have outrun conception; we have eaten more than we can digest. The cultivation of those sciences which have enlarged the limits of the empire of man over the external world has, for want of the poetical faculty, proportionally circum-scribed those of the internal world; and man, having enslaved the elements, remains himself a slave.

6

From *Prometheus Unbound* to *The Portal of Initiation*: Shelleyan Themes in Steiner's Mystery-Play

It may be interesting, since we have referred to Rudolf Steiner's descriptions of visionary states and his understanding of the shaping myths of Lucifer and Ahriman, to examine his treatment of imaginative themes in his own extraordinary poetic drama, *Die Pforte der Einweihung* (first produced in Munich in the Schauspielhaus in 1910). He designated the work a 'mystery-play'. This may usefully point our attention toward the genre, say, of *Die Zauberflöte*, or to the contemporary dramatic experiments such as the 'Rosicrucian' drama of Villiers de l'Isle Adam, or Maeterlinck, or even the 'musical' and visionary plays of Strindberg, of which Steiner seems to have been aware. There is also, perhaps, something Wagnerian in the scale and symphonic complexity of Steiner's 'lyrical drama', whose structure again owes much to frankly musical forms and can be studied in terms of sonata-like alternations of exposition and development (transformation).

Precedents also lie in literature outside drama, and in particular the relationship of *The Portal of Initiation* to Goethe has been much discussed. The basis of discussion is not the tumultuous drama of *Faust*, but the oddly fascinating *Märchen* (fairy-tale, parable) of *The Green Snake and the Beautiful Lily* which seems to have arisen out of Goethe's Rosicrucian and alchemical interests, as well as his response to the theories of Schiller on human freedom and the central role of free 'play' in creativity. The links between the mystery-play and *Das Märchen* are certainly deep. But it is worth remarking how completely the elements of the fairy-tale have been imaginatively transmuted into the substances of drama: characters, relationships, events of personal life. Steiner himself denied that the play had its 'origin' in the story by Goethe. 'Quite the opposite!' he said to one of the original actors. The play drew upon the same archetypal happenings, spiritual events, and realized them in the fuller form possible at a later date and in an extended dramatic mode. At the same time, he often talked about the connection and shared significance of the two works, and was so far from feeling that *The Portal of Initiation* was of his own devising that he inscribed on the title-page not 'by' but 'through' Rudolf Steiner.

If, then, Steiner's mystery-play attempts to penetrate the truths of imagination that had earlier expressed themselves in a modern fairy-tale by a contemporary of the English Romantics, and in the closely related writings on aesthetics by his friend Schiller, we might also be justified in looking for parallels and illuminating analogies within English Romanticism itself. We have frequently mentioned parallels between Goethe and Shelley, and Shelley's preoccupation with Rosicrucian and alchemical symbolism, and with themes of initiation. It is not unlikely, therefore, that Shelley's poetry and Steiner's drama should cast an interesting light upon each other.

It is the depth of the analogy which is important. Nevertheless, the case is rendered intriguing by the additional possibility of actual influence, improbable as it may seem, from Shelley's poetry upon the Austrian dramatist. Shelley's disastrously short university career, coupled with the reputation for atheism and immorality which attended his name and his absence in Italy when he wrote his greater verse, meant that he had little effect upon English poetry. His influence is detectable later on, and also in some surprising continental quarters. 'One curious and unexpected influence', says Richard Holmes, 'was on the German Expressionist writers of a century later, who wrote in the climate of social upheaval and desperation of the years 1917–22.'* And they in turn had their roots in the thought of anarchists and individualists at the turn of the century. Rudolf Steiner mixed in such circles in the 1890s in Vienna and Weimar, where he was working on an edition of Goethe. Hence it is not too startling, perhaps, when we find him writing in a letter of 1891 about his pleasure 'in meeting someone with such exact knowledge and enthusiasm for one whom I revere and reckon among the foremost minds – Shelley'.

It was doubtless Shelley's political ideas and the rhetoric of his verse which made the greatest impact on Steiner's anarchist

---

*Richard Holmes, *Shelley: The Pursuit* (London, 1976) p. 402.

friends. Steiner's interest, however, was more inward and meta-
physical. Whereas the epic *Revolt of Islam* and the dogmatic *Queen
Mab* had the status almost of canonical works in Chartist and
revolutionary circles, Steiner knew *Prometheus Unbound* and
apparently some of the lyrics, which he later recommended for use
in the Waldorf educational system at an appropriate stage. The
lady with so much 'exact knowledge' of Shelley who probably
aided his interest in the English poet was Helene Richter. It is in a
further letter to her that he discusses *Prometheus Unbound*, com-
paring it (inevitably) with Goethe's *Prometheus*, and noting that
there is such agreement between them that Goethe, had he
extended his treatment from the bound to the unfettered Titan,
would necessarily have treated the episode in substantially the
same way as Shelley. The issue, for Steiner, was the unfolding of
man's self-consciousness – his potential for wisdom and love.

The Luciferic figure Jupiter is a 'false God' (*Pseudogott*) and the
liberation of Shelley's Prometheus takes place, says Steiner, spon-
taneously when he realizes his full potential for life; at that
moment the fetters fall away. He adds:

> At the same moment he sees that the shackles he bore were only
> those of a false God. They fall from his limbs. And Jupiter, who
> is the God of the man who has not yet awoken to full
> self-consciousness, dissolves away in his own nothingness.

> (Letter to Helene Richter, 29 August 1891)

Later, when he came to write his own drama of the progress of
man toward Promethean self-consciousness, it seems likely that
Prometheus Unbound came to mind once more as the prototype of a
poetic drama, and helped to shape his approach to the theme. The
action of *The Portal* may deal with less theological perspectives, but
it certainly has to do with the achieving of that *höchste Daseinspotenz*
he already speaks of in the letter. And it seems that the parallel was
explicit, at least in the scene where the hero, Johannes, is dis-
covered in a rocky landscape. He is then on the brink of self-
transformation, recognizing the source of his struggles to lie in
himself. He calls up from his own inner depths an image, like the
Phantasm, an 'appalling form':

> There, from the murky abysm –
> what creature stares?

> What are these shackles that I feel
> that fetter me to you?
> Prometheus on the crags of Caucasus
> was not more tightly chained
> than you to me.
> Appalling form! what may you be?

But we anticipate the action of the play, and the workings of the imagination with which it is concerned.

Steiner's controlling vision has in common with Shelley's the determination to hold together the world of ordinary consciousness and the realm of archetypal forces transcending and yet working within it. The subject of the play is the attainment of imaginative vision beyond the 'painted veil', which must be achieved without allowing the equilibrium of the self and its grip upon reality to be disrupted. The central character, Johannes, is an artist and the central theme the relationship of love and frustration which exists beween him and Maria.

Early in the first scene, the theme of the 'destructive power of imagination' emerges, seeming to echo the ideas of *Alastor*. Johannes seeks in Maria not only the satisfaction of his quest for love, but also his desire for knowledge: for imaginative truth. When they first met, it had seemed like a dawning of friendship in which his own creativity could flourish. He opened himself whole-heartedly to the fiery spirit she embodied – only to find that the energies of his soul were arrested, frozen. Like the estranged poet–hero of Shelley's poem after he has seen the vision of his ideal, he fell gradually into an abyss of doubt and uncertainty about himself and his artistic vision, even about his love. We encounter him thus broken when, in Scene 1, he finally pours out his troubles to Maria. Unable to comprehend the effect her love and encouragement has produced, she can only admit confusedly that her spiritual path turns into its opposite whenever it touches upon another's life. He feels himself wandering in the darkness of the spirit, a death-in-life he must endure while the unreal shapes of the ordinary world play about him.

Meanwhile we meet other characters. Among the most prominent are Professor Capesius and Dr Strader: they represent the intellectual search for truth which parallels the artistic quest of Johannes. In them the dialectical poles are embodied. Capesius – a historian – turns out to be a Luciferically inclined character wrapped up to a considerable extent in his own mind, feeling there, as he puts it, the 'firm support of judgment' in the face of any experience. He speaks about his subject with warmth; but to him it is essentially a realm of thought, capable of inspiring men's minds and even actions, yet oddly lacking in concrete reality. And although he is disinclined to follow the argument through, he all but admits that his approach to things directly implies the complementary view represented by the rationalist and empiricist, Strader. The latter seizes on his words, agreeing that the truth of an idea has nothing to do with its value for human life, or for bringing warmth to the heart. Truth, Strader claims, must meet the verdict of pure reason and scientific evaluation. It is significant that he too must therefore acknowledge, like Capesius, that ultimate questions lead beyond his sphere. Beyond, however, he sees only a nothingness in which our steps would sink and yield no support.

The dramatic interest lies less in the theoretical dialogues of Capesius and Strader, or indeed in the views of the other personalities; rather do we grow increasingly mystified about the underlying connection between all these divergent characters and what brings them together. Those connections are the real subject of the play. Their ramifications extend, layer upon layer, life upon life, into surprising domains whose revelation at climactic moments of the drama goes hand in hand with the growing self-knowledge of the central figures. But for the moment, in Scene 1, the sense of connection is exactly what Johannes lacks. He is torn between the numerous stand-points represented; he finds expressed in them the opposing powers wrestling for his own soul. Both directions draw him and he can maintain no inner unity, no self-consciousness by means of which to resolve them. Instead he finds himself estranged – outside life, though still suffering in it:

> To bind in one the many sides
> of life, to make one self –
> I entered boldly on the path
> they taught me here.
> It's made a Nothing of me now!
> Of course, I know
> the failings of them all.
> But then I know
> they stand in life:
> I flounder in this Nothingness.

The dialectic of the two spirits completes the pattern of *Alastor*: the avenging Spirit of Solitude has tracked down the searcher for ideal knowledge and love.

We have seen that such a moment of conscious self-recognition – however negative – may become the flash-point for an initiatory transformation. But now, just as in *Prometheus Unbound*, a Luciferic temptation is made in purest form, like the offer Mercury made to Prometheus of 'voluptuous joy' among the gods. A force of psychic resistance asserts itself, the mind making a desperate attempt to preserve its illusions. Moved by pity, Helena comes to comfort Johannes. Or rather, she comes to persuade him that an error lies at the root of his troubles and that he ought to yield himself to the unequivocally joyful raptures of a wisdom which, she claims, can gaze with tranquillity on the depths of human nature:

> To look into the abyss of Being
> wakes no desires
> that can torment!

But Johannes, like Prometheus, is beyond the reach of a suggestion such as this. A single glance reveals its falsity.

The mountain heights of *Alastor* led Shelley to those where Prometheus hangs tormented. Scene 2 of Steiner's play transports us to an open, rocky place with streams. It is openly described as representing the soul-condition of Johannes, analogous to the mental landscapes of *Prometheus Unbound*. In his meditation Johannes experiences the full intensity of the Ahrimanic alienation, the spirit of solitude. Solitude had once meant to him an easeful withdrawal into his own spirit, but has now become a painful facing of emptiness, like the 'black and watery depth' felt behind nature. Johannes gives himself up to the phenomena of nature, following their shifts and changes, which now rob him of any real identity, until even his own body seems alien to him, a mere shell. It is now that, Prometheus-like, he confronts the 'appalling form' from the abyss. He asks its identity of the elements. But outer nature can give him no direct answer, no certainty. The rocks and springs merely echo back to him, 'Acknowledge your own being, Man' ('O Mensch, erkenne dich!'). Just so the elements dared not utter the curse which Prometheus had to hear in order to retract. He too was compelled to summon it up from the depths of his self-knowledge.

The admonitory echo out of the darkness of nature guides

Johannes back 'to the spheres of his own being': but he sees himself dehumanized, a monstrous dragon sprung from lust and greed. This is the horrible phantasm which confronts him from the abyss – his own lower self. It asks him implicitly, as it asked Shelley and his Prometheus, whether he is content with what he has become. The shadowy veil which sheltered Johannes from the deepest forces of his lower nature is torn aside as if by the Furies. He is blinded by the experience, but not completely overcome. He has the strength to acknowledge the vision as himself, in much the same way that Prometheus unexpectedly began the process of transformation when he acknowledged the Phantasm of Jupiter. The beast is overcome in the very act of self-recognition, and in a visionary climax Maria enters the scene, like the ideal of love which was imaged for Shelley in Asia.

The path is yet far from clear of thorns. The dialectic of the inner life has many further twists. Maria too must undergo a development before she can adequately embody the spiritual truth of Johannes' ideal, and for him this means a further trial. She too must achieve a separation from those elements which are not truly herself. In their polarization, Johannes is left to hear the powers of Luciferic illusion and inflation speak through her lips: only by overcoming illusion in the sense-world, it transpires, can he be united with her on the plane of spiritual truth. The irony is akin to the careful confusion of Prometheus and the Phantasm, who is really his own shadow-side. Johannes learns to distinguish true being from the manifold assertions of the daemonic powers, so that he may hold a firm course toward inner freedom. He triumphs, though with great pain. In the next scene (Scene 4) the figures of Lucifer and Ahriman stand revealed at opposite sides of the stage, and are recognized by Johannes.

Here then he faces the twin destinies of the wandering soul, which weave their tapestry over the abyss. Each claims to lead the human spirit to ultimate truth:

> *Lucifer*
> Acknowledge your own being, Man;
> but, Man, experience me!
> Self-estranged, self-separated
> from the guiding Spirit's hand,
> you have fled
> to earthly freedom.

Self-pursuing, self-exploring
in earth's tumult,
self-possession
proved your payment,
proved your fate.
Me you found there!
Guiding Spirits willed from far
to shroud your senses with a veil –
till I ripped their curtain wide.
Guiding Spirits willed from heaven
to act through you their purposes –
till I made your will your own.
Acknowledge your own being, Man;
but, Man, experience me!

Ahriman

Acknowledge my existence, Man;
experience, Man, yourself!
Self-released, self-liberated
from the oppressive Spirit's night,
you have found
Earth's radiance.
Absorb my stability
imbibed from Truth's unflinchingness!
For I congeal the solid ground,
Guiding Spirits willed from heaven
to bar you from the thrill of sense.
For I contrive all sense-delights,
condensing even the light!
I draw you on
to touch the very truth of things.
Acknowledge my existence, Man;
experience, Man, yourself!

Lucifer

Time was there never
when you did not feel me within you;
through ages and births
I've pursued you, I've filled you
with strength from your selfhood,
with infinite self-sufficiency's joy!

Ahriman

Time was there never

when you did not see me around you;
through aeons and worlds
you've beheld me, you've bid me
exult in my arrogant beauty,
in ceaseless manifestations' delight!

Johannes, however, attains gradually to a hard-won clarity of vision.

The Spirit of the Elements makes an appearance in a further vision-sequence. Like the Silenus or Pan of Shelley's elemental forest, he rules over the immense process of cosmic development, the coming-to-be and passing-away of all things like an endless river. Natural things come spontaneously into existence, revolve, subside and swell. From man, however, the Spirit demands a return for the freedom from nature which man has won through selfhood. Neither Capesius nor Strader understand this. But Johannes has come far enough to see – as Goethe, Coleridge and Shelley had seen – that man's liberation from nature is at once the highest point of nature's development, and a breach produced by self-consciousness which can therefore only be overcome by man, from within. 'We receive but what we give, / And in our life alone does Nature live': only thus can the Spirit of the Elements be repaid as he demands. Towards the end of the play, that 'life of nature' will become Johannes' artistic experience of himself and his world, as it becomes the Promethean universe of Shelley's Act IV.

Beyond this point, the details of the initiation, the descent into the depths and the finding of the hidden source, do not directly suggest Shelley's voyages. The descent leads to a subterranean Temple where the four Hierophants stand at the compass-points; they are revealed as the archetypes of Wisdom, Love and Action, and a fourth 'mixed' power compounded of them. But this cavern in the depths has little in common with the Cave of Demogorgon, whose terrors have been overcome in the reaching of this remote sanctuary. The task of the initiate is to raise this Temple to the daylight – to achieve a spiritualization of consciousness like that of the transfigured Asia. Its result will be an integration of human life and experience with the cosmic forces of nature. The forces of Lucifer and Ahriman are overcome, but at the same time mastered and retained in a redeemed form.

One of the ways in which the Spirit of the Elements can be repaid is through the stories told by Felicia Balde, a countrywoman with a deep and entirely spontaneous feeling for nature. In the modern world, however, such imaginative apprehension must face the sceptical resonances of the developed consciousness: a curious voice from behind the scenes parodies Felicia's tale, which is not thereby devalued, though it is made part of a more complex modern reality. Strangely, in both there are odd similarities at moments to Shelley's poem *The Two Spirits*. It also seems possible that the tale was partly prompted by the lyric in *Prometheus Unbound* Act I (lines 723–36) where a spirit tells how it has come from beside a sage's bed:

> And the lamp was burning red
> Near the book where he had fed,
> When a Dream with plumes of flame,
> To his pillow hovering came,
> And I knew it was the same
> Which had kindled long ago
> Pity, eloquence, and woe;
> And the world awhile below
> Wore the shade, its lustre made.
> It has borne me here as fleet
> As Desire's lightning feet:
> I must ride it back ere morrow,
> Or the sage will wake in sorrow.

Felicia's tale represents one of Steiner's few direct excursions into the *Märchenhaft* in the play:

> There was a Being once, that flew
> from east to west, and ever chased
> the footsteps of the Sun.
> And over land and over sea
> it flew, and from the height surveyed
> (so far below!) the lives of men.
> It saw the tenderness of love,
> it saw the bitter schemes of hate.
> But nothing made that Being pause,
> or linger on its swift-winged way,
> for love and hatred breed the same
> a thousandfold in dreary round.
> But then, above a certain house,

the Being hesitated.
Inside there sat a weary man,
who contemplated human love
and contemplated human hate.
His meditations had inscribed
deep furrows on his lonely brow
and blanched his ageing hair.
And high above his care-worn head
the Being lost its guide, the Sun,
to hover round this man.
Long within his room it strayed,
until the Sun sank down;
and when the Sun returned again
the spirit of the Sun-disk whirled
the Being back upon its way.
Again it saw the multitudes
of ceaseless loves and ceaseless hates
on earth ever revolving.
And as it drew a second time,
chasing the Sun, above the house
its distant gaze
beheld the man lie dead.

Then comes the sardonic echo:

Once there was a Man, who trudged
from east to west, by deep desire
of knowledge lured incessantly,
traversing sea and land.
According to his wisdom's code
he scrutinized the lives of men.
He saw the tenderness of love,
he saw the bitter schemes of hate.
But every instant he beheld
his wisdom at an end.
For how it is that hate and love
forever rule this earthly world
could not be locked in any law.
He reckoned countless instances,
but missed the Grand Hypothesis.
This dry researcher, shuffling on,

next met a Being, born of light:
and yet its life was burdensome,
because it struggled endlessly
with a dark shadow-form.
'Who are you, then?'
the dry researcher asked of them.
'Oh, I am Love,'
the one replied;
'And I its tracking shadow,
Hate,' the other said.
In vain, the Man no longer heard,
already far away.
A deaf researcher, without rest,
the Man trudged on from east to west.

In accordance with the individual scale of his play, Steiner does not offer a final vision of a millennial world redeemed for all, but the passage of his central character through 'the portal of initiation'. The light of spiritual vision is not granted indiscriminately from without, but must be won in freedom by each human being. The play ends with Strader, still unable to rise toward this condition, wandering in doubt. The seeress Theodora prophetically sees a radiant human image shaping itself from his breast, which says that the power of reaching the light has been attained. She ends the play by exhorting Strader, and us with him, to trust in ourselves.

When the time comes, we ourselves will speak the words.

*   *   *

Having surveyed the events of Steiner's drama and the principal characters of the play, we are in a position to return to the musical analogy I mentioned at the outset. A full treatment would demand extensive comparison of passages; I aim to do no more here than draw attention to a powerful forming element in the work, and, for the rest, the 'musical' process is perhaps better appreciated as a background to the conscious interest we normally feel in the surface of a drama, the presentation of action and ethos.

The first three scenes of *Die Pforte der Einweihung* do not serve only to map out the chief relationships, and problems, of Maria and Johannes, Strader and Capesius: they delineate the three worlds through which the action moves. Scene 1 ('A Room') takes place on the mundane level, the social universe and the plane of personal desires and hopes. It includes the debates of the two thinkers, the fairy-tales of Felix Balde and his wife, the odd humour of the parodist German, and a good deal more. In fact, the sense throughout the scene of constantly shifting groups of individuals with no understanding of the bonds that bring them together fills the pained consciousness of Johannes and seems to distintegrate him too. The basic themes or root-problems of the play are all laid out. Much that will be significant flits undeveloped before us. Benedictus, the guiding force in Johannes' crisis and recovery, appears only briefly in the doorway, passes a few words with Felix Balde and Capesius, then disappears. He leaves his desperate pupil without a word. We later learn that this is part of the strategy of his care, and that Johannes must lose and find himself before Benedictus can intervene. But perhaps against the background of this strategy we can also understand the outburst of Maria against Benedictus later on as the inevitable recriminations of the lower selfhood. She is 'possessed' – but then we have all been 'possessed' by such feelings at moments in our lives, and what we witness is essentially a heightened realization of a normal event. Benedictus' role must necessarily incur the hostility of ordinary, self-regarding parts of our mind, since he serves the higher self and the urge toward purgation.

However, Johannes' solution is first sought in the subjective, psychic realm of Scene 2. Johannes' soul-world now literally fills the whole area of consciousness. The recurring refrain of the Rocks and Springs suggests realms of rhythmic or cyclical movement. But Johannes is unable to touch any firm truth – rather as if the music underlying the scene were in no definite key, but keeps changing – until he comes to the imagination of Maria, which in Johannes' struggle at last coincides with a real person.

Scene 3 moves convincingly in realms of real relationship: but seen now as a hidden world to which as yet only Benedictus has full access. Here, in the Meditation-room setting, the inhibitions and knots of the characters are brought to crisis-point and the note of resolution is first triumphantly sounded. Benedictus ends the scene with his long mantric verse, and invocation ('O now you spirits who are visible to man'), answered by the mystic Spirit-Voice from above.

It is not hard to conceive of these three scenes as the Exposition section of a sonata-movement, such as has been used in symphonic first movements. Scene 1 is the First Subject, containing the germ of much that will unfold; Scene 2 the Transition section bringing a phase of indeterminacy and the establishing of a different key; Scene 3 the contrasting Second Subject, which yet is inwardly related to the First, as spirit to body.

The middle part of the play would then correspond to the central Development section of sonata-form, as portrayed in Figure 3. The emphasis is indeed on metamorphosis, a symphonic transformation of the earlier statement of themes. In many sonatas and symphonies the seemingly functional Transition passage turns out to be a rich source of ideas for the Development. In Steiner's musical-dramatic sonata the setting of Scene 2 is taken up in Scenes 4 and 6: as if the Voice that echoed from the rocks and Springs now takes on definite form as the Spirit of the Elements. He is essentially a 'transitional' figure, whose work is located on the border-line of the natural and the spiritual. (His counterpart in Goethe's *Märchen* would be the Ferryman across the river which divides the two lands.) Various new features emerge from the Development too. In Scene 4 the opposing poles of all human experience are seen, as Lucifer and Ahriman, appearing at the sides of the stage while Johannes sits in solitary meditation. In the same scene, the rhythmic repetition of the Voice from Rocks and Springs is paralleled by the violent outbursts of thunder and lightning from elemental heights and depths; in the answering Scene 6, the Spirit of the Elements is placated by the first (and perhaps still the best) of the fairy-tales which are a feature of other Steiner mystery-plays too. Scene 5 may best be discussed a little later. Scene 7 brings the Development to a fully orchestrated climax, focussed on the relationship between Johannes and Maria.

EXPOSITION	DEVELOPMENT	CONDENSED RECAPITULATION	CODA
(1) A Room		(8) A Room	
	(4) Soul-world		
(2) Soul-world	(5) Sun-Temple	(9) Soul-world	(11) Sun-Temple
	(6) Soul-world		
(3) Meditation-room	(7) Devachan	(10) Meditation-room	

Figure 3.   The Eleven Scenes of *Die Pforte der Einweihung* as a Sonata-Movement.

The language of the scene forms the lyrical high-point of the play, especially in the concerted passages with Maria and her three mysterious companion-beings, Philia, Astrid and Luna. Devachan, where the scene is set, might be called the world of essential relationships. It is another of Steiner's terms for the world beyond the blissful realm of spiritual images, the world that includes tragic pain as well as paradisal joy. It is the reality whose closest analogue is not the word or image, but music, to which all here is almost transmuted. Benedictus ends the scene in undiminished lyrical vein with a metamorphosed version of the mantric verse that brought the Exposition to an end.

Scenes 8 to 10 are a condensed Recapitulation, again corresponding to the classical sonata arrangement. Scene 8 is set once more in the Room of Scene 1, and the world of the action is again the ordinary physical and social one: Johannes, Maria, Capesius and Strader (i.e. the central figures) are present, and we discover that the resolution of one set of problems is the starting-point of critical developments for another. Now it is Strader who belatedly comes to see the knots of destiny he must learn how to untie. Scene 9 reproduces the soul-landscape of Scene 4, and there is once again the rhythmic utterance of the Voice from Rocks and Springs; this time it is through Johannes' own imaginative strength that he finds Maria and is able to share his experience with her. Scene 10, however, though it takes place in the Meditation-room and echoes Scene 3, shows that the tendency of the dramatic, linear structure of the play is ill at ease with the pure musicality of a Recapitulation. Instead of emphatically re-establishing the pattern of Scene 3, Scene 10 begins to break up. Johannes is struck with new uncertainties and contradictions. Lucifer and Ahriman threateningly and unexpectedly reappear. Steiner resists a mechanical transposing of a musical form, and, rather than impose it, lets the drama burst its banks, to snatch a still-more-musical victory out of potential chaos with the Coda of Scene 11.

The Sun-Temple had already featured in the drama in Scene 5, mentioned but not discussed in the summary above. There, however, the Temple was still 'underground' – it did not work into the consciousness of the protagonists, but was buried in the darkness, though it was not less a source of power. The raising of the Temple and its glorification is an important part of Goethe's *Märchen*; but Steiner's treatment is less visual and more essentially symphonic. Since Beethoven, the Coda has often stood as virtually a second Development, and the idea of basing it upon new ideas that made a first appearance in the Development was perhaps also originally his. Steiner ends the drama with an assured touch of processional and ritual solemnity, his main characters gathered within the Temple: the glimpse of the powers who govern human growth and retardation from the dark centre of the play now unfolds into the sunlight of awakened consciousness at the end.

The contrast between the dark, submerged Sun-Temple of Scene 5 and the illuminated scene at the conclusion of the play prompts a deeper idea of sonata-form than the mere alternation of development and achievement we have so far considered. The sonata-principle is fundamentally based on the tension between contrasting tonalities or key-centres – normally between the First and Second Subjects in the Exposition. Such contrasts are extended in the Development, and in the Recapitulation unity is achieved: the two Subjects are now played in the same key. Within Steiner's *Die Pforte der Einweihung* the contrast of key-centres corresponds to nothing less than the opposition between the physical and the spiritual worlds. In a profounder sense, therefore, the developmental process of the drama consists in the tension between and finally unification of the spiritual and earthly natures of man. At the play's beginning, the characters find themselves in a world where the real motivating powers working through them are hidden. In various ways, through the drama, they find a way to their own occult depths. But the finale of the play celebrates not the occult but the manifest. In the world of the raised Temple the characters will live in the world we know, and still have human difficulties to face, doubts to overcome. They have found the meaning of their lives not in 'another' world, but in this world spiritually seen and understood.

Like all our visionary poets, therefore, Steiner finally asserts that the world of vision is not 'somewhere else' or 'other' than the world we know. It is a reorganization of experience – just as in music the same sounds can be differently centred, organized around another key-note. The fulfilment of Steiner's Rosicrucian mystery does not mean a renunciation of the natural world. Steiner accepts that world as the stage of human action. But in the process of inner awakening its reality is transposed into another key, it is brought into relation with the 'symphonic' wholeness of man's experience. The music of Steiner's poetry, and the musical form of the play, may be perhaps its deepest message.

7

The Two Lives of W. B. Yeats

I was confirmed in this opinion, that he who would not be frustrate of his hope to write well hereafter in laudable things, ought himself to be a true poem . . .

– Milton

Perhaps it is a part of Yeats' modernity that, in contrast to the visionary poets studied in earlier chapters, it proves impossible to understand his poetry except as an aspect of his life's work. It is not only that much of his poetry springs from occasions, places, people, possessions and events. His poetry is the record of his struggle to be a particular kind of man: to make his own personality. It acquires greater depth when seen alongside Yeats' other activities, which were many. He was an agent in the birth of Ireland as a nation and as a cultural force in the twentieth century, indeed a Senator of the Irish Free State who looked one day and found himself 'a sixty-year-old smiling public man'. This was the more surprising since he was always painfully shy, and since he was temperamentally inclined to solitude and inner work. He would for much of his life have rejected the approach to his verse proposed here, feeling that

> The intellect of man is forced to choose
> Perfection of the life, or of the work.

But in the last analysis it is Yeats' striving for what he would later term 'Unity of Being' which works like a submerged force in his artistic development and eventful outer life alike. And it was, I think, his sense of that concealed force which best explains his other great interest: magic and occultism.

The powers hindering his way toward 'Unity of Being' were formidable, and though they figure in his biography under various guises they can be grouped according to what are recognizably the 'daemonic' tendencies of Luciferic and Ahrimanic, dream and reality, temptation and power. They met him with especial intensity through his sustained and unsatisfied longing for Maud Gonne, the Irish patriot and beauty whom he never married, his Helen of Troy who filled his soul with yearning images and made him dream of *The Land of Heart's Desire*; and through his father J. B. Yeats, a painter but a sceptic and rationalist, an enormous influence on his son yet impatient of his son's religious and emotional nature, a constant challenge to Yeats' self-confidence and so one source of his painful self-consciousness, an attendant spirit whom the poet found it extremely hard to exorcize. Yet the dichotomy can be traced back still further into the realm of Yeats' origins. For he was descended on his mother's side from the Pollexfens of County Sligo, where he spent much of his childhood, and they were a family rooted in the traditional Irish past with all its legendry and its mystic sense of the holiness of the land. Richard Ellmann, to whom everyone who wishes to know of Yeats' life is deeply indebted, points the contrast between the restless intellectual talk and constant unproductive work of J. B. Yeats and the quiet mother who, he says, 'is difficult to describe. She had few opinions about anything, but liked best of all to exchange ghost and fairy stories with some fisherman's wife in the kitchen. Sensitive and deep-feeling but undemonstrative, she always considered her birthplace, the romantic country of Sligo, the most beautiful place in the world.'

Thus Yeats grew up with a sense of incompatible yet coexistent values, of belief and scepticism, unity and personality, natural and mystic. It is scarcely to be wondered at that as he grew to a young man he felt a kind of strange detachment: known to many in modern life but experienced with painful force by the poet. His friend Katherine Tynan recalled that 'he had an uncanny faculty of standing aside and looking on at the game of life as a spectator.' He himself later described the labyrinthine self-doubt and paralysing effect of his perpetual self-distancing consciousness. Ellmann connects this with his 'premature decrepitude', or early tendency to imagine himself an old man, his race already run and pondering a long life. But it is also a source of Yeats' awareness of the problem to be solved, the need to attach himself to life and community. He was always to retain a critical, sceptical portion of his father's mind. But he regained too his lost youth and flaunted it as a victory among the bodily defeats of old age in his astonishingly energetic late poems.

His dual origin and aim of establishing spiritual certainty without abandoning critical consciousness recalls Rudolf Steiner, with whom his development is curiously intertwined, as we shall see. Steiner was likewise born, at almost the same time, his biographers are fond of pointing out, in a village and was first brought up in traditional ways. That was on the shifting borders of the Austro-Hungarian empire. But already in the late 1860s the great world of technology had found its way there in the shape of the railway, with which Steiner's father was employed. It brought in its wake modern and scientific ideas, and a freeing of social structure. And Steiner, like Yeats, grew up with a sense of different realities, subtle conflicts and the need for new solutions. His diagnosis of the *Bewusstseinsseele* (consciousness-soul) or 'onlooker' mentality parallels Yeats'; they came together also through the esoteric interests we have mentioned, albeit in a rather indirect way. And there were moments when the link became rather more direct.

Yeats' drive toward 'Unity of Being' involved him in many 'vacillations'. One of the most confusing aspects of his work is his ability to adopt different viewpoints on virtually anything he may have said. The 'phases of the moon' became a central symbol of his later poems, and certainly his inner life had its shifting phases all along. Yet the problem arose from his wishing less to reject modernity and scepticism in his quest for relationship and beauty, than to include them all, somehow, in a kaleidoscopic whole. He crystallized his ideas eventually around the finding of opposites. 'Unity of Being' shows itself in the seer's achievement of the right inner perspective. He is tentatively enabled, as Yeats wrote in *A Vision*, 'to hold in a single thought reality and justice' – where 'justice' means essentially poetic justice, satisfying the soul's desire for a world where all is meaning and in harmony with man's demand for rightness, truth and beauty. Reality – meaning essentially the world that forces itself upon us and demands that we be changed – is not lost here, though it becomes only part of the artistic whole. Contrarily, the poet's dream of desire fulfilled has to be chastened, its luxuriant flowers to wither into truth. Luciferic and Ahrimanic energies are to be caught up in a visionary perspective where both are retained yet revalued, as when Yeats says that he has sought 'some moment of intensity when the ecstasy of the lover and of the saint are alike, and desire becomes wisdom without ceasing to be desire'.

Yeats achieved that vision sometimes: balancing or fusing a kind of lover's satisfaction in the presence of the beloved with the saint's passion for the world to come; the world as it is must be acknowledged and affirmed, yet it is seen in the light of what it could be and what man might make of his own raw material, in response to the pressure of change from the world. At such moments the cosmic dance includes the dancer, the flower and branch are already there in the root of the tree, and the only 'labour' is blossoming and dancing. But the vision came only through a lifetime's search. Indeed, so long a search, combined with Yeats' odd 'premature decrepitude' can best be described as two lives, not parallel but placed end to end. One of them seemed about to fizzle out in despair when the second one began. At the centre of both was poetry, and the poet's belief in the importance of a kind of Masonic magic, or magical Masonry, which intimated the possibility of the vision he sought. He kept his sense of its importance through most of his two lives, and its 'Rosicrucian' spirit helped him to insights similar to those we have found in Milton and the Romantics.

Steiner's part in it was, I suggest, a crucial axis around which the later story revolves – though Steiner's involvement with such Masonico-mystical practices, we should remember, was much shorter (spanning less than a decade between 1906 and 1914) and his final judgment upon them less positive. He felt the attraction, as Hella Wiesberger suggests, of continuity.* After all, his whole approach to the spiritual life was historical and developmental. He would have preferred to remould existing forms and symbols rather than break with the real feelings rooted in them. But in the end – that, however, is still almost a lifetime away.

There is much that could be said about Yeats' early explorative years: his involvements with Theosophy, the Hermetic Order of the Golden Dawn, and, more importantly, the kind of poetry he was enabled to write by means of his long meditations on their symbols. One could mention too those ventures, originally esoteric, which bore fruit in more accessible cultural forms, such as the

*See Rudolf Steiner, *Zur Geschichte und aus den Inhalten der ersten Abteilung der Esoterischen Schule. Briefe, Rundbriefe, Dokumente und Vorträge* hrsg. von Hella Wiesberger (Dornach, 1984). See also Steiner, *Zur Geschichte und aus den Inhalten der erkenntniskultischen Abteilung der Esoterischen Schule* (Dornach, 1987).

project for the founding of the Irish Mysteries which somehow turned into the famous Abbey Theatre. Such cases deserve study, not only because they show that the culture of the late nineteenth century was remarkably open to occult and magical influences; it has been less clearly understood that the kind of spiritual philosophy Yeats was seeking in those years embraced not only an inner, meditative approach but also a practical, out-going emphasis. The Golden Dawn adept Florence Farr, a well-known actress, affirmed the Rosicrucian ideal of keeping in contact with the sorrows of the world, explicitly rejecting the ideal of Nirvana or mystic self-negation. Likewise Yeats in his meditation and occult poetry was seeking to define 'a movement downwards upon life not upwards out of life'. The contradictions some have supposed to exist between his occultism and his aims in poetry are often resolved when we realize the character of the Western (Hermetic and Rosicrucian) teachings he avowed.

But I am less inclined to go into detail, both because 'Golden Dawn' studies of Yeats are already extensive, and because Yeats came to reject the path of men whom he was to describe as 'otherwise worthy', but who 'claimed a Rosicrucian sanction for their fantasies'. After many years of serious involvement, he steered the remaining group of adepts towards a thinker who came to occupy, as it seems to me, an important and neglected place in his inner life. In doing so he discovered a path of his own that took him out of their company. And it is afterwards that he wrote some of the really magnificent poems for which he is most often remembered today. He overcame the disillusionment which caught up with him in the early years of the twentieth century, and it is the later story of his search that I shall try to tell.

His disillusion was not restricted to the Golden Dawn. He was on the verge of rejecting visionary poetry itself as a mode of approach to reality. His collections *The Green Helmet and Other Poems* (1910) and *Responsibilities* (1914) experimented instead with the harsher, more colloquial modern style. He had himself been rejected, unequivocally, by Maud Gonne; and the death of his hope for her love had also been the death of his idealistic dreams for Ireland, with whose spirit she had somehow become blended in his thoughts. It was truly the end of his 'first life' amid 'the stir and tumult of defeated dreams'.

Yet there are, of course, continuities: notably the great themes of reality and dream themselves. To find the sources of Yeats' subsequent development – his 'second life' as I shall call it – we must look back before the moment of rebirth itself, his marriage in 1917. We must glance at events in the Golden Dawn as far back as 1900, for it was in the years that followed that a certain Dr R. W. Felkin became prominent in the Order. He was an intelligent man, with medical degrees from Edinburgh and Marburg and experience in Africa as a medical missionary. The Order needed his talents, having been depleted and undermined by a series of crises, inner and outer. Above all, it acutely needed a source of authority and further teaching, for it had been forced to expel MacGregor Mathers, its original 'Chief', and it was through him that it had received the forms of its rituals and instructions. (Indeed, some would say that he had simply concocted them: but the truth is harder to recover and the real sources may never really be known.) The so-called 'Cypher Manuscript' did not provide rituals or teachings for the higher grades of initiation. Felkin's problem, therefore, was how to advance the Order beyond its present stage, and put it once more in touch with Rosicrucianism. He has been much criticized for his attempt to do so, yet after all that was the whole basis of the Order, at least of its claim to be more than a band of bold occult experimentalists. Dr Felkin's researches soon pointed to Germany, and focussed in particular on Dr Rudolf Steiner.

Yeats supported the move toward Steiner. After all, the alternative could only be the 'fantasies' propounded by the other factions. He continued to preside over the Isis Urania Temple in London during the time of prolonged negotiations with Steiner over the next decade and more, and, as we shall see, the results deeply affected his poetry and thought. The results also drastically changed his personal life, for finally despairing of Maud Gonne he began to fall in love with a young anthroposophist called Georgie Hyde-Lees.

By the time he married her in 1917, Yeats was fifty-two years old, and could hardly have known that a further twenty-two years of poetic (and other) achievement still awaited him. Georgie, or George Yeats as she soon became known, made a crucial difference to his domestic security and the fulfilment of his earthly love. She had also been studying Steiner seriously for at least three or four years, and although it was no part of her purpose to establish herself as Yeats' teacher, the knowledge and the patterns of thought she had thereby acquired turned out to be extraordinarily important. To her own amazement, she became the vehicle of the revelation he had spent a first 'lifetime' seeking. But the story of her role, and more generally of the impact of Steiner's ideas, directly and indirectly, upon Yeats, cannot be resumed until we resolve some of the questions raised about the Golden Dawn by Dr Felkin. And we must examine also Rudolf Steiner's activities as an esotericist in those first decades.

It may seem to delay grappling with Yeats' difficult poetry, but we shall come to his work in the end with a proper sense of its background, the visionary strivings of the poet and his contemporaries. Steiner, like Yeats, felt that these needed ritual expression in addition to his teachings, and had evidently decided as early as 1906 to develop a 'symbolic and cultural' activity of a rather Masonic kind.* It was specifically devoted to Rosicrucian symbolism, the same imaginative vision he would dramatize in *Die Pforte der Einweihung*, embodying a Christian self-awareness. The Golden Dawn, of course, had a similar Christian–Rosicrucian basis. Steiner took care to ensure the 'historical succession' attaching to his rite, but the actual forms employed in his 'Mystica Aeterna' Lodge were new creations, fashioned for the symbolic and cultural life he intended to foster. The episode was relatively short in Steiner's career, since by 1914 at the latest he had abandoned any attempt to link up his own basically new ideas with traditional fraternities such as Freemasonry. But it does shed considerable light on the spiritual needs of the time, the needs which came to expression in Yeats' life and poetry. Steiner's esoteric practice did not come to an end in 1914: he continued it in a different guise within the Anthroposophical

---

*Steiner acquired the warrant for a rite of 'high-grade Masonry', the Rite of Memphis and Misraim, from Theodor Reuss, a figure whose interests run parallel to Steiner's own. According to Martin Green in *Mountain of Truth* (Hanover and London 1986, p. 176), Reuss 'had been a regular Freemason in London (1896–1899), and a member of the Socialist League there from 1885 until he ran afoul of Eleanor Marx and William Morris'.

Of Reuss' 'Order' he adds: 'It seems that there were also some specifically feminist features to this ... We note that Alice Sprengel (1871–1941), Reuss' secretary, was head of the Locarno branch as late as 1937, and Ida Hofmann says that several significant women were members. That would explain why Laban had his dancers inducted.' Steiner (also discussed by Green) had of course mixed in anarchist and socialistic circles in Vienna at the time of writing his *Philosophy of Freedom*. And like Laban, Steiner was interested in developing a new art of movement, or Eurythmy, first employed in performances of his mystery-plays. Steiner's Lodge too was open to *sorores* as well as *fratres*. He never had any connection with the so-called 'Ordo Templi Orientis' that grew up out of Reuss' activities.

Society; and it lived on in something like its earlier form through the exertions of Dr Felkin in the framework of the Golden Dawn. The latter is especially important for us, as it establishes the context for Yeats' reception of anthroposophical thought, which stands at the centre of his 'second life'.

The 'Stella Matutina' comprised that portion of the Golden Dawn *adepti* who had followed Felkin in search of Rosicrucian masters, to obtain the missing 'higher grades' left unprovided by the Cypher Manuscript. He had been trying several methods of communicating with them, including questions to a medium (still unidentified). It was in the latter way that he obtained directions from so-called 'Sun Masters', whose communications are fortunately preserved along with other Golden Dawn materials. Whatever clairvoyant faculties may have been involved, these 'Masters' seem to be in some sense projected personalities of Dr Felkin himself, and their answers reflect his own search for an adequate solution to the Order's problems. Meanwhile in 1903 A. E. Waite had led a further secession from the Golden Dawn with his own group of adepts who desired a less magical and more mystical approach. His faction was to include the celebrated writer on mysticism Evelyn Underhill, and the rivalries of these different splinter-groups and differing estimates of Felkin's line perhaps helps explain her strangely hostile account of Rudolf Steiner in her best-known book *Mysticism*.

In 1907 Felkin was still asking his 'Secret Chiefs' and 'Sun Masters' for the higher grade-rituals. In 1910, however, he travelled to Germany, and questioned Wilhelm Hübbe-Schleiden, who had been first President of the Theosophical Society's German section, about the possibility of acquiring such Rosicrucian rites. Evidently it was then that he learnt about Steiner's new ritual activities. Here suddenly seemed to be the very thing he was looking for. Obtaining Steiner's address from Hübbe-Schleiden, Felkin met him and was immediately convinced that he could supply what the Stella Matutina lacked. Steiner, as we gather from Chapter 36 of his *Mein Lebensgang*, was willing to help if he could, and permitted Felkin to watch the Rosicrucian rites he had evolved.

On his return to England, Felkin consulted the trance Masters again, asking their approval. One of them said: 'Have nothing to do with Mathers. Go on with Steiner which is the ultimate end of search.' An associate of Felkin, one Neville Meakin, was made

Felkin's representative and travelled back and forth to Berlin. Steiner was unhappy with this arrangement, and with many subsequent intermediaries; he later asked complainingly for 'any sensible person' to be sent over to consult him. It seems that Felkin also tended to exaggerate Steiner's interest in the Order and to interpret Steiner's concessions to him in a highly personal manner. With a need to have a clearer 'inside' knowledge of events, Steiner asked H. Collison to join the Stella Matutina with a watching brief. Much later, looking back on the period in a letter of 1921, Collison explained:

> Dr. Felkin was a spectator at one of Dr. Steiner's ceremonies in Munich several years ago. No grades have been given to him by Dr. Steiner. No grades were given to him in Munich. But Dr. Steiner gave Dr. Felkin a great deal of instruction, such as he gives to other people who desire it . . . Dr. Felkin was anxious to get a charter from Dr. Steiner and made many attempts to gain this and be appointed his sole representative in England . . . Dr. Steiner said that he was unable to grant this request.

Steiner also felt it would be necessary to put the Order on a different footing, although he did not actually condemn its old form. Collison wrote:

> Dr. Steiner cannot say that the forces in the Order are good or bad, but in all spiritualistic practices under the old form of clairvoyance which is resorted to in the Felkin Order, self-deception is very possible and forces may enter which are beyond the power or understanding of those physically present.

Felkin had come to regard Steiner as the sole candidate to head the Golden Dawn. His effort to hand him the insignia of the Order was, however, politely declined. Steiner apparently told Felkin to remain where he was and work to transform the Order – an innocent instruction which Felkin may later have interpreted as making him equivalent to 'Magister Templi' in England, as he claimed Steiner had authorized in 1914. Steiner was still interested in possible connections between the Anthroposophical Society and the Stella Matutina at that time. He was closing down his own 'symbolic and cultural' section, and perhaps saw it as a way of satisfying those who wanted ritual and pictorial forms as a means of spiritual instruction. In 1916 three new Temples were founded by the Stella Matutina in England: one of them was specially set aside for members of the Anthroposophical Society. A separate Temple was necessary, wrote Felkin, 'because they have been working on different lines to the Stella Matutina and would undoubtedly cause confusion in the Stella Matutina Temple.'

Felkin had obtained certain 'Continental processes' from Steiner the preceding year, enabling work in the Order to go forward at last beyond the Cypher Manuscript's rituals. Along with other *adepti*, W. B. Yeats was duly initiated into the higher stages of Rosicrucian vision in the years that followed.

These obscure yet fascinating events establish the setting for Yeats' encounter with Steiner's teachings. It would be surprising if, during the years of negotiation, Yeats did not make some effort to acquaint himself with Steiner's writings and lectures. Most probably he had intensive discussions with his wife. And indeed there are signs in the period 1911–1917 of innovations in Yeats' thought, which may best be traced to Steiner's influence. And then, there is the more complex issue of *A Vision*, the theoretical basis of his later work.

In 1912, for example, Steiner had given lectures that were published under the title *Reincarnation and Karma: Their Significance in Modern Culture*. He had suggested several exercises, including one which was intended to 'evoke with the utmost energy' a certain inner experience. Imagine, says Steiner, all the events which come to meet us in the course of life, obstructing our smooth passage and requiring us to extricate ourselves from difficult situations. As a karmic exercise, in order to grasp the meaning of our 'destiny', he proposes, we can inwardly reverse the position:

> We can say: I will imagine that the position from which I disentangled myself was one in which I deliberately placed myself with the strongest determination of will. Thus we bring before our souls the very thing which was repugnant to us . . . We do so in such a way as to be able to assert: I will bring before my soul the picture of a man who willed something like this with all his might . . . If we do this repeatedly, forming a living idea of a man who has willed everything that we have not willed, we shall find that the picture will not leave us; it impresses us to a striking extent as though it really had something to do with us . . . When we evoke such an image from memory it remains,

ordinarily, simply an image; but when we practise the exercises of which I have spoken there is an element of feeling which comes to life in the soul, an element connected with moods of the soul and not so much with the images. We feel a definite relationship to this picture. The picture is itself of little account, but the feelings we have make an impression comparable to images of memory.*

Yeats was fascinated by the idea of reincarnation, and appears to have taken up the idea enthusiastically in the years around 1912. Steiner's book forms an obvious source for his thought at this period. The central theme of his meditations became precisely the attempt to conjure up 'the man who has willed everything we have not willed' in the way Steiner suggested. In 'Ego Dominus Tuus' (composed in 1915) he announced:

> By the help of an image
> I call to my own opposite, summon all
> That I have handled least, least looked upon.

In his dramas such as *The Player Queen*, which he worked at over many years, his themes take shape around the characters' quest for their 'antithetical self' and so for the mastery of their destiny. He had carried the exercise into his 'magical' life, too: in the two or three years before 'Ego Dominus Tuus' he had worked with a medium in Hampstead – still seeking the practical evidences Madame Blavatsky had denied him! Once more, the results of mediumship seem to have stemmed largely from Yeats' own mind. The spirits virtually admitted as much, saying: 'We are the unconscious as you say or as I prefer to say your animal spirits formed from the will, & moulded by the images of Spiritus Mundi.' What is interesting is that from his mind intent upon its antithetical self his trance researches came up with a spirit-personality who claimed, with considerable supportive evidence, to be the ancient geographer Leo Africanus.

The spirit was surprised to find that Yeats did not know him, since he was none other than Yeats' *daimon* or attendant spirit. The surprise, we may assume, was mutual. What could Yeats have to do with this pedantic geographer who had tramped over the globe,

*Rudolf Steiner, *Reincarnation and Karma* (Vancouver, 1977) pp. 24–5.

his gaze fixed firmly on the earth? But that was just the point: Leo was his complete antithesis, an image which had intensified into the presence of a contrary self. Leo claimed that by association they 'should each become more complete', as though together they would form a personality greater than either of them individually. He was, on a deep level, Yeats himself. 'Yet do not doubt', he added, 'that I was also Leo Africanus the traveller.'

Was Leo simply a projection of the unconscious? A real personality? Or his own previous incarnation? Yeats was never quite sure, but the encounter gave him the starting-point for his own later vision. As yet, however, the experience was personal and idiosyncratic, hardly the material for poetry with a claim to universal appeal. Yeats still needed to find a mode of arriving at a balancing of judgment in his visionary world, a centre of self-consciousness such as was inevitably by-passed in trance researches with a medium.

Yeats never quite succeeded in raising the potencies of imagination into consciousness fully, in the measure achieved by a poet such as Shelley. He did succeed, however, in establishing an intermediate level of communication, a somewhat unstable solution involving an element of automatism along with a demand for active intelligence and vigilance of mind. And again it was a breakthrough connected intimately though obscurely with Steiner's teachings. Already in his earlier poetry he had moved away from that 'possession by the image' characteristic of the Symbolist poet, to make room for the conscious faculties of the mind and, thereby, build a bridge to include the 'objective' world. In the system of *A Vision* (first ed. 1925), originating partly in his wife's automatic writing, Steiner's mythic polarities of Luciferic and Ahrimanic re-emerge in a novel form to make possible a precarious self-conscious imagining. The result was to serve Yeats well for the whole of his 'second life', and we must examine how it was achieved.

Mrs Yeats was not a practised automatic writer. Some days after their marriage, she tried to divert Yeats from his psychological difficulties (perhaps he was still thinking of Maud Gonne) by attempting it, almost in the spirit of a parlour-game. 'There were a few meaningless lines', says Richard Ellmann who later knew Mrs Yeats well, 'and then suddenly she thought that her hand was seized by a superior power. In the fragmentary sentences that were scribbled on the paper her amazed husband saw the rudiments of the system which he had spent his early life trying to evoke through vision, and his middle age trying to formulate through research'. The 'Instructors' had introduced themselves into his life, and over the next few years expounded an extraordinary symbolism founded on the phases of the moon correlated to a range of human types or 'incarnations'. Later, the cycles – or 'gyres' as Yeats preferred to call them – were linked to such matters as the life after death and the ebb-and-flow of history. But above all they pointed toward a poetic vision of the world. 'We have come to give you metaphors for poetry', the Instructors engagingly declared.

The material from the Instructors eventually became *A Vision*, and the odd phenomena associated with Mrs Yeats' trance-states are described in the Introduction to the revised edition. There were spectral scents and sounds, signals that the communication was about to begin. There were odder phenomena, too, suggesting that the sense of strangeness was felt on both sides of the threshold: verbal or auditory communication soon replaced the automatic writing, and while the couple were in a garden at Oxford the process was interrupted by an owl hooting. The communicator asked if he might be silent for a while. 'Sounds like that', he said, 'give us great pleasure.' Sometimes the spirits insisted that the system itself was 'the creation of my wife's Daimon and of mine, and that it is as startling to them as to us'. Yeats often thought it might be a sort of shared dream. I shall suggest that Mrs Yeats' *daimon* played a central and neglected role.

It would be a mistake to suppose, however, that *A Vision* is primarily the product of mediumistic dreaming. Basing himself on the geometrical symbols of the communicators and their instructions, Yeats was required to fill out the abstractions of spiritual geometry with the detail of poetic life. He was encouraged by them 'to read history in relation to their historical logic, and biography in relation to their twenty-eight typical incarnations ... and if my mind returned too soon to their unmixed abstraction they would say, "We are starved" '. Moreover, the transmission of the system would not have been possible simply as dictation. We learn that other agencies were able from time to time to disrupt the communicators, and to counteract this only Yeats' own waking intelligence could be used. He named the Luciferic sources of disruption 'Frustrators': 'the automatic script would deteriorate, grow sentimental or confused, and when I pointed this out the communicator would say, "From such and such an hour, on such and such a day, all is frustration." I would spread out the script and he would cross all out back to the answer that began it, but had I not divined frustration he would have said nothing.' Thus the responsibility for the continuing validity of the system rested ultimately with Yeats. One may see in the extraordinary spiritual configuration of *A Vision* an intermediate stage between the possession of the mind by symbolic revelation, and the conscious imagination of Steiner's fully Rosicrucian path.

If the experience underlying *A Vision* was shaped consciously by Yeats' questions and his vigilance against frustration, it was certainly shaped too by the unconscious powers of Yeats and his wife. Yeats noted that the communicators took up his theme of the 'antithetical self' from *Per Amica Silentia Lunae*, his previous book. We may add that they took their meaning of 'primary' from Wordsworth, and their concept of 'deformity' from Shelley's *The Triumph of Life*. Above all, the ideas of the book suggest the thought of Rudolf Steiner, which was no doubt latent in Mrs Yeats since she had been studying Steiner and joined the Anthroposophical Society in 1914. Or, to put it another way: Steiner's concepts were used unconsciously by Mrs Yeats to shape the experiences which thrust themselves upon her, and to give the material of the 'communicators' (whoever or whatever they were) a form in which it would be useful to Yeats. *A Vision* shows the effect of unconscious moulding in this way, indeed the effect of a patterning and commutative faculty that is probably beyond the scope of the conscious mind. It seems unlikely that the mind could consciously have toyed with the multiple variables in the interpenetrating gyres of the basic symbol so as to conceive of the twenty-eight types, or could have juggled with history so as to approximate the cycles with historical change. Far from reproducing Steiner's ideas in a jumbled state, Mrs Yeats' unconscious mind somehow, in conjunction with her husband, had completely redisposed them to suit the character and needs of his imagination.

The idea of arranging all possible world-views in a circle and playing them off against each other, for example, which makes *A Vision* able to generate the views of all its critics and include them, most probably derives from Steiner's lectures on *Human and Cosmic Thought* given in 1914. There Steiner described a dynamic, multiform kind of thinking, and set out twelve possible world-views in developmental series around a circle. Mere logical possibilities, however, are not yet living frameworks of thought. The twelve systems are only the beginning. Taking them as a figurative 'zodiac', Steiner proceeded to characterize predominant 'moods' of thought which can be conceived, planet-like, to move through the world-views in succession. His account of these 'mental Zodiac signs' and the moods which affect them is couched in appropriately solar imagery, and applied to generating the essential attitudes of philosophers such as Leibniz, Schopenhauer, etc. Other types, such as Meister Eckhardt, are also discussed. Steiner concludes:

> Just as the sun, if we adopt the Copernican view of the world, passes through the signs of the zodiac to illuminate the earth from twelve different directions, so we must not adopt one standpoint . . . we must be in a position to go all round the world (of thought) and accustom ourselves to the twelve different standpoints. In terms of thought, all twelve standpoints are fully justifiable.*

At times, the twelvefold solar structure of the metaphor glimmers through *A Vision*. But in general the idea has been given a thorough lunar transposition – suiting the twilight or border state between conscious and unconscious in which it was unfolded. And the world-views, though important to the purpose of *A Vision* are more subordinate to an interest in character than appears in Steiner.

Central to Steiner's concept of freedom and conscious vision is the idea of a balance between opposing forces. The result of equilibrium in his thought is always further development, not stasis: the moment of freedom is constantly to be achieved, never simply given, always slipping away through the force of circumstance, demanding concession or extrication. In broadest terms we have seen the forces struggling with man's free ego as Lucifer and Ahriman. All poets who wish to attain a valid perspective, a truth of imagination, must necessarily wrestle against these fundamental powers of mind. And we have seen the solutions – not all successful, indeed perhaps none wholly so – of the 'visionary poets' of a great tradition as well as Steiner's vision. We can still recognize Steiner's contraries in the system of Yeats' revelation; but it is remarkable how the axis of resolution, of balance, is displaced. The possibility of an established conscious centre is

---

*Rudolf Steiner, *Human and Cosmic Thought* (London, nd) pp. 39–40.

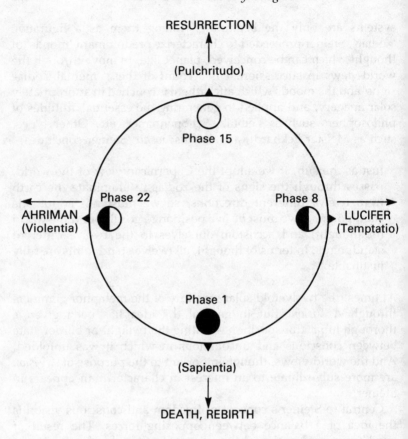

Figure 4. Imaginative Polarities, Phases of the Moon. After Yeats, *A Vision*.

subtly ignored to be replaced by a restless oscillation, the endless
gyration or 'phases of the moon'. Once again, the solar, day-
waking side of Steiner's symbolism is neglected for a moony
half-light and the working of unconscious processes into the free
area of consciousness.

The contraries are clearly visible in the pseudo-Giraldus illustra-
tion of the system, invented for the first edition of *A Vision* when
Yeats did not feel he could give the real story of its origins. (See
Figure 4.) If we put 'Phase 1' to the bottom we can immediately
distinguish two axes, a vertical and a horizontal. The horizontal is
defined by what is recognizable as Steiner's Luciferic–Ahrimanic
polarity, Yeats' *temptatio* and *violentia*. The vertical axis joins

pulchritudo at the full moon with *sapientia* at the new: running between beauty and knowledge, that is to say, in both of which the disparity, the conscious gulf between wisdom and desire is annulled. We learn from the text of *A Vision*, however, that this axis of equilibrium has no human incarnations: man's ability to accept the given for what it is (*sapientia*) and the adequacy of man's vision to his hope (*pulchritudo*) are denied final realization. Where Steiner saw the possibility of dynamic equilibrium as a source of freedom, Yeats finds uncertainty. He is left to swing perpetually back and forth, rather than hold the *daimons* consciously by the reins. Denis Donoghue points to Yeats' constantly changing opinions as an unstable part of his character: 'Sometimes one side of a question will hold Yeats' affection for years, but sooner or later conflict begins again.' Steiner felt that man could affirm the validity of many ways of thought; but it is as if Yeats is compelled dream-like to believe in each of them singly and in succession.

An examination of *A Vision's* text for the twenty-eight phases confirms that Yeats is dealing with materials of the Luciferic and Ahrimanic mythologies. A good way in to the book is the poem 'The Phases of the Moon', included in it. It is cast as a dialogue beween Yeats' old familiars, Robartes and Aherne. Yeats himself is a lonely student in a high tower like Milton's Platonist (from *Il Penseroso*) or Shelley's visionary youth (*Prince Athanase*). It is late at night, but:

> that shadow is the tower,
> And the light proves that he is reading still.
> He has found, after the manner of his kind,
> Mere images . . .

Robartes, however, almost to mock the emblem of conscious 'wisdom won by toil', agrees to recite the phases of the moon, the elusive revelation from the unconscious *daimon* or spirits of *anima mundi*. His recital brings out something that the prose Yeats never admits about the circuit – namely, the extent to which the phases suggest the course of a single life.

In the first phases man is simple and childlike. The dream, or longing which leads him beyond himself, is merely a 'summons to adventure', and he is 'always happy like a bird or a beast'. In the phases approaching the full he becomes an adolescent hero and chooses the most difficult paths in order to prove himself, whether physically or intellectually as a Nietzschean revolutionary. Soon enough, however, a more inward turn of mind takes the adventure out of things and 'sets the soul at war / In its own being', opening the possibility of deeper maturation. In the second half of the cycle man no longer seeks self-expression, but takes upon himself the tasks of the world. Aherne remarks of the soul:

> Before the full
> It sought itself and afterwards the world.

Now the world's pressure predominates. Henceforth the dream is no more the object of desire but a nightmare of retreat or escape.

Soul is 'deformed' from its own inherent beauty by the force of outer reality. Yet inner growth is still possible, since 'there is no deformity / But saves us from a dream'. The metaphor takes its origin from Shelley's *Triumph of Life* and the figure in the Chariot 'as one whom years deform', showing that the underlying concept here is that of ageing, itself a long-familiar Yeatsian theme. Once again, however, Mrs Yeats' *daimon* was drawing on Steiner's ideas of evolution. For Steiner rejected the linear notion of evolution as endless improvement, reasserting the importance of rhythmic processes. Darwinian evolution is a theoretical construct, whereas Steiner is basically a phenomenologist. In all the organic developments we actually see, there is a rhythmic building-up followed by disintegration. 'We forsake reality', insists Steiner, 'if we believe that evolution constitutes a continuous ascent. This is the view of Haeckel, under the influence of the delusion that simple beings are followed, as evolution progresses, by increasingly complex, increasingly perfect beings *ad infinitum*. This is nonsense. Every progressive evolution also regresses ... every ascent bears in itself the germ of the descent.'* He embodied his views on form artistically in the remarkable capitals for the interior columns of the First Goetheanum. There each column was not a repetition but a transformation of the foregoing one, showing increasing complexity up to the middle of the series. Thereafter, the complex form began to break down again: the cycle thus includes both formation and deformation, growth and an inherent tendency to die away. In the final simplifications, however, a powerful spiritualization can be felt. The end of the cycle is both a return to formlessness and an

---

*Rudolf Steiner, *Die Sendung Michaels* (Dornach, 1962); English translation (New York, 1961) pp. 45–6.

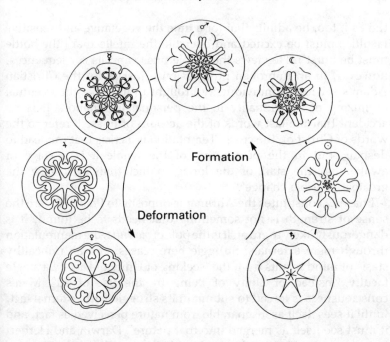

Figure 5. Rudolf Steiner, Planetary Seals. A sequence illustrating the evolution and simplification of forms (Goethean metamorphosis).

intimation of a matured 'innocence' and wisdom of acceptance. Yeats' lunar phases of formation and deformation contain a similar ambiguity, as we shall see. (See Figure 5.)

The crucial points in the Luciferic–Ahrimanic oscillation, the dialectic of dream and deformity, reveal their reworking of traditional myth in the longer explanations of *A Vision*'s prose text. Phase 8 is the turning towards individuality ('the beginning of strength') and corresponds to the pole of *temptatio*. Its typical virtue is that of Milton's Luciferically aspiring hero, 'courage unbroken through defeat'. Every codification of morality, says Yeats, as codification rather than as the aim of desire, must now be broken up, 'the soul must lose all form received from the objectively accepted concience of the world.' We recognize behind such a soul the mythic Adam who broke the commandment by eating the fatal and forbidden fruit. Yeats sees this myth re-enacted in the seizure of freedom, 'the war between individuality and race' which is the conscious preoccupation of the phase. As in traditional versions of the Fall, too, he admits that for a time the vegetative and sensitive faculties must be excited and overrule the intellectual ('the bottle must be burst'). He views the whole phase and its consequences, however, in an unbroken progression – just as for the Christian Adam's seizing of individuality brought in its wake the eventual divinizing of individuality in the personal Incarnation. It is no accident that the last words of the account of Phase 8 refer to the words of Christ on the cross. Temptation is a crisis that can lead to despair, but in the perspective of the whole it is a stage of awakening, the start of the inner conflict that 'can make the greatest possible change'.

Phase 22 constitutes the Ahrimanic opposite to Phase 8. Here the sense of strength is not something that needs to be found. It is dangerously likely to erupt. It is the pole of *violentia*, the manipulation through mere externals. Struggle here ceases, and an unhealthy stasis of mind results from the 'seeking of Unity of Fact by a single faculty, instead of Unity of Being by the use of all'. Man's consciousness is forced to submit in its struggle with external fact, 'until it sees itself as inseparable from nature perceived as fact, and it must see itself as merged into that nature'. Darwin and Herbert Spencer were of this phase, though the peculiar conditions of imagination it imposes were taken up, Yeats claims, by Flaubert and Dostoievsky. Personal power is broken. Submission to the existing takes its place, and in later phases still this may be transmuted into the religious submission of the Saint. But here also man meets the limits of his attempt to grasp only the external and objective: 'confused and weary, through trying to grasp too much, the hand must loosen'.

Phases 8 and 22 stand for the extremes of imagination in its relationship with the world, the confrontation with Lucifer and Ahriman. What we normally mean by 'subjectivity' and 'objectivity' can be defined as lying between these poles. But it is a clue to the strangely unstable character of Yeats' system that he posits them, not as outer limits, but rather as the mid-point of the gyres he calls 'primary' and 'antithetical'. These terms he associates with 'subjective' and 'objective' values – but in an idiosyncratic way that can mislead the student of *A Vision*, especially about Phases 1 and 15. Phase 1 is certainly not absolute objectivity in our normal sense: but rather an unformed 'doughy' plasticity, the starting point of spiritual development that can respond to any stimulus, take any form and lose it as readily. Nor is Phase 15 what we normally mean by absolute subjectivity, like the loss of all external form at Phase 8. It is rather the balance, the body still bodily yet purified of all that resists the desire of the spirit. Yeats connects it with what he calls in 'The Completed Symbol' the clarified or 'Celestial Body'.

Here he alludes obviously to the Christian idea of the glorified Resurrection-body, memorably described by Paul:

> There are Celestial Bodies as well as terrestrial; but the glory of the celestial is one, and the glory of the terrestrial is another . . . So also is the resurrection of the dead: it is sown in corruption, raised in incorruption, sown in dishonour, raised in glory, sown in weakness, raised in power, sown a psychic body, raised a spiritual body.

Eternal life is not the liberation of soul from the corrupt body, but the transmutation of both into a spiritual unity. Man retains his bodily identity, yet makes it utterly transparent to spirit, all physical limitations purged away. Harold Bloom claims to be baffled by Yeats' 'Celestial Body': but it is as vivid an imagination of human fulfilment in Pauline terms as any we possess. The Christian symbolism of Phase 15 also shines strongly through the remaining solar imagery of Steiner's thought when the phases are divided, as Yeats directs, among the twelve months. Phase 15 takes March. And of course, the Easter festival of resurrection still takes its date from the cosmic event of a full moon in March, or the next Sunday as soon after the Spring Equinox as possible. However, before exploring the finest poetic realization of Phase 15 we must make a few remarks on the historical and some other aspects of *A Vision* and its gyres.

The Instructors had given Yeats the series of twenty-eight phases first, and finished this exposition around November of 1917. They spoke next of the life after death:

> And then just as I was about to discover that incarnations and judgment alike implied cones or gyres, one within the other, turning in opposite directions, two such cones were drawn and related neither to judgment nor to incarnations but to European history. They drew their first symbolical map of that history, and marked upon it the principal years of crisis, early in June 1918, some days before the publication of the first German edition of Spengler's *Decline of the West*, which, though founded upon a different philosophy, gives the same years of crisis and draws the same general conclusions.

The standard double-cone came to include classical and Arab history too, and dates were attached to the turning-points and phases of the gyres. Although Yeats was struck by the startling resemblances to the unread work of Spengler as he came to know it later, the significant dates are again those mentioned and discussed by Steiner in many of his lectures.

Taking the commencement of the Christian era as a fixed point, for example, Yeats' cycles yield 1450 AD as the climax, or Phase 15, of the Christian impulse. Thereafter follows the ascendancy of the dark phases, whose gyre is still expanding in our own day. Steiner described the period of the 'Consciousness Soul' beginning about the middle of the fifteenth century – although for him this was by no means the exhaustion of the Christian evolution of man's consciousness. He too saw the dimming of man's spiritual awareness, and foretold some of the grimmer aspects of the end of the twentieth century. His vision is reminiscent of Yeats' dark prophecy of an Ahrimanic incarnation as the dark gyre widens to its furthest extent, in a world losing its coherence:

> Turning and turning in the widening gyre
> The falcon cannot hear the falconer;
> Things fall apart; the centre cannot hold;
> Mere anarchy is loosed upon the world,
> The blood-dimmed tide is loosed, and everywhere
> The ceremony of innocence is drowned ...

Yeats feels that 'some revelation is at hand' – a 'second coming' which gives the poem its ironic title. But the one who appears is no Christ in glory, but an image from the dark depths of the mind:

> The Second Coming! Hardly are those words out
> When a vast image out of *Spiritus Mundi*
> Troubles my sight: somewhere in sands of the desert
> A shape with lion body and the head of a man,
> A gaze blank and pitiless as the sun,
> Is moving its slow thighs, while all about it
> Reel shadows of the indignant desert birds.
> The darkness drops again; but now I know
> That twenty centuries of stony sleep
> Were vexed to nightmare by a rocking cradle,
> And what rough beast, its hour come round at last,
> Slouches toward Bethlehem to be born?

Yeats seems to suggest that this incarnation is of the dark penumbra of Christianity, the shadow cast into unconsciousness by the light of the Christian revelation. And for Steiner, too, the balance of evolution required that the Christian self-consciousness be required to face the challenge of the Ahrimanic manifestations of modern times.

Another significant date 'pricked' upon the cones by Yeats' spirits is 1875. For Steiner this marked the approximate beginning of a further development in human consciousness. He associated this period with the image of the Archangel warring with the dragon, the emergence of an 'apocalyptic' consciousness. Nevertheless, the character of the new 'Michaëlic' age could not be adequately rendered by the old mythology of the Apocalypse, essentially derived from Jewish revelations and apocrypha. The struggle has become less external, Steiner argues, in modern times and the symbol must change. We must imagine that the Archangel gestures at times toward the more spiritual significance of the life-against-death struggle in which he is engaged. That struggle took on a different meaning in the light of the death-and-life on Golgotha. In Yeats' diagram of the historical double-cone, the Will, i.e. the conscious self of man is shown as having just passed in our time this critical beginning of a new phase. It is classed as a Phase 22, a confrontation with the Ahrimanic dragon.

Other correspondences might be indicated. In general, much that is genuinely illuminating can be found mapped out on the intersecting gyres, however odd we may find the mechanism. Yet in this respect Yeats' critics not unnaturally show a degree of partiality. Richard Ellmann claims that 'esoteric Yeatsism' has a coherence and grip upon the factual surpassing other, similar systems. In reality, however, to turn from Steiner's evolutionism and dynamic thought to Yeats' cumbersome sacred-and-profane-love-machine is very much like a regression from the ellipses of Copernican astronomy to the proliferating cycles and epicycles of the old geocentric universe:

> the Sphear
> With Centric and Eccentric scribl'd ore,
> Cycle and Epicycle, Orb in Orb,

as Milton's Raphael put it in *Paradise Lost*. The lunar transposition of Steiner's 'evolution of consciousness' produced by the circumstances of *A Vision* must be admitted to contain an element of the quirky. As for the striking conjunctions with Spengler, these are perhaps to be explained too by the presence in Mrs Yeats' unconscious of her reading of Steiner on the 'turning points' of history. Steiner and Spengler evidently shared a common milieu of Central European thought. At any rate it is the unconscious use of Steiner's far-reaching occult thought which, here as elsewhere, accounts for the strange coherence of *A Vision*.

A final remark on the correspondences between *A Vision* and Steiner. In the last (1937) edition of the book, Yeats spoke much of a principle which runs counter to the determinism of the gyres. And since the symbolism reverted periodically to solar numbers when it was not dealing with the twenty-eight incarnations, he or his Instructors posited beyond the twelve vortices an entity called 'the Thirteenth Cone'. Ellmann concludes that it is, in effect, Yeats' God. It is freedom, for it intervenes incalculably in the process of the gyres; it is the unknowable, ungrounded, the 'somewhat' that may change any constellation of events and give them a new meaning. Once more the basis of the idea goes back to Steiner, who had distinguished, from around 1909 onwards, between the work of the 'Bodhisattvas' and of Christ. Elaborating on the significance of the Eastern term, Steiner depicted the Bodhisattvas as a sort of culture-heroes, bringing to first fruition human qualities and abilities which later become the common property of mankind. They are the creation and the creators of their times: they speak clearly for the first time what is trembling on everybody's lips, and the forces which find a voice through them are the shaping-powers of a civilization or epoch rather than their own. Therefore in Eastern thought they appear in cyclic succession, emerging from the revolutions of destiny at once to express its essence and to show the way of release. A great deal of thought is indeed the thought of the age thinking itself through us. Yet that thought always appears through a definitive thinker – and it is in him that we must seek the clue to mastery, rather than enslavement to ideas. Against this 'Eastern' truth, however, Steiner sets the Christian concept of a unique intervention, God's radical changing of the course of the world. The Incarnation is the type of such intervention, and in the sphere of the individual its meaning is freedom. Beyond the traditional circle or cycle of the twelve Bodhisattvas, therefore, Steiner sets the Thirteenth – the intervention of freedom, the Christ. I have been informed that in his later years Yeats spoke much with Iseult, the daughter of Maud Gonne, about Steiner's teachings. That must have been the time of his slow revision of *A Vision*, with whose determinism he had been basically unsatisfied, and the disturbing entity of the Thirteenth Cone probably reflects his following of Steiner's path beyond the cyclical thought of the East. Perhaps he also recalled the mysterious Thirteenth Aeon of the Gnostic treatise *Pistis Sophia*, whose translator G. R. S. Mead he had once known.

A Vision thus continued to occupy Yeats almost to the time of his death. A complete edition of the book ought really to include all the poetry Yeats wrote, with a new confidence and sense of power, in connection with its themes. *The Wild Swans at Coole* (1919) already included the poem on 'The Phases of the Moon'; *The Tower* (1928) gathered together much material which derived its deeper meaning from the Instructors, as well as revivifying the old Hermetic and Miltonic image of the lonely tower. Indeed, 'the tower' became Yeats' literal possession when he moved permanently into Thoor Ballylee around 1920 after years of restoration work. As Ellmann remarks, the far-off symbols of his youthful verse now stand, grow or lie familiarly about him, a man of property and self-assurance. The perfection of life and work have turned out after all not to be irreconcileable.

The Winding Stair (1933) is again the spiral stair of his ancient Norman tower as well as the turning gyres of his master-symbol. In the last collections of verse he wrote in the 1930s, Yeats tested his vision ever and again against greater obstacles and challenges to the imagination. He spoke to his time with oracular power. Sometimes, as in 'News for the Delphic Oracle', he seems to parody his own message. With the framework of his Instructors behind him, he can afford laughter and make parody itself serve the ever-changing perspectives of the gyres. *A Full Moon in March* (1935) takes its title from a central symbol of Phase 15. The concluding poem of *Last Poems*, 'Under Ben Bulben', is still running on 'gyres', and draws together nearly all of Yeats' life-long concerns: his own detachment, the significance of being Irish, the search for occult reality, death-in-life and life-in-death. It is fitting that the poet gripped in his twenties by premature old age should write, aged seventy-three, his own youthfully defiant epitaph there:

> Under bare Ben Bulben's head
> In Drumcliff churchyard Yeats is laid.
> An ancestor was rector there

> Long years ago, a church stands near,
> By the road an ancient cross.
> No marble, no conventional phrase;
> On limestone quarried near the spot
> By his command these words are cut:
>> *Cast a cold eye*
>> *On life, on death.*
>> *Horseman, pass by!*

*   *   *

'I think if I could be given a month of Antiquity', writes Yeats somewhat whimsically in Book Five of *A Vision*, 'and leave to spend it where I chose, I would spend it in Byzantium a little before Justinian opened St. Sophia and closed the Academy of Plato'. In a deeper sense, Byzantium became a part of his life in later years – not only the historical city but a state of mind, or image of the soul at the moment of greatest possible perfection, with the richness of both Christian and pagan worlds. The Byzantium poems are justly admired instances of Yeats' art, and by examining them as examples of his work after *A Vision* we shall need to draw upon all the themes of his early and later poetry alike. I shall concentrate on 'Byzantium' (written in 1930), but touch first upon 'Sailing to Byzantium' of four years earlier because it illustrates, among other things, how Yeats' poetry has become an art of perspective. Interpreting Yeats has become a matter above all of finding the proper perspective of the endlessly shape-shifting soul.

Both poems are about the search for wisdom. 'Sailing to Byzantium' is also about ageing: reminding us of the increasingly deformed phases on the approach to the pole of *sapientia*. In a much earlier poem on 'The Coming of Wisdom with Time' Yeats had written:

> Through all the lying days of my youth
> I swayed my leaves and flowers in the sun;
> Now I may wither into the truth.

For the poet of 'Sailing to Byzantium', however, the interlocking gyres provide the possibility of a contrary vision whilst admitting to the inevitability of physical decay:

> An aged man is but a paltry thing,
> A tattered coat upon a stick, unless

> Soul clap its hands and sing, and louder sing
> For ever tatter in its mortal dress,
> Nor is there singing school but studying
> Monuments of its own magnificence.

He can still describe his heart, his natural selfhood, 'sick with desire / And fastened to a dying animal'; but he also feels the power of the imagination strong within him to create a more real self. His pursuit of his opposite in the meditations of many years gives him the sense of mind able to exert a far greater control and enter with greater depth into reality than the ordinary intellect in its organizing of sense-perceptions and ideas. He invokes the Byzantine mosaics as images or 'masks' of this greater strength. This is both because of the higher truth on which their staring eyes look and which they make us feel; and to express the inadequacy of the dissecting intellect, for when we try to analyse the artist's work we disintegrate the precious wholeness of effect – we are left only with the rough-hewn fragments. Both wholeness and disintegration are important for Yeats, since they bring us to the bounds of the physical, the world of the senses and the sense-bound mind. The senses register only the diverse impressions, the mosaic pieces; the 'mask' is immanent yet eludes the scrutiny of consciousness.

Those themes will be taken up in 'Byzantium'; but for the moment Yeats is content to evoke the Sages, calling upon them to reveal the hidden power behind, the turning cones: 'Come from the holy fire, perne in a gyre, / And be the singing-masters of my soul.'

But how can Yeats advance beyond the disintegrating world of his natural heart? The Sages behold worlds we cannot see, inhabiting as they do the supersensible, the Blakean energy of God's holy fire burning round them. In earlier days Yeats might have tried through sensual emblems to lay hold of the transcendent. He would have entered the familiar round of Luciferic projection and the inevitable backlash of doubt or despair. Already in this maturer poem, on the other hand, Yeats has rejected the treacherous dream – or not so much rejected it, as adopted such a view that in an astonishing revision of perspectives the Luciferic vision coincides with the material earth:

> That is no country for old men. The young
> In one another's arms, birds in the trees
> – Those dying generations – at their song,

The salmon-falls, the mackerel-crowded seas,
Fish, flesh, or fowl, commend all summer long
Whatever is begotten, born, and dies.
Caught in that sensual music all neglect
Monuments of unageing intellect.

It is the earth to which Yeats bids farewell. Yet it is the common earth transfigured by the dream of fulfilment, full of the 'honey of generation', the lover's pursuit of unattainable beauty realized in retrospect in the mythical Ireland now being abandoned.

Shelley, in the third stanza of the *Ode to the West Wind*, sees the best of the world he is leaving behind, reflected in the purity of the image on the calm sea. The invisible power of the wind, however, ruffles the water and even penetrates into the occult depths to bring death-and-rebirth into contact with elemental forces of regeneration. Yeats likewise turns from the play of sensual images. But his mind hovers at the brink, incorporating the moment of dissolution into the 'mosaic' metaphor. What lies beyond is characteristically suggested by half-waking, half-unconscious states. The Emperor is drowsy and slipping toward sleep, yet kept awake by the play of symbols; the bird 'of hammered gold and gold enamelling' is so realistic that the lords and ladies of Byzantium might stop to see whether it is singing. And yet it is doubtful whether they can really hear its message of 'what is past, or passing, or to come'.

'Sailing to Byzantium' depicts a thrust of consciousness toward the supersensible. At the upper limit of the perceptible the images crumble away. An intenser reality is strongly felt beyond; yet it lives only at a level of feeling or half-consciousness, and to this extent the poem reflects exactly the nature of *A Vision* and its system. The equilibrium of full waking is declared to be unattainable on the axis of Beauty (Phases 1 and 15). Hence the poem is a journeying and an expectation rather than an achievement, and the poet still looks forward to the stage when he will be 'out of nature' as is the supersensible reality he apprehends.

Yeats was not wholly content, however, with the result of 'Sailing to Byzantium', and four years afterwards, in 1930, he wrote 'Byzantium'. No longer does he remain on the verge of transcendence, hovering between dream-like voyage and the consciousness of arrival at the destined spot. Indeed, Yeats exceeds in the poem the scope of the *Vision*-framework that enabled him to write it: for he speaks now out of an undiminished consciousness, a source of strength not only to overcome the Luciferic dream but also to confront in full consciousness the limits of perceptual reality and gaze into the beyond. Yet he could not have composed the poem without the 'intermediate' half-lit consciousness manifested in *A Vision* – nor for that matter without his studies of Steiner and the continuing work with the Stella Matutina. For 'Byzantium' had been maturing in Yeats' mind for many years, and the final effort of raising it into the full light of consciousness represented a climax of inner work as well as poetic achievement.

We recall that Dr Felkin had found a way of continuing the 'Golden Dawn' and its Rosicrucianism. He had obtained certain 'continental processes', i.e. the ritual forms developed by Steiner, with which initiation into the higher grades of the Order could finally proceed. In accordance with Steiner's directions for the rite, Yeats was initiated in 1915 to the grade of Adeptus Exemptus. It was from this initiation-experience, as Richard Ellmann points out, that Yeats drew the inspiration for his first sketch of the poem that later became 'Byzantium'. It was as yet only a sketch, and the Byzantium-symbolism drawn from the historical gyres of *A Vision* was still lacking:

> We are weighed down by the blood & the heavy weight of the
> bones
> We are bound by flowers, & our feet are entangled in the
> green
> And there is deceit in the singing of birds.
> It is time to be done with it all
> The stars call & all the planets
> And the purging fire of the moon
> And yonder is the cold silence of cleansing night
> May the dawn break, & gates of day be set wide open.

The sense of being 'captives on earth' (*erdbezwungen*) was to be expressed also by Steiner in meditative verses, using imagery of flowers, metals, moon and planets in addition to men.

> Ich schaue in die Blumen;
> Ihre Verwandschaft mit dem Mondensein offenbaren sie;
> Sie sind erdbezwungen; denn sie sind Wassergeborene.

Ich denke über die Metalle;
Ihre Verwandschaft mit den Planeten offenbaren sie;
Sie sind erdbezwungen, denn sie sind Luftgeborene.

Ich erlebe die Geheimnisse des Tierkreises
  in der Mannigfaltigkeit der Menschen;
Die Verwandtschaft dieser Mannigfaltigkeit
  der Menschen mit den Fixsternen
  steht vor meiner Seele;
Denn die Menschen leben mit dieser
  Mannigfaltigkeit erdbezwungen;
  sie sind Wärmegeborene.

They appeared in connection with his 1923 course on *Mystery Knowledge and Mystery Centres,* and so cannot be a source of Yeats' poem directly, but perhaps Steiner had used similar forms of expression earlier in esoteric circles. At any rate, such were the thoughts suggested to Yeats by Steiner's ritual. The poem, however, took some fifteen years to mature.

In the meantime Yeats had left the Stella Matutina. He had had enough of wrangling and secessions, and the automatic writing of his wife had suddenly given him more work than enough for his inner life. The date of his resignation can be put at about 1922. Steiner too had long since closed down his 'symbolic–cultural' activity. His verdict on the Golden Dawn, we gather from the memorandum of H. Collison, was that its limitations and complications exceeded its usefulness. For Steiner, he wrote in 1921, 'the Order is decorative and useful to those who need it and are able to distinguish between mere ornament and reality'. This was hardly a charter for further collaborations.

Ellmann has pointed to a further stage in the evolution of 'Byzantium' – a poem called 'Images' from around 1926. The object of the quest is now the sacred mountain Abiegnos, a Rosicrucian and alchemical symbol in its specific Golden Dawn form. Attention again focusses on images and the limits of imaging, but still the poem does not quite cohere. The rehumanized figures caught up in the mountainous ascent lapse back into animal guises and the cyclic round of incarnations; man's power to create himself through image-making is defeated.

It is only the association with Byzantium that brings the completed pattern of the poem, when Yeats realizes that the work he is trying to write is the fulfilment of the earlier poem, 'Sailing to Byzantium'.

'Byzantium' in its finished form is Yeats' most powerful poem of visionary affirmation, despite its resolute confrontation with the 'mire and blood' of man's physicality – imagined in terms perhaps the most bitter since Blake's in the *Book of Urizen*. Whereas 'Sailing to Byzantium' renounced the dream of Ireland and a sensual world heightened through poetic dream, in 'Byzantium' Yeats must renounce the crutches of the external world in a final act of self-confident vision. He then faces the full force of his own scepticism: a material universe that does not point beyond itself. The poet accepts this most difficult of truths. To ascend from the given world to some intenser reality there are no ladders: it demands nothing less than total transformation, an imaginative leap to a new ontological level. No continuation of the existing, no projection of contingencies into absolutes, no metaphysical jugglery can succeed in describing the transcendent in terms of the immanent. And so, in a way that is unusual – perhaps unique – in Yeats' poetry the material world and the body are grasped in their physicality. The earth is affirmed in its own right, although with sombreness, yet wholly and without flinching.

The link with a higher world is man himself, a captive on earth even though it is in his power to affirm the earth and to give it meaning. Ahriman is given his due, not permitted to encroach into the human spirit. Thus Yeats does not overturn his scepticism, but incorporates it and accepts it as the very ground on which to assert the power of the human imagination. How does he achieve this in concrete terms? How can he transcend in language the sensual association of words themselves? These are questions that must be answered by a detailed look at the poem itself.

The subject of the poem is really the image-making power of man, and when the poem begins the merely given ('unpurged') images of unreflective man's perception are already dying away. At the very outset, Yeats stands at the point he reached at the end of 'Sailing to Byzantium' with its drowsy Emperor. The soldiers – men of action determined by the laws of the outer world – are asleep. External reality persists as the remote serenity of the starlit dome, seeming to tower over man with his tangled thoughts and questioning mind, reducing him by its greatness to infinite littleness.

> The unpurged images of day recede;
> The Emperor's drunken soldiery are abed;
> Night resonance recedes, night-walkers' song

> After great cathedral gong;
> A starlit or a moonlit dome disdains
> All that man is,
> All mere complexities,
> The fury and the mire of human veins.

Yeats always connected the cosmic spaces with that 'purging fire' mentioned in the original initiation-sketch. In *A Vision* he described the progress of the soul through the astral regions and its purification from – precisely – 'Complexity'.

Although the universe of external colour and sound has died away like the echo of the cathedral gong, leaving man to confront the simplifying emptiness of the inhuman cosmos, man's image-making power remains strong. Indeed it grows stronger as it feels the infinite emptiness, and desires to populate those spaces with a self-made world. Yeats takes as emblems once more the 'burning' mosaics, the images of art in the deserted Byzantine streets. From this juncture in the poem, he is examining images made by the spirit in answer to the Ahrimanic meaninglessness of the world, and analysing the creative process in search of the justification of art – the truth of imagination.

At first, however, Yeats is struck above all else by the fearful demands made by the vision for the annihilation of the natural man. The image that floats before him is a shade rather than a man, and the horror of death informs the entire second stanza:

> Before me floats an image, man or shade,
> Shade more than man, more image than a shade;
> For Hades' bobbin bound in mummy-cloth
> May unwind the winding path;
> A mouth that has no moisture and no breath
> Breathless mouths may summon;
> I hail the superhuman;
> I call it death-in-life and life-in-death.

The typical inner process of the poem is first uncovered in this stanza, the winding and unwinding through which 'image' is defined and enriched: as 'man', as 'shade', and then returned, stripped bare of sensory content as less than man, less than shade. We are made uncomfortably aware of the unsupportedness of the image at the boundary of knowledge. We feel behind it the intensity of the vacuum. But the winding and unwinding also generates an energy, like an electric charge accumulating, which survives the reversal or unwinding of the image and will enable us to confront the supersensible without losing ourselves in nothing-ness. For Yeats the winding–unwinding process of imagination hints at the solution of man's inner complexities.

If these can never be satisfied by our experience of the living world, it is inevitable that they seem to our unregenerate eyes to participate in death; yet the poet may be content to let the world fade away and twine himself in such thought:

> Such thought, that in it bound
> I need no other thing,
> Wound in mind's wandering
> As mummies in the mummy-cloth are wound

as he puts it in the 'Epilogue' to *A Vision* ('All Souls' Night'). The second stanza is thus a further in-volving of the mind. Leaving behind the 'images of day' it withdraws into its own gyrations. Yet still in its helplessness, even while it hails the 'superhuman' power of creativity, it still clings to identification with the natural to the extent that it feels the withdrawal to be death-in-life, recalling the nightmare figure in Coleridge's *Rime of the Ancient Mariner*. Its state is also a ghostly 'life' in the realm of death – but no further progress is possible until the natural heart will give itself up for lost. The imagination must now renounce its identification with the natural entirely and trust itself to the supersensible source of all images, to its own indescribable source of power within. The winding–unwinding is given a further turn:

> Miracle, bird or golden handiwork,
> More miracle than bird or handiwork.

'I shall find the dark grow luminous, the void fruitful', said Yeats, 'when I understand I have nothing' – and once more he connects that realization with death, an initiatory putting-off of identity: 'the ringers in the tower have appointed for the hymen of the soul a passing bell'. In the knowledge of the natural self 'having nothing', he is struck now by the sheer miracle of the creative imagination. He returns to the intricately wrought Byzantine golden bird for his example, unable to decide whether it is more wondrous as 'bird',

i.e. the achievement of the essence of a bird by art, or for the
incredible fineness of workmanship itself. Yet he again unwinds
the accumulated associations and leaves us staring at its sheer
miraculousness. It stands for the illimitable, indefinable possibil-
ities of imagination.

The third stanza is all brightness in the acceptance of miracle and
rebirth. It is for this dawn that the 'cocks of Hades crow',

> Miracle, bird or golden handiwork,
> More miracle than bird or handiwork,
> Planted on the star-lit golden bough,
> Can like the cocks of Hades crow,
> Or, by the moon embittered, scorn aloud
> In glory of changeless metal
> Common bird or petal
> And all complexities of mire or blood.

Here it is no longer the material splendours of the cosmos which
scorn man in his littleness. It is the creative spirit of man which is
able to look back with disdain. Yet even as he looks back from this
new perspective, Yeats is able to admit all the unresolved
complexities and the irremoveable physicality of man's nature: but
he is not daunted by it. It no longer seems to make a mockery of
man's aspirations. In the intermediate poem 'Images' he said of his
dehumanized brutes, with quasi-Darwinian overtones, 'These
chuckling & howling forms begot the sages'. But now the
'changeless metal' appears to him to take primacy, to constitute the
essentially human; man with his creativity is not a Darwinian freak
of nature but a miracle, though captive on earth in a mortal body.

The fourth stanza takes us into the realm of essences. On the
path of the spirit through the stations of the night we have reached
the furthest point. If we suppose that the course is also that of the
discarnate spirit, we have reached the point when the spirit turns
again to look upon the earth and to fashion a new life there in the
working out of its destiny. All has been purified to the self-existent,
expressing not the contingencies of sense-perception but the
innermost energy of thought. The flames imaged on the Byzantine
Emperor's famous pavement, says Yeats, are as bright at midnight for
the imagination as they are in natural light. Moreover, though they
do not singe a sleeve, they embody the nature of flame more
intensely, more single-mindedly than any 'real' flames. They are not

burning wood, nor sparks from steel, but 'flames begotten of flame' – referred only to their own inextinguishable archetype. In their realm at last the 'blood-begotten' spirit of man can fuse all his energy into the re-creation of himself.

> At midnight on the Emperor's pavement flit
> Flames than no faggot feeds, nor steel has lit,
> Nor storm disturbs, flames begotten of flame,
> Where blood-begotten spirits come
> And all complexities of fury leave,
> Dying into a dance,
> An agony of trance,
> An agony of flame that cannot singe a sleeve.

That 'dance' is perhaps the creative-and-destructive dance of Shiva, the trance that of self-collection, the gathering of energy before the final assertion.

When that final assertion comes it is with an amazing image, or metaphor: the dolphin-leap of the spirit from the sea of mire and blood.

Many elements always go into the making of a poet's metaphor. Perhaps somewhere behind this one is the 'salmon-leap' of the Irish hero Cuchulain; the critic Norman Jeffares quotes also a passage from Mrs Strong's *Apotheosis and the Afterlife* mentioning dolphins.* Yet the image was shaped by a Shakespearean vision of the afterlife more than by Byzantine or Nabataean dolphins. In *Antony and Cleopatra*, Act V, scene ii, Cleopatra beholds a vision of her dead Antony transfigured, a cosmic being:

> His face was as the heavens, and therein stuck
> A sun and moon, which kept their course, and lighted
> This little O, the earth ...
> His legs bestrid the ocean, his rear'd arm
> Crested the world: his voice was propertied
> As all the tuned spheres ...

Such a vision is, Cleopatra urges, 'past the size of dreaming' and must be real, a truth of the imagination. In a subtly displaced argument about nature and fancy, reality's inability to vie with

*A. N. Jeffares, *A Commentary on The Collected Poems of W. B. Yeats* (Stanford, 1968) p. 359.

imagination in creation (at least in the creation of strange forms) seems in Shakespeare less to undermine the power of vision, rather to constitute a challenge to reality to prove adequate to man's hopes. An existing Antony would then be nature's master-piece, 'condemning shadows quite'. All this is of interest in the case of Yeats because the visionary Antony is an image of exuber-ance, or more than natural creative power:

> For his bounty,
> There was no winter in 't: an autumn 'twas
> That grew the more by reaping: his delights
> Were dolphin-like, they show'd his back above
> The element they lived in.

Antony's super-reality was no doubt as important to the formation of Yeats' image as the dolphin-delights themselves. Yeats' purified though blood-begotten spirit is also part of an argument between imagination and nature, of life and death, and is resolved finally by that initiatory dolphin-leap.

All the images fuse in the astonishing last stanza – the dolphin-spirits, the artist-smithies (now golden like their handi-work), the marble mosaics which are the floor of the dance. The energy of the Emperor's artists is able to withstand and even to 'break the flood', the Ahrimanic dark waters which surge round and buffet the soul, filling the eyes with salt blood as in 'The Delphic Oracle upon Plotinus'. The mosaic patterns again break in 'bitter furies of complexity' as if the boiling, raging sea of the world were lashing upon the pavements of Byzantium. The disintegra-tion of the outward image is complete: but Yeats does not now yield to twilight states or moony intimations. Consciousness reaches an apocalyptic intensity.

In his refusal to yield to Ahriman, his determination to face the power of material reality and to assert that 'leap' of the spirit into the supersensible, Yeats is the poet of what Steiner hailed as a new Michaelic age. The old pattern of apocalypse is radically internal-ized. The dolphins, after all, are not monsters of the deep like those tamed by the creator-God or by the warring Archangel. Consciousness is seized upon by the poet in the very moment of creativity, as the source of the self-sustaining images which are essential being. But consciousness also looks out in archangelic power, with mingled scorn and exhilaration, upon the wild surface of life's dark ocean:

> Astraddle on the dolphin's mire and blood,
> Spirit after spirit! The smithies break the flood,
> The golden smithies of the Emperor!
> Marbles of the dancing floor
> Break bitter furies of complexity,
> Those images that yet
> Fresh images beget,
> That dolphin-torn, that gong-tormented sea.

Epilogue
The Tower

For Yeats the Tower is a symbol of the conscious soul struggling toward the difficult achievement of wisdom. Indeed, it becomes an image sometimes for the essential loneliness of human life in our age of the 'consciousness soul': the sage or poet in his necessary isolation, at midnight burning his solitary light while his creations move through the world with a freedom he himself lacks, perhaps mocking him slightly as do Aherne and Robartes in 'The Phases of the Moon'. Milton's Platonist lives on here, and in the painting of Samuel Palmer to which Yeats refers. But we must now pose a last question. Is it really the visionary knowledge Milton attributed to his lonely sage which still feeds the modern sensibility of a Yeats? The former brooded on 'thrice great *Hermes*' and summoned:

> The spirit of *Plato* to unfold
> What Worlds, or what vast Regions hold
> Th' immortal mind that hath forsook
> Her mansion in this fleshly nook.

His was a knowledge of daemons, planets and elements. Has this visionary wisdom still a place in the universe of modern man?

Yeats' achievement in 'Sailing to Byzantium', his treatment in the context of a farewell of what Wordsworth had called 'The consecration and the Poet's dream', can be related to the characteristic structures of modern philosophy – specifically the strain that begins in the eighteenth century with John Locke and provides the presuppositions for scientific realism. That philosophy drew attention to the subjective or 'secondary' nature of the qualities we suppose to invest the external world: scent, colour, sound, warmth, etc. These exist, the Lockean philosophers declared, only in relation to our sense-organization, our eyes, noses, ears and skin (the boundary of our tactile and warmth-sensations). In the world strictly as it is, there are only the 'primary' qualities of extension, bodies in space and their movements. The latter world can be described by means of mathematics and geometry, the great instruments of scientific understanding. This idea was part of a great change – and it did not happen all at once – from the traditional universe, the world-made-for-man by the Creator. The intellect of man aspired to comprehend the world as it is in itself. Formerly, the world had been understood to point beyond itself – to the Creator as its cause, and to man as its purpose. Around man and God the imagination had woven vivid mythologies. What place for the human imagination in the new 'realistic' world?

The eighteenth-century writer Addison already accepted the philosophers' distinction between primary and secondary qualities, and his reaction strikingly anticipates the imagery of the Romantic poets, notably Keats:

> What a rough, unsightly sketch of nature should we be entertained with, did all her colouring disappear, and the several distinctions of light and shade vanish? In short, our souls are at present delightfully lost and bewildered in a pleasant delusion, and we walk about like the enchanted hero of a romance, who sees beautiful castles, woods and meadows; and at the same time hears the warbling of birds, and the purling of streams; but upon the finishing of some secret spell, the fantastic scene breaks up, and the disconsolate knight finds himself on a barren heath, or in a solitary desert.

Behind Addison's description of the modern 'bewildered' mind lurks the myth of diabolic illusions and temptations, and ultimately the story of Lucifer in Eden. For it was Lucifer, as we have seen, who tempted man to grasp at ultimate knowledge. But the effect was to make Paradise a delusion and let 'killing Truth', as Shelley said, destroy it. The biblical emphasis falls on the lesson of man's creaturely limitations, his dependence on the greater Giver who made him and the world. And coming at the beginning of the scriptural narrative, the point is intended to be made once and for all. Early modern philosophy, however, by challenging the traditional view of the external world, brought the myth once more closely into focus. Addison found himself again in a paradise of delights, and at the same time reaching out with his reason to grasp at reality beyond. The result in his case too was a fall: he wakes from his dream to find himself in a barren, solitary world of mere form and extension.

But the myth has been taken up on a different level. For Lucifer is not now an actor in a divine drama wherein man has only the role of dependent and succumber to external temptation. He is a power that man must control in his own mind. He begets manifold illusions, yet he is at the same time a power in whom man may take an active delight. Indeed, Addison is prepared to think himself 'in a pleasant delusion', for all his acceptance of the 'barren' truth. The later Romantics, with the benefit of hindsight, the experience of the Industrial Revolution and its social ravages, the alternation of idealism and tyranny which broke up the 'Age of Reason', were not to find the position so easy.

For purely intellectual reasons, Addison's untroubled tone proved hard to sustain. As philosophical thought proceeded, the distinction between 'primary' and 'secondary' qualities came to seem less clear. After all, extension and motion could not be perceived without our sensory organization, so that it is problematic to see how they really differ from the 'secondary' qualities. What remained clear was a realization of the active part played by the mind in perceiving and knowing the actual world. Here again different trends soon appeared. There were sceptics like Hume who denied that we could know anything at all outside the 'pleasant delusion' of our mental constructs. Others tried rather desperately to prove the necessity of there being external objects; others clung to the object and tried the relatively novel exercise of arguing away the mind instead. Crises came relatively soon in the philosophical domain, but in many ways they have only begun to affect the practising scientist in our own century, where the problems surface in concepts such as 'relativity', 'indeterminacy', etc. Relativity made its *debut* around the beginning of the century. At the same time the concept of the imagination as 'fantastic scene', as thoroughly divorced from reality and rational discourse, climaxes in the pure 'image' of the Symbolists.

The idea that the imagination could treat of things in their wholeness, in the richness and immediacy of their experienced reality when man's faculties are active, yet intensely 'open' to that 'freshness of sensation' Coleridge described – any such idea has largely been ignored. Yet it asserts itself again in our time, both as a recognition of the role of the 'irrational', of history and imagination in science and scientific discovery, and as a necessary response to the abysses of scepticism and relativism to which our cultural and intellectual traditions have led us. The question of man's Luciferic aspirations, the proper scope of his creativity, have again become crucial.

In 'Sailing to Byzantium', Yeats sets out to explore the scope of man's imaginative contribution. That the pursuit of the Luciferic dream – what Wordsworth termed 'The light that never was, on sea or land' – could lead the poet into a delusive paradise of his own fabrication was something that Yeats knew well. When he fuses that dream with the landscape of earth, of Ireland, therefore, in that beautiful first stanza of the poem, we may take it as his answer to the dilemma of the post-scientific imagination. He knows that the glamour of beauty is imparted by the perceiving mind, the 'young / In one another's arms' who see ideal beauty in their own beloved. As an 'old man' he sees through the illusion and sternly prefers the 'monuments' of thought. Yet as the poet he himself creates the 'sensual music' which charms them, and his is the creative artist's enjoyment of the dream he has evoked. Lucifer is not rejected outright. Yeats seems to be saying that there is a need for that kind of imagination: in fact, its scope is the creation of the actual world. It does not need fantasy realms, the enchanted bowers of Addison's old romances. The philosophers, strangely enough, have brought this quaint faculty into the process of knowledge itself. The poet vouches that the Luciferic imagination can be profoundly fulfilled in painting the colours of earth. Not only Palmer, but the great Romantic artists of landscape add a parallel testimony. It is since the eighteenth century that landscape painting in its modern sense has become a self-subsistent domain of imagination. Through Turner and Constable the imagination has been engaged by the qualities of the earth around us, and found a fulfilment there not known to the painters of epic history and of domestic detail who preceded them.

Landscape brings us back to Wordsworth. Yet Wordsworth's imagination, powerful though it was, was singularly lacking in the qualities of romance, the erotic and supernatural elements which featured so strongly in the work of the other Romantics. His experiment with the limits of the natural therefore took another course. In Addison's terms, his imagination did not survive, and he spent his latter years on a poetic 'barren heath' or 'solitary desert'. He had looked for an ultimate reality in nature. Yeats perhaps evades his fate because he looks there rather for a field of human creativity, a bower in which to dream. His own departure from the dream-land he so brilliantly depicts is a tacit assertion that he does not pin there his hopes of finding the answer to the riddle of himself. His leave-taking symbolizes an inner freedom from the temptations of the Luciferic dream – the dream which, once taken for truth, forebodes the shipwreck of the soul.

Yet, so far from being radically novel, Yeats' solution looks back to Milton, another sensual dreamer though often miscast as an abstractionist and worshipper of 'unageing intellect'. It echoes ultimately those marvellous and disturbing passages in *Comus* where Milton allows his Tempter to address the virtuous Lady. Comus assails her with nothing other than Milton's acknowledgement of the natural glories of earth. Surely here man can, indeed surely should, find satisfaction:

> Wherefore did Nature pour her bounties forth
> With such a full and unwithdrawing hand,
> Covering the earth with odours, fruits and flocks,
> Thronging the Seas with spawn innumerable,
> But all to please and sate the curious taste?
> And set to work millions of spinning Worms,
> That in the green shops weave the smooth-haird silk
> To deck her Sons, and that no corner might
> Be vacant of her plenty, in her own loins
> She hutchd th'all worshipt ore and precious gems
> To store her children with; if all the world
> Should in a pet of temperance feed on Pulse,
> Drink the clear stream, and nothing wear but Freize,
> Th'all-giver would be unthankt, would be unprais'd,
> Not half his riches known and yet despis'd.

A typical Luciferic excess follows. (If it is not true ecologically that the restraint of man's presence and participation prevents the riot of nature, it is certainly true on the level of imagination where man must control the forces at work within him. Here, too, Milton looks forward, not back to older myth.) Nature, continues Comus:

> would be quite surcharg'd with her own weight,
> And strangl'd with her waste fertility;
> Th'earth cumberd, and the wingd air darkt with plumes,
> The herds would over-multitude their Lords,
> The Sea o'erfraught would swell, and th'unsought diamonds
> Would so emblaze the forhead of the Deep
> And so bestudd with Stars, that they below
> Would grow inur'd to light, and come at last
> To gaze upon the Sun with shameless brows.

Comus, and his Luciferic excess, must be controlled – and is controlled, by the Lady's sense of her latent self, the destiny she 'chastely' reserves herself in order to fulfil.* But Milton does not unsay the poetry of sensual splendour he gives to the 'unwithdrawing' bounty of nature. It is only that it has no power to hold the soul captive to its enchantments. Like Yeats with his gesture of farewell, Milton utters the greatest praise of nature in the act of transcending it.

Now all this is not too unlike the Hermetica which Milton studied. In that main tractate, the *Poimandres*, which influenced Blake as well as scientific thought of the seventeenth and eighteenth centuries, beauty is the reflex of the 'form of God', imaged in the waters of creation. Nature herself falls in love with it; and man, 'seeing this form, a form like to his own, in earth and water, loved it, and willed to dwell there'. For those of a Gnostic disposition, like some of the Hermetic enthusiasts, this could be seen as pre-cosmic temptation and fall; for others, the phrasing 'willed to dwell there' stressed man's ultimate, metaphysical freedom. Hermetic thought at any rate agreed with Milton (in what is indeed a strictly Hermetic rather than Platonic allusion at the end of *Comus*) that man's destiny was not down here among the revolving spheres. The realm of spiritual values was infinitely greater, far 'Higher than the Spheary chime'. Man wished to dwell on earth, and nature's beauty was the reflection of his own divine origins. In so far as the Hermetic universe expressed man's 'trapped' consciousness, on the other hand, it formed a salutary warning of the dangers of man explaining himself by means of an elaborate system he had himself (according to the myth) constructed.

Visionary poetry establishes that our experience of the natural world can never be tied down to the fixities isolated from experience for the purposes of 'science'. Imagination always intervenes. The barest reality is always mediated to us by a framework, a schema of the mind, attended by desire, hope, expectation, nightmare, or religious awe. Actuality exists against a backdrop of myth, of patterns of possible relation, contrary interpretations. Without any myth, without any preliminary framework, we would not have a pure, 'objective' world before us: we would have no intelligible experience at all, but that senseless and

*See the brilliant essay on 'Milton's Early Poems', in J. Broadbent (ed.), *John Milton: Introductions* (Cambridge, 1973) pp. 258–97, especially pp. 268–82, by Lorna Sage.

shapeless plasticity of Yeats' Phase 1. The line of visionary poetry has accepted and explored the mythic backdrop, those Hermetic mirages of divine beauty which Nature herself as we see her embraces and loves. And it has affirmed, often in opposition to the prevailing philosophies, the value they hold for the exploration of the 'real' itself – a value which modern thought is only beginning to understand. It has shown that the world around us, far from meeting us as a mere 'given', offers us a field for infinite enrichment and deepening of experience. Of this the imagination is the only adequate instrument we have.

There is no reason that science should not co-exist with such an approach. Indeed, the old argument between the 'facts' of science and the 'fictions' of imagination is already outmoded. The cruder materialism of solid lumps, the knocking-together of atoms which Coleridge had to contend with in the 'Corpuscularian philosophy' of his day, has largely gone. We can see the world in terms of possibilities of meaning – whose sum is not likely to be comprehended in the relations between a number of irreducible particles. Rather, scientists are learning to think of complexly interacting systems, where the behaviour of the whole may have very little to do with the classic materialist's question 'What is it made of?'*

What seem to be needed in the present situation are more lines of communication, more awareness of parallel concerns – also, perhaps, a greater resistance to the reduction of imaginative experience for short-term or immediate ends, especially in the field of education. Openness is needed alongside even the most detailed scrutiny of evidence. That openness is imagination, potential new meaning and relations 'hitherto unapprehended' but which yet may be grasped. If it is denied, we have seen from Blake as from Wordsworth how it may become a haunting spectre, or yawning void of meaninglessness.

Imagination is not something, therefore, which can be relegated to the underworld of the Freudian 'Unconscious'. It is not mere 'fantasy', nor can its awareness of new, perhaps subversive meanings behind our ordinary experience be treated as 'overdetermination', the accidental fusing of layers of significance which has no meaning except for the pathologist. It embodies rather the deep-lying assumptions which make experience a shared reality.

---

*There is an interesting popular presentation of some of these approaches in C. H. Waddington, *Tools for Thought* (St. Albans, 1977).

For all the emphasis on the loneliness of the sage in the Tower, we should recall those images from earlier literature, influenced perhaps by the Hermetica, where the Tower stands for community (*ekklesia*). It appears as such in the *Visions of Hermas* (the Mystery-god in Christian guise?), and in Langland's great mediaeval vision-poem of *Piers Plowman* rises high above the 'field full of folk'. The perspective of the Tower includes society, and the common aspirations of men and women, not just their private dreams. Steiner's Goetheanum, in some ways his version of the Tower, built high on the Dornach hills above Basel, is not only a centre for study, but a theatre, conference-hall and much else besides. Yeats' Thoor Ballylee not only has its foundations far in Irish history, but its symbols are rich in associations with Yeats' life and friends.

It is, however, at the frontiers of awareness that the poet stands alone, a 'borderer', perhaps even a legislator for times to come. This is the setting for the achievement in Yeats' other Byzantium poem, defending that conscious struggle to grasp the 'hitherto unapprehended': the supersensible which can only be intimated through the mutual 'begetting' of images, and the winding–unwinding tensions of the poem. Despite its symbols of Byzantine piety, its magical allusions, its hints at Platonic teaching on the soul when it has forsaken its 'fleshly nook', its recalling of ancient initiations, 'Byzantium' faces an essentially modern dilemma of consciousness. It asserts the possibility of that ultimate openness which for Yeats points to the Thirteenth Cone, his unknown God. Again, the visionary tradition retains its vitality and its relevance unimpaired. After all, 'Byzantium' is a poem in the tradition of initiation-poems like Blake's *Book of Thel*, pioneered as a response to the vision of the material world, the modern cosmology. Blake recognized in its most negative aspects the manifestation of the 'consciousness soul', and England's special role in its emergence:

The banks of the Thames are clouded! the ancient porches of
                                                    Albion are
Darken'd! they are drawn thro' unbounded space, scatter'd upon
The void in incoherent despair! Cambridge & Oxford &
                                                    London
Are driven among the starry Wheels, rent away and dissipated
In Chasms & Abysses of sorrow, enlarg'd without dimension,
                                                    terrible.

                                            (*Jerusalem* 5, 1–15)

It was thence that he drew the realization of his great task – 'To open the Eternal Worlds, to open the immortal Eyes'. Yeats inherited Blake's struggle with the Ahrimanic mind, the false divinity Urizen.

Like Blake, Yeats managed to assert the strength of the imagination not to become what it beholds – not to take the little portion of experience man can organize, and analyse, for the whole. The 'terrible Starry Wheels' appear to enclose everything, define everything, generate everything. But in the face of them and their Gnostic 'archons', or demonic rulers, Blake asserted the Romantic sense of infinity, the openness of the mythic dimension. This is the primacy on which science itself is finally dependent, as Blake clearly saw when he wrote:

> If it were not for the Poetic or Prophetic character the Philosophic & Experimental would soon be at the ratio of all things & stand still, unable to do other than repeat the same dull round.

He did not see so well, perhaps, that while his Gnostic vision provided a thoroughgoing solution in the battle with Ahriman, the problems of the Luciferic struggle were bound to assert themselves once more from within (though in his last huge 'prophetic book' *Jerusalem* one can see the beginnings of a new awareness).

Yeats absorbed much from Blake, whom he studied in an intensive if not always exact fashion. Nevertheless he was confronted nearer at hand by the inner crises of the Symbolist imagination, and in the longer term his structures of thought cannot be understood purely in terms of Blake's influence. His poetry was shaped rather by the whole of the 'visionary line' since Milton, and indeed by Spenser farther back. His 'apocalyptic' consciousness in 'Byzantium' has a manifoldness, a multifaceted quality that does not derive from Blake, but the explorations of Shelley and the philosophical dialectics of Rudolf Steiner.

For Blake's failure to place himself in the historical process, or to appreciate the historical conditions of vision, had ultimately to be supplemented. Steiner began his career as a Goethe scholar in Weimar, and from the beginning was influenced by the historical awareness of the author of *Wilhelm Meister*, the poet who juxtaposed a 'Romantic' devil with classical Helen of Troy in *Faust* – who was at the same time the exponent of the *Colour Theory* and *Metamorphosis of Plants*. These works are now being scientifically re-evaluated.* Science itself, Steiner believed, needed a sense of history. Consciousness was subject to historical change or evolution; the conditions of knowledge were not for him invariable and fixed, but part of a changing relationship in which consciousness inserted itself into the world, establishing a balance of forces that allowed particular aspects of reality to appear. 'Subject' and 'object' were not *a priori* necessities, but results of this insertion. Reality was polarized into thought and thing by man's cognizing organization – a view echoed in *A Vision* where Yeats describes reality as a Sphere, which is however known to man only through the opposing gyres, the double cones. Yeats' sense of history remained tenuous, always too likely to revert to legend or outright myth. But to the extent that his Thirteenth Cone is the God of Steiner's moral individualism he is also in some degree a God of history.

Steiner was an esotericist and occasionally poet–playwright as well as a critic and philosopher. He taught at a time of greater acceptance in wide circles of the possibility of the unseen: in the decades following the foundation of the Society for Psychical Research by prominent minds, cultural and scientific; the overthrow of 'classical' physics and the exploration of the mind by new theories, suggesting novel syntheses; the influence of esoteric thought on great artists and writers and musicians, from Kandinsky and Mondrian to James Joyce and Strindberg, Holst and Scriabin. Yeats felt a 'trembling of the veil', as he put it in his *Autobiographies*. That sense of imminent revelation has not survived. But it is unfortunate that its retreat has obscured Steiner's importance – not so much as a literary figure on the basis of his musical–dramatic experiments, but as the latest full inheritor of Romantic thought, the 'Romanticism come of age' characterized by Owen Barfield. I have tried, in a modest effort to link the themes and form of his play with Shelley's idea of 'lyrical drama', to indicate his continuity with the concerns and solutions of earlier Romanticism, and to suggest the especial value of this when Shelley's feeling for balance and the complexity of consciousness went largely unappreciated and exerted little influence on the post-Romantic tradition at large. I have also tried to suggest his role as a transmitter of ideas to the last great student of the lonely light of the Tower in English poetry.

Yeats through *A Vision*, Steiner through his insight into the

*See F. Amrine, F. J. Zucker and H. Wheeler (eds), *Goethe and the Sciences: a Re-Appraisal* (Dordrecht, 1987).

evolution of consciousness, achieved a *rapprochement* with the massed particulars of history. All literature is, of course, markedly of its period and betrays its origins. Whilst it clearly does emerge out of a specific setting, however, the striking thing about literature is surely the extent to which it resists contextualization. The poets and novelists of a period – like its musicians and artists – still speak to us with considerable directness and immediacy, when the effort to place ourselves in the scientific or philosophical thought of their time might be a laborious task that only specialists would willingly undertake. That is surely because, as I tried to say at the outset of this book, the imagination is not so much a product of specific times as the instrument by which any period tries to put itself in the context of the widest, richest human experience. It is the very means by which the writer tries with as little reduction as he can to establish the context in which contemporary knowledge and customs stand.

Shelley offered the insight that 'poets . . . painters, sculptors and musicians are, in one sense, the creators, and, in another, the creations of their age'. Wordsworth saw the poet as:

> In part a fellow citizen, in part
> An outlaw and a borderer of his age.

But their insights have been taken up in a highly unequal manner by modern criticism. Relevant results from sociology and history have certainly illuminated literature – but the concept of the 'unacknowledged legislator', the border explorer who opens up new ways of seeing, unnoticed affinities and unremarked relations that will become important to men of the future, has met with little recognition. Yet perhaps here is the link between myth and history, a road to accommodating the knowledge offered by both. The myth connects human life with the greater unknown, the sense of obscure 'sublimity' without which it sinks to Blake's 'dull round'; reality itself can only be plotted against the backdrop of such a mythic dimension, and yet the myth is constantly evaporating, escaping into the rarity of the supersensible. One extremely widespread myth is that of 'Paradise Lost'. The nostalgia for Paradise is to be found even in the most archaic, seemingly 'unfallen' cultures.* The myth's existence implies that Paradise can be recaptured, or at least remembered fitfully, like Shelley's 'echoes of an ante-natal dream', or Wordsworth's inklings of a

---

*See M. Eliade, *Myths, Dreams and Mysteries* (London, 1968) ch. III, 'Nostalgia for Paradise in the Primitive Traditions'.

similar pre-existence. Yet all attempts to live the myth here and now, to identify the Garden with the present state of the self, are inevitably disastrous – Luciferic in the traditional terms of Western myth itself. This is the remaining mythological wisdom, fixed by Milton in his definitive literary rendering: the age of paradisal myth is over and gone. And yet it must constantly be evoked, if only to explain why it is that man has set out instead upon the course of his history, seeking for his identity and the meaning of his actions.

No poet since Milton has achieved quite the poignancy of Milton's concluding lines in *Paradise Lost*, Book XII. But the visionaries whom we have studied all recognized the crucial necessity of myth. The defeat of Lucifer is the beginning of history, in which man is joined to the earth securely by his will to act and to find himself through action. The defeat of the Ahrimanic lapse into meaninglessness, however, requires the taking over by man's self of mythic creativity. The most strident solution is apocalypse: the myth of divine intervention. All the visionaries who followed Milton have invoked some form of the apocalyptic scenario of the 'End of the World'. Blake achieved a remarkably full rehabilitation of the myth in his special Gnostic form. By bracketing the Ahrimanic universe in a dualistic vision he achieved the pure space of imagination in which to unfold his amazing mythology. Others, however, felt the need to retain man's existence in history and could not put the historical setting in parentheses. Like Blake, they have all displaced the strident forms of apocalypse from cosmic disaster into inner crises of consciousness, but they have sought at the same time to see this as the genesis of a new historical process rather than an individually achieved *gnosis*.

At the risk of being misunderstood, one may suggest that it is elements in the Christian world-view, with its simultaneous grasp of myth and history, that have offered most to the circumstances of the Romantic and post-Romantic imagination. Christianity attributed to an event of history the sustaining and transforming power, the depth of meaning reserved before for the grandiose myths of creation and destruction. It had the same ability to redefine the nature of the world, making meaningful the bold statement that the death on the cross was the death of God, an agony whose reverberations were felt through the whole of the cosmos. Christian teaching connected the agony by a further paradox with an act of love. The classic statement is in the Gospel of St. John: 'For God so loved the world that he gave his only-begotten Son . . .'; but it is less with statements that we have to deal than with implicit imaginative attitudes and ways of seeing. I have suggested that Shelley reveals a spirit highly 'Christian' in this sense, despite his lack of formal acceptance of any beliefs; and there is a strong Christian side to Yeats, using the term to mean an extension of essentially Christian attitudes into modern imaginative experience. There is necessarily a struggle to be fought here with the limits of historical Christianity: we witness that struggle in all the poets we have studied. We also see how out of that struggle emerge forms of knowledge, and modes of self-awareness that are not mere acceptance ('faith') but achievement, truths of the imagination. According to such an attitude, we might say: just as the overcoming of Luciferic dream is history, so the overcoming of Ahriman, the Lord of power, is knowledge – or in a deeper sense, love.

Visionary poetry does not suggest an order beyond human experiential range, whether of an objectivist or a mystical kind. Its determination to hold fast to the fulness of human experience leads it rather to base its 'truth of imagination' on the possibilities of meaning it finds there. Modern philosophy has learnt that absolute objectivity proves vacuous if conceived as the pinning down of an ultimate 'given' truth. But we can work to exclude from our understanding the distortions of Luciferic self-love and self-centred vision. Conversely, the human 'ego' – the essential self – is threatened with extinction in an Ahrimanically conceived universe. The self takes its place at the centre of knowledge if knowledge is conceived as the loving acceptance which allows an object to unfold its qualities, and communality as the generous impulse of the imagination to share its joys. All our visionaries express aspects of these struggles. The emphasis of the 'visionary line' has not been that of Wordsworth when he spoke, in the title of a Book in *The Prelude*, of the 'Love of Nature leading to Love of Man'. Their question seems rather to be whether mankind can extend its proper love of itself to the world it is shaping, depleting and transforming all too often without love, without imagination. Our poets suggest that this is the road to greater self-knowledge, as well as to the deeper truth.

The imaginative tasks they have placed before us are open to the future and largely unfulfilled. The light still beckons from the Tower. Its light, they claim, is sufficient to our sense of reality, as well as to our sense of beauty and of our humanity.

Appendices

Appendices

Appendix 1
Ranters and Poets

The Ranters have been mentioned several times in this book: from the passages devoted to them it should already be obvious that they were a sect of radical religious thinkers, enthusiasts who like other groups at the time of the Civil War claimed a new revelation. Their popular name (by analogy with the process by which the spiritually stirred Friends became 'Quakers', or Baptists became 'Dippers') was Ranters, and as such they are still known.* But what to some was ranting, to others was inspiration, and to some it suggested a new kind of poetry. Milton can be seen as a pioneer of the kind of poetry that developed from the 'new revelation', the new consciousness of the seventeenth century. Blake can be seen to continue it. Shelley has also been linked with the Ranter line, though with less plausibility.

The Ranters flourished from the 1650s onward, and appear to have lingered on into the nineteenth century as an active, if progressively more isolated spiritual force. It is significant that the Ranters did not emerge into prominence, or produce any of their major protagonists, in the earlier phase of development when the ideas of the various radical sects actually seemed on the verge of being put into practice. By 1650 the tide of events had turned, and a spiritual reform of society seemed definitely thwarted, or at least severely compromised. The Ranters attracted considerable attention thereafter, it seems, precisely because of their Gnostic character. They did not believe in an 'apocalyptic' realization of the spirit through historical events, but in the attainment of an inner illumination beyond good and evil, or any other of the delusive oppositions forged by the mind (one of the Ranter texts to survive is a meditation on *The Light and Dark Sides of God*). Norman Cohn has speculated that they were carrying on the Gnostic tradition which he traces through the mediaeval Brethren of the Free Spirit, and which leads back through Cathars, Bogomils and other esoteric groups to ancient Gnosticism and Manichaeism. In this he

*Evidence about the Ranters, and a selection of surviving texts from the Ranters Bauthumley, Clarkson, Salmon and Abiezer Coppe, is conveniently available in Norman Cohn, *Pursuit of the Millennium* (London, 1970) pp. 287–330.

may be correct; but from our point of view it is at least as important to ask why the Ranters came into prominence just when they did. We must ask what contribution they made to the visionary imagination, what use the great poetic writers were able to make of Ranter visions and ideas.

'If we were not so over-awed by Milton the great poet', writes Christopher Hill, 'we should long ago have recognized his role as a precursor of the Ranters'.* He goes on to mention many convincing points at which Milton and the radical enthusiasts agree, where Milton echoes Bauthumley or agrees with Winstanley and Coppe in his numerous pamphlets and essays. Examples are forthcoming, too, from the later poetry. In fine, Milton is not only a precursor but could have learnt from the Ranters and was engaged in a kind of dialogue with their fundamental ideas throughout his life and inner development. On Milton's symbolism of light and darkness, for example, Hill says: '*Pace* M. Saurat, this underground tradition seems to me a more plausible source than the *Zohar*, though Milton may have read that too. He could have learnt that sin is the privation of light from Bauthumley's *Light and Dark Sides of God*, and the light/darkness antithesis pervades the thought of many other radicals as well as of Milton.'

Now the Ranters were fairly consistent Gnostics, and followed through their ideas to reach startling religious formulations, close to those of ancient Gnostic thought. They regarded the Old Testament God as a Demiurge – a 'God–Devil'. This God presides over the divided material universe (where spirit and matter are at odds) and is worshipped by divided, corrupt society (where man is at odds with his 'fellow creatures'). The 'true God' is to be found in knowledge which leads beyond these dualities: a knowledge for which matter is the immediate expression of spirit – indeed does not exist in separation from it at all; he is in all creatures and in the whole Creation. This God the Ranters invoked by typically Gnostic names: 'They call him The Being, the Fulnesse, the Great Motion, Reason, the Immensity.'

Milton certainly was drawn by such a drastic imaginative solution to the crisis of the radical revolution. But he resolved it in his poetry in a more complex way, giving up the dream of the millennium yet not losing grip on man's historical situation and his task of self-transformation. Likewise, he experienced the divided,

*Christopher Hill, *The World Turned Upside Down* (Harmondsworth, 1975) p. 395.

Ahrimanic cosmos (the 'Universe of death'), but also envisaged a process of redemption in which man's physical nature and that of the world around him would share. The most valuable insights presented by Hill, therefore, are those where he sees Milton absorbing the ideas of Ranter thought, but struggling to convert them into a somewhat different and more complicated structure: 'If we think of Milton as living in a state of permanent dialogue with radical views which he could not altogether accept, yet some of which he valued very highly indeed, it may throw light even on the great poetry.' I believe this to be true, and in the chapter on 'Milton's Christianity and the Birth of the Ego' I have attempted to delineate the forces with and against which Milton struggled, and to sketch the more complex resolution which begins to emerge. I am also inclined to accept, however, that this resolution was never completely achieved, but appears fitfully in his verse, at moments of self-transcendence and uniqueness.

On Milton's avoidance of a Gnostic solution, Hill is quite clear. 'If Milton had allowed himself consciously to accept the view of Winstanley, Erbery and some Ranters, that the God whom most Christians worshipped was a wicked God, his life would have lost its structure, would have fallen in ruins about his head like the temple of the Philistines . . . No Ranter could have written *Paradise Lost*: the tension would have been lacking.' The tension is definitely there in Milton, and if his imagination did not wholly succeed in its enormous labour of creating a self-conscious vision, he did open new paths where the Romantics and later visionaries could follow. Milton himself was swayed by other modes of thought besides Ranterism, of course. Though that was one ingredient, a temptation rather than solution,* in his inner struggle, I have suggested that the current of 'Rosicrucianism', with its Christianization of the occult tradition and its more modern, rather than Gnostic, evaluation of the conscious self, played an important role in providing the essential pattern of Milton's epic.

The Ranter element, on the other hand, does a good deal to explain what Blake found in Milton; and the connection of Blake with the Ranters or their successors has been well argued, above all by A. L. Morton.†

---

*Cf. Empson's observation that Gnostic-Manichaean ideas are attributed by Milton to the fallen angels: *Milton's God* (Cambridge, 1981) pp. 85–8.

†A. L. Morton, *The Everlasting Gospel. A Study in the Sources of William Blake* (New York, 1966).

Blake, during his major creative period, is a Gnostic visionary who went far beyond the Ranters is recreating the spirit and the mythology of ancient Gnosticism. It is possible that he read some of the Ranter literature. But more likely, he lived in his youth with artisans and tradespeople among whom radical and Ranter ideas were still diffused. Certainly his Gnosticism meets us as a living tradition, and could hardly have been derived by patchwork from the surviving fragments of *gnosis* quoted by the Church Fathers and retold again in the eighteenth century by Unitarian preachers. The problem is that it is very hard to explain how Blake did manage to achieve so complete a fusion of Gnostic ideas. In my study of 'The Gnostic Imagination of William Blake' I examined the range of agreement between Blake and ancient Gnostic sources, and also the extent to which this could have been the result of Ranter influence. My conclusions were that the Ranters can account for only a part of this remarkable spiritual phenomenon, even if we assume their influence to have been very strong indeed. I showed that patterns of inner experience must be invoked – of the type discussed in this book under the heading of 'initiatory' patterns – and that deep similarities of outlook and inner experience must be presumed if we are to understand how Blake brought together so much out of Radical tradition, the Bible, Neoplatonism, etc. and moulded it into a coherent vision.* The kind of inner experiences Blake decribed, and the historical pressures with which he contended, have alike been discussed in the Blake chapter of this book. But certainly we may see the doctrines of the Ranters as stepping-stones on the way to Blake. And we may suppose that Blake sympathized deeply with them, as with all Gnostics: 'because they kept the Divine Vision in time of trouble'.

---

*Andrew J. Welburn, 'The Gnostic Imagination of William Blake' (Cambridge Ph.D. thesis, 1980).

Appendix 2
The Gnostic Lyric: Blake and Baudelaire

Tout enfant, j'ai senti dans mon coeur deux sentiments contra-
dictoires, l'horreur de la vie et l'extase de la vie.

– Baudelaire

I have suggested that Blake's Gnostic vision, embodying his sense
of contradictory levels of experience, originated in his personal
'initiatory' experience yet at the same time expressed a solution to
the tensions between natural and spiritual reality, between human
aspiration and the Ahrimanic universe of the natural philosophers
– tensions existing in European culture as a whole and forming a
phase in the history of modern consciousness. In this book there is
no space to document that view on the scale it would require, or
even to deal with the major figures. Yet it could easily be thought
that within such a perspective, Blake's case is too unrepresenta-
tive. His Gnosticism was shaped, albeit on the foundation of deep
and universal feelings, by his involvement in mystical, Swedenbor-
gian and Neoplatonic circles, and by a recognition of his affinity to
the ancient heretics, severely limited as knowledge of their views
could be in the late eighteenth century. In this short appendix I
hope to show that another visionary imagination of tremendous
importance in European poetry, that of Charles Baudelaire, crystal-
lized its attitudes and insights around a similar Gnostic structure of
vision.

At first sight there are many differences between Blake and
Baudelaire. Baudelaire lacks the explicit mythological and cosmo-
gonic dimension of the 'prophetic books'; he writes intense and
disturbing short lyrics, full of ironies and contradictions, but
aspiring toward a reality that is not to be found either in the world
of things or in his own consciousness, so clearly aware of its
self-indulgence, hypocrisy and lethargy. Yet he arranged many of
his lyrics in the famous volume *Les Fleurs du Mal* *(Flowers of Evil)*
with the express aim of depicting a whole world, or rather the

'procession de l'imagination humaine' including birth and death, aspiration and defeat – one might say 'the Contrary States of the Human Soul'. Critics have disagreed about how to categorize Baudelaire, whether as a mystic or a decadent, social critic or probing psychologist. Some, like Alison Fairlie in her excellent study of the *Fleurs du Mal*, have noted the 'undertones of religious ritual, its litanies of supplication, worship and terror' in the apparently inappropriate contexts of poems of love and of loathing. Though clearly not an orthodoxly Christian poet, his imagination includes a spiritual reality, is even obsessed by religious themes. That unstable fusion of humanistic and religious, sensual and mystic is what we find in Gnosticism, which regards such disjunctions as necessary in a divided world, and it is that label, if any, which fits both Blake and Baudelaire.

We find in Baudelaire as in Blake the frequent perception of 'This World' as impediment or hindrance to the fulness sought by the imagination. It is:

Un monde où l'action n'est pas la soeur du rêve.

And here man is ever liable to linger, to have his desires frustrated even while they seem assuaged, his will paralysed by the half-willing indulgence in sin. Time is felt, as in Gnosticism generally, in its infinite slowness, as a dimension separating man from his creative self:

Quand le ciel bas et lourd pèse comme un couvercle
Sur l'esprit gémissant en proie aux longs ennuis

recalling the oppressive 'Ages on ages' which roll over the gloomy world of Urizen, himself 'bound in a deadly sleep'. Beauty breaks in both as the awakening of trancendent desire, of the sudden glimpse of infinity, but also as torment, mercilessly uncovering the ambivalence of man's wish to aspire but not to relinquish, his hopelessly divided and contradictory nature. In Gnostic fashion the glittering, impersonal stars become an image for the object of his passion, so high and bright and clear, but without warmth. His hymn to his adored mistress, 'I worship you like night's pavilion' ('Je t'adore à l'égal de la voûte nocturne') makes us remember Blake's goddess of night and its cold spaces, Enitharmon: and Baudelaire will likewise round upon her suddenly as 'all creation's concubine', or a bizarre and ever-unsatisfied divinity like the whoring Wisdom of Gnostic myth.

Within Baudelaire's universe there is one power which epitomizes the all-pervasive presence of 'Satan Trismégiste', his demiurge who holds the strings of our puppet-destiny. More than all the menagerie of our vices it holds us impotent on earth. It is 'Ennui' – the boredom of a civilization whose knowledge, vast as it is, can only reveal a wasteland of meaninglessness and is unable to fire the will of man: 'Il ferait volontiers de la terre un débris'. Blake's Urizen too can only explore the deserts of alienation he himself has made: our knowledge is bounded by our own state of mind, and our own willingness to forge connections, to respond to the subtle '*correspondances*' which otherwise pass unregarded.

But man possesses imagination, *gnosis*. For to Baudelaire poetry is knowledge and power: power to accept our bizarre situation and knowledge of our transcendence. It is 'la recherche de l'absolu', though it reveals no divinity whose home is not in the human breast. Its knowledge is exact, since it reveals to us what we ourselves are. Indeed, 'l'imagination est la plus *scientifique* des facultés'. It enables us to accept our situation by altering the conditions of our knowledge, so that even the revelation of squalor and ugliness becomes a moment in the awakening of beauty. 'C'est un des privilèges prodigieux de l'Art que l'horrible, artistement exprimé, devienne beauté.' For it shows shabby reality as a pole in the dualism of apathy and spiritual longing, 'Spleen et Idéal'. The very force of the contrast is the energy which sustains Gnostic consciousness.

The early poems in the sequence 'Spleen et Idéal' (the first large division of *Les Fleurs du Mal*) map out Baudelaire's awareness of the poet's position. The famous 'L'Albatros' describes the lordly birds, 'vastes oiseaux des mers', caught by sailors for their amusement on a long voyage: once on deck they stumble about ridiculously, trailing their great wings with shame:

> À peine les ont-ils déposés sur les planches,
> Que ces rois de l'azur, maladroits et honteux,
> Laissent piteusement leurs grandes ailes blanches
> Comme des avirons traîner â côté d'eux.

Then, having spelled out the mixture of sadness and derision we feel for these temporarily deposed kings, Baudelaire intervenes in his own voice to point the analogy with the poet, exiled here on earth among the shouting crowds:

> He cannot walk, for he has giant's wings.*
>
> Ses ailes de géant l'empêchent de marcher.

Alison Fairlie sees the intervention as a relic of a cruder technique from the French Romantics; but the break in narrative is necessary to express the violent discrepancy between the awkward stumbling bird and the inspired lyric poet, the contrast being here the very point of the analogy between them. The disjunction could not attain its full force without the shift of emphasis and voice.

The ironic 'Bénédiction' expands the theme of that discrepancy in direct terms, charting the birth and development of the poet on earth:

> Lorsque, par un décret des puissances suprêmes,
> Le Poëte apparaît en ce monde ennuyé,
> Sa mère épouvantée et pleine de blasphèmes
> Crispe ses poings vers Dieu, qui la prend en pitié.

This is like:

> My mother groan'd! my father wept.
> Into the dangerous world I leapt:
> Helpless, naked, piping loud:
> Like a fiend hid in a cloud.

Both Blake and Baudelaire stress the treachery of the earthly world, the selfishness and enmity the child innocently encounters and cannot understand, the whole conspiracy of the world to make him forget all that is precious in childhood. And yet in the end the world is powerless against the 'supreme decree'. As for Blake 'the soul of sweet delight / Can never pass away', but only be clouded and obscured, so for Baudelaire 'ce monde ennuyé' cannot corrode the essential being of man. The poet thrives and grows ruddy in the sunshine and wind, converses with the clouds and speaks mysteries which those who cannot understand envy and hate him for. His wife turns against him because he can be satisfied with

---

*In the version by Joanna Richardson, in Baudelaire, *Selected Poems* (Harmondsworth, 1975).

nothing mortal, looking to the vision of infinity. There God still keeps the Poet's place in the hierarchies of the blest.

The Gnostic vision includes an element of man's essential loneliness – hence its understanding for the alienated and oppressed. It would be wrong to suppose that it is lacking in sympathy. The world for which it aspires, on the contrary, the world for which the poet would set sail on an inner journey, is precisely one in which all otherness, all painful separateness, has been overcome. Such a world is intimated by nature itself, seen as the repository of the secret *'correspondances'*, the harmonies of sense and soul to which the poet is sensitive.

Baudelaire is temperamentally unlike Blake, and his inner voyages lack the energy and fantastic invention of Blake's. Since they are a letting-go of self-will, they are touched rather by an oriental languor, as in the wonderful 'L'Invitation au voyage'. The Blake of the more relaxed visions – the sun and sea of the south coast in his verse letters to Butts, for example – sometimes comes close. And sometimes, as in the heavenward sweep of 'Élévation', Baudelaire approaches a Blakean rendering of the Gnostic ascension. Here he launches himself most boldly into the infinite regions of man's spirit beyond the cramping contradictions below, like a 'swimmer, ravished by the sea'. With extraordinary vividness and power the poem captures the vision of swimming in immense heights. But his spirit does not lose itself in the abstract spaces, the 'bleues immensités' of his frigid goddesses. His vision expands to ensoul and fill even the humble and mute creatures he abandons on earth, 'Le langage des fleurs et des choses muettes'.

Appendix 3
Yeats, the Gyres and a Learned Jesuit

A Vision was composed in such an extraordinary manner that in any discussion of 'sources' we must first establish the level of significance on which we intend to treat the work. Thanks to the publication of transcripts and other documents relevant to the book's development, we now know in some detail what the 'Communicators' said and how Yeats interpreted it.[*] The meaning of the whole, I have argued, cannot be separated from the needs and the intuitions of Yeats' imagination. The poet had laboured for most of his life to close the gap between imagination and reality, life and justice. Perhaps his deepest intuition was that of the unity of life behind its many-sided appearances: a unity rooted in the 'unseen' yet accessible to the image-making, 'masking' power of the mind. The prime 'source' of *A Vision* is Yeats' poetic faculty. Of that there is no doubt. I have further suggested that Yeats was aided in articulating his vision by the philosophy of Rudolf Steiner. This is a 'source' of *A Vision* in another important sense, in part through Steiner's intervention in Golden Dawn activities, fashioning rituals which deeply affected the poet, in part through Mrs Yeats' *daimon*, unconsciously shaping the 'system' which came through her trance writings and speech. At the same time, Steiner's ideas and even the general cast of thought were modified in the process to suit Yeats' imaginative requirements, to give him the needed 'metaphors for poetry'.

The content of *A Vision* deriving from Steiner seems to me especially important, since it includes fundamental concepts: opposites (polarities), the dialectic of world-views, cosmic thought, reincarnation, destiny, rhythms of history. Nevertheless, Steiner is far from being the only source of the book. Indeed, characteristic of the unconscious creativity underlying it is a tendency to garner from dispersed and forgotten fragments of mental life generally. Images, ideas, events are invested with symbolic value; personal accidents become grist to the mill of the unfolding vision.

[*]*The Making of Yeats's 'A Vision'*, ed. G. M. Harper (2 vols) (London, 1987).

When Mrs Yeats began her sessions of automatic writing in 1917, for example, her script suggested to Yeats earlier materials he had received from automatic writing by Lady Edith Lyttelton some years earlier (1913 or 1914), and a vision by his friend Horton concerning the myth of the soul in Plato. Both these had mentioned black and white horses, which became a crystallization point for the system of contraries expounded by the new scripts.* On some level we have to do once more with 'sources', and it even seemed to Yeats that the whole system had developed from the earlier hints and Horton's prophetic vision. Certainly the former images, from trance and vision, facilitated the language of contraries in the Communicators' texts. Yet it also seems clear that the minds of Yeats and his wife were able to resuscitate these mental fragments and incorporate them because there was now, unconsciously, a latent pattern in their minds which would gradually be made explicit. The unconscious seized upon useful images, like the mention of black and white horses, because they help symbolize that latent whole. Until Mrs Yeats entered the picture and began her writing, there is no evidence that these scraps were starting to generate a system, and it is hard to see how they could do so.†

Richard Ellmann's doubts about the ultimate relevance of Yeats' 'sources' are therefore well-founded. Even when clearly relevant somehow, they often serve to point out the originality of Yeats' imaginings rather than their derivativeness. I hope that in dealing with Steiner's influence I also showed how the ideas were necessary, consciously or otherwise, to articulate Yeats' imagining and how they were changed in the process of his 'shared dream' into something essentially Yeatsian. In dealing with the following instance of derivation, I am aware of once more tracing the use of an image seized because it fitted the deeper purposes of his mind, not a source which is able to explain *A Vision*. So far as I know it has not been pointed out that the system of contrary gyres and the phases of the moon was the idea of a famous Jesuit scholar and scientist, Athanasius Kircher. It was illustrated and discussed in his *Ars Magna Lucis et Umbrae* (Rome 1646 and later editions). (See Figure 6.)

*See G. M. Harper, *W. B. Yeats and W. T. Horton. Record of an Occult Friendship* (London, 1980) pp. 59–61.
†The ability of the unconscious to construct a system of 'mystic science' out of commonplace words and materials was interestingly demonstrated by a patient of Jung: cf. his *Psychology and the Occult* (Princeton and London, 1977) pp. 42ff, 87ff.

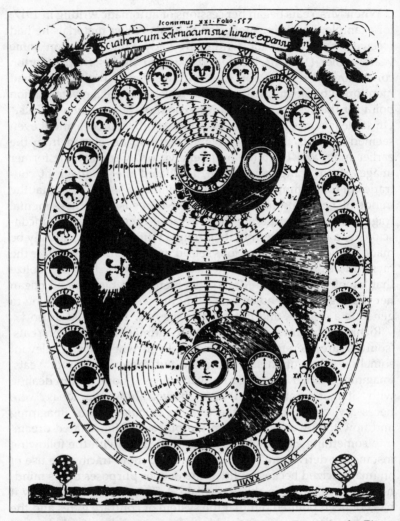

Figure 6. Athanasius Kircher, The Gyres of the Moon. Engraving by Pierre Miotte from *Ars Magna Lucis et Umbrae* (1646).

Through whom did it enter the 'shared dream' of *A Vision*? Either Yeats or his wife could have seen it, perhaps, in the learned Hermetic circles they frequented. For Kircher was the heir to Renaissance Hermetism and esoteric wisdom. Indeed he represents the most audacious attempt to win this knowledge for the Church and fit it into the frame of orthodoxy. Alternatively, we might recall that in Ireland there was no shortage of Jesuits or those interested in their achievements. However it came to the attention of the seekers after vision, it was presumably forgotten: for there is no mention of Kircher or any analogous system of calculating the lunar phases in *A Vision* itself. (The pre-Socratic and other philosophical 'gyres' discussed there offer only remote parallels where they seem similar at all.) At some stage, the forgotten image was revived as offering the fullest possibilities for a lunar vision of polarities, equivalent to Steiner's solar 'mental astronomy'.

The illustration to *Ars Magna* vividly depicts the double gyres, studded with numbers which enable the times of the moon's phases to be calculated. Ideally, points out Kircher, the two tails of the gyres should be thought of as coinciding. Within the gyres, and also set out around the edge in an elongated circle, are the twenty-eight phases, with Phase 1 at the bottom and Phase 15 at the top. The two halves, and the two gyres, are distinguished with the words *luna crescens* and *luna decrescens*. The whole is decorated with small symbols of day and night, and with clouds and a scroll-title.

The diagram of the phases, with its gyres coinciding at the extremes, must surely be the source of Yeats' unusual association of gyres with the moon at the basis of the mechanism of his symbol in *A Vision*. The probability is at any rate increased by the presence in works of Kircher of the 'double cone' image, the interlocking of light and darkness which is the Communicators' other favourite representation. It is striking, however, that the figure in *Ars Magna* lays no claim whatsoever to mystic symbolism. It is simply a means of calculating the hours of visibility and the occurrence of the phases of the heavenly body orbiting round the earth. It is, then, a 'source' of *A Vision*: yet a purely naturalistic device for working out the phases of the moon has been taken up by Yeats' imagination for quite other ends. We can trace the 'origin' of the image on the level of books and illustrations. But the spiritual import of Yeats' work needs to be borne in mind independently, and the use of the figure to help create a remarkable body of modern poetry is scarcely a subject to be approached along those lines. Images borrowed from conscious or unconscious memory are caught up into a process both more important and much more elusive.

A tantalizing 'mystic' connection from Kircher, also connected with the moon's phases, perhaps also deserves to be mentioned. It might conceivably have been an ingredient in the rich mixture of *A Vision*, given that the link with Kircher has been established. In his

Turris Babel (Amsterdam, 1679), Kircher argues that all systems of
pagan theology derived from the worship of sun and moon in
various aspects. The different religions exalted one or other of
these aspects, or worshipped them in different groupings. The
restored complete system or *Theotechnia Hermetica* is thus, on a
cruder level, a device for generating all known systems of ancient
theology, as Yeats was to generate all characters and modes of
thought. It works, however, by reducing all mythologies to a
supposed common denominator, and is hardly a match for the
psychological sophistication or the developmentalism of Steiner. It
is interesting here because it aligns the active and passive powers
with the phases of the moon (inner circle), and these in turn with
the twelve annual stations of the sun. We recall that there are
passages in *A Vision* too where the lunar symbolism seems to
revert to a more primary, solar pattern. Kircher's system, on the
other hand, does not suggest the important polarities of *A Vision*.
Although the powers are divided into actives and passives, these
do not correspond to opposites on the wheel; rather they are
correspondences between the inner (moon) circle and the outer
(sun) circle. And once more, Kircher's approach is basically
naturalistic. His Apollo is nothing more interesting than the
'power of heat' (*vis calefactiva*); Minerva, the goddess of his Phase
15, is the healing quality of colour. One senses that the pretensions
of Hermes and his theotechnic are being kept within bounds. They
are hardly on the way to begetting a new mystic vision.

Bibliography

In the following sections I offer suggestions for further reading on visionary poetry and imagination. It makes no claims to completeness (the bibliography of Milton alone would be vast); indeed it is often frankly eclectic, listing works with some similarity or obvious relevance to the approach adopted in this book. Needless to say, I do not intend to detract from the merits of historical treatments, source-criticism, biographical analyses of poetry, etc. in their own terms. Works not specifically identified in a footnote when quoted in the text are those listed under their author in the appropriate section. An asterisk * here denotes a work of a more difficult, detailed or advanced kind rather than an introductory one.

GENERAL

Abrams, M. H. *Natural Supernaturalism. Tradition and Revolution in Romantic Literature* (New York, 1971).

Abrams, M. H. *The Correspondent Breeze. Essays on English Romanticism* (New York, 1984).

Barfield, O. *Poetic Diction. A Study in Meaning* (London, 1952).

Barfield, O. *Saving the Appearances* (New York, n.d.).

Barfield, O. *Romanticism Comes of Age* (London, 1966).

Barfield, O. *What Coleridge Thought* (Oxford, 1972).

Beer, J. B. *Coleridge's Poetic Intelligence* (London, 1977).

Beer, J. B. *Wordsworth in Time* (London and Boston, 1979).

Blackstone, B. *The Lost Travellers* (London, 1962).

Bloom, H. *The Visionary Company* (Cornell, 1971).

Burwick, F. *The Damnation of Newton: Goethe's Color Theory and Romantic Perception* (Berlin and New York, 1986).

Coleridge, S. T. *Selected Poetry and Prose* ed. D. Stauffer (New York, 1951).

Coleridge, S. T. *Biographia Literaria*, ed. J. Engell and W. Jackson Bate (Princeton, 1983).

Fairlie, A. *Baudelaire: Les Fleurs du Mal* (London, 1960).

Faulkner Jones, D. E. *The English Spirit*. With an Introduction by Owen Barfield (London, 1982).

Ford, N. F. *The Prefigurative Imagination of John Keats* (London, 1951).

Hartman, G. *Wordsworth's Poetry 1787–1814* (London and New Haven, 1977).

Hepworth, B. *The Rise of Romanticism. Essential Texts* (Manchester, 1978).

Hirst, D. *Hidden Riches. Traditional Symbolism from the Renaissance to Blake* (London, 1964).

Hungerford, E.   *Shores of Darkness* (New York, 1941).
James, D. G.   *Scepticism and Poetry* (London, 1937).
Jones, J.   *John Keats' Dream of Truth* (London, 1969).
Keats, J.   *Selected Poetry* (with letters) ed. Paul de Man (New York, 1966).
Keats, J.   *Letters* ed. R. Gittings (Oxford, 1975).
Kermode, J. F.   *Romantic Image* (London, 1971).
Kermode, J. F.   *Renaissance Essays* (London, 1973).
Knight, G. W.   *The Starlit Dome* (London, 1959).
Levere, T. H.   **Poetry Realized in Nature. S. T. Coleridge and Early Nineteenth-century Science* (Cambridge, 1981).
Prickett, S. (ed.)   *The Romantics* (London, 1981).
Prickett, S.   *Coleridge and Wordsworth. The Poetry of Growth* (Cambridge, 1970).
Raine, K.   *Defending Ancient Springs* (Ipswich, 1985).
Shaffer, E. S.   **'Kubla Khan' and The Fall of Jerusalem. The Mythological School in Biblical Criticism and Secular Literature 1770–1880* (Cambridge, 1975).
Taylor, R.   *The Romantic Tradition in Germany. An Anthology* (London, 1970).
Wasserman, E.   *The Finer Tone. Keats' Major Poems* (Baltimore, 1953).
Wordsworth, J.   **William Wordsworth. The Borders of Vision* (Oxford, 1982).
Wordsworth, W.   *William Wordsworth* ed. S. Gill (The Oxford Authors) (Oxford, 1984).
Wordsworth, W.   *Letters* ed. A. G. Hill (Oxford, 1984).

MILTON

Milton, J.   *Poems* ed. B. A. Wright (London, 1973).
Milton, J.   *Selected Prose* ed. K. M. Burton (London, 1955).

Broadbent, J.   *John Milton. Introductions* (Cambridge, 1973).
Curry, W. C.   **Milton's Ontology, Cosmogony and Physics* (Lexington, 1966).
Hunter, G. K.   *Paradise Lost* (London, 1980).
MacCaffrey, I. G.   *Paradise Lost as Myth* (Cambridge, Mass., 1967).
Martz, L. L.   *The Paradise Within* (New Haven, 1964).
Roston, M.   *Milton and Baroque* (London, 1980).
Saurat, D.   *Milton, Man and Thinker* (London, 1944).
Wittreich, J. A. (ed.)   *Milton and the Line of Vision* (Madison, 1975).

BLAKE

Blake, W.   *Complete Poetry and Prose* ed. D. V. Erdman with commentary by H. Bloom (New York, 1982).
Blake, W.   *Complete Writings* ed. Sir G. Keynes (Oxford, 1972).
Blake, W.   *The Complete Graphic Works* ed. D. Bindman (New York, 1978).
Blake, W.   *The Illuminated Blake* annotated D. V. Erdman (Oxford, 1975).
Blake, W.   Illuminated colour editions:
    Songs of Innocence and Experience ed. Sir G. Keynes (Oxford, 1970).

The Marriage of Heaven and Hell ed. Sir G. Keynes (Oxford, 1975).
The Book of Urizen ed. K. P. and R. R. Easson (London, 1979).
Milton, A Poem ed. K. P. and R. R. Easson (London, 1979).
(not colour): *Blake's Job* ed. S. Foster Damon (New York, 1969).

Beer, J. *Blake's Visionary Universe* (Manchester, 1969).
Bindman, D. *Blake as an Artist* (Oxford, 1977).
Damon, S. F. *A Blake Dictionary* (London, 1973).
Frye, N. **Fearful Symmetry* (Princeton, 1947).
Nurmi, M. K. *William Blake* (London, 1975).
Raine, K. *Blake and Antiquity* (London, 1979).
Sola Pinto, V. de *The Divine Vision* (London, 1957).
Tannenbaum, L. **Biblical Tradition in Blake's Early Prophecies. The Great Code of Art* (Princeton, 1982).

GOETHE

Goethe, J. W. von *Selected Verse with Prose Translations* ed. D. Luke (Harmondsworth, 1964).
Goethe, J. W. von *Faust. Eine Tragödie*. Kommentiert von E. Trunz (Hamburg, 1963).
Goethe, J. W. von *Faust. Parts I and II* trans. P. Wayne (Harmondsworth, 1949/1959).
Goethe, J. W. von *Great Writings of Goethe* ed. S. Spender (New York, 1958).

Biesantz, H., Greiner, W., Blume, M. and Roggenkamp, W. *Faust am Goetheanum* (Stuttgart, 1982).
Cottrell, A. P. **Goethe's Faust. Seven Essays* (Chapel Hill, 1976).
Cottrell, A. P. *Goethe's View of Evil* (Edinburgh, 1982).
Eppelsheimer, R. *Goethes Faust. Das Drama im Doppelreich* (Stuttgart, 1982).
Gray, D. **Goethe the Alchemist* (Cambridge, 1952).
Raphael, A. *Goethe and the Philosopher's Stone* (London, 1965).
Steiner, R. **Geisteswissenschaftliche Erläuterungen zu Goethes Faust* (2 Bände) (Dornach, 1967).
Steiner, R. *et al. Das Faust-Problem anthroposophisch beleuchtet* (Dornach, 1981).
Wilkinson, E. M. and Willoughby, L. A. *Goethe, Poet and Thinker* (London, 1962).

SHELLEY

Shelley, P. B. *Poetical Works* ed. Hutchinson, rev. G. M. Matthews (Oxford, 1971).
Shelley, P. B. *Selected Poetry and Prose* ed. K. N. Cameron (New York, 1951).

Shelley, P. B.   *Selected Poetry and Prose* ed. H. Bloom (New York, 1966).
Shelley, P. B.   *Shelley on Love* ed. R. Holmes (London, 1980).

Cronin, R.   *Shelley's Poetic Thoughts* (London, 1981).
Richter, H.   *P. B. Shelley* (Weimar, 1898). Also translated *Prometheus Unbound* (Leipzig, 1887).
Wasserman, E.   **Shelley. A Critical Reading* (Baltimore, 1971).
Webb, T.   *Shelley: A Voice not Understood* (Manchester, 1977).
Webb, T.   **The Violet in the Crucible. Shelley and Translation* (Oxford, 1976).
Welburn, A. J.   *Power and Self-consciousness in the Poetry of Shelley* (London, 1986).

STEINER

Steiner, R.   *Mysteriendramen* (2 vols) (Dornach, 1973).
Steiner, R.   *Four Mystery Plays* trans. A. Bittleston (London, 1983).
Steiner, R.   *Kosmische Dichtungen* (Dornach, 1982).
Steiner, R.   *The Essential Steiner* ed. R. A. MacDermott (New York, 1984).

Fletcher, J.   *Art inspired by Rudolf Steiner* (London, 1987).
Hutchins, E.   *Introduction to the Mystery Plays of Rudolf Steiner* (London, 1984).
Pusch, H.   *Working Together on Rudolf Steiner's Mystery Dramas* (New York, 1980).
Steffen, A.   *Über den Keimgrund der Mysteriendramen Rudolf Steiners* (Dornach, 1971).

YEATS

Yeats, W. B.   *The Poems* ed. R. J. Finneran (London, 1984).
Yeats, W. B.   *Autobiographies* (London, 1955).
Yeats, W. B.   *Mythologies* (London, 1959).
Yeats, W. B.   *A Vision* (London, 1937).

Bloom, H.   **Yeats* (Oxford, 1970).
Donoghue, D.   *Yeats* (London, 1971).
Ellmann, R.   *Yeats: The Man and the Masks* (Oxford, 1949).
Ellmann, R.   *The Identity of Yeats* (Oxford, 1954).
Harper, G. M.   **Yeat's Golden Dawn* (London, 1974).
Harper, G. M. (ed.)   *Yeats and the Occult* (New York, 1975).
Raine, K.   **Yeats the Initiate* (London, 1987).
Whitaker, T.   *Swan or Shadow. Yeats' Dialogue with History* (Chapel Hill, 1964).

Index

Addison, Joseph   203, 204, 205
Ahriman, Ahrimanic   35–42, 48,
   59, 60, 83, 85–95, 118, 120, 121,
   125–6, 127, 128, 130, 132, 133,
   134, 136, 138–41, 144, 146–7, 149,
   154, 155–7, 162, 166, 167, 176,
   179, 180, 181, 183, 184, 186–7,
   195, 200, 210, 213, 214, 219, 221
Anthroposophy, see Steiner,
   Rudolf   4, 26, 147, 171–2, 173, 178
apocalypse   2, 18–22, 39–40, 77,
   78, 105–6, 200, 210, 213, 217
Aristotle   29

Bacon, Francis   13
Barfield, Owen   13, 23, 24, 26, 111,
   211
Baudelaire, Charles   221–5
Beer, Gillian   11
Beer, John   17, 113
Berkeley, George   101
Blake, William   1, 2, 3, 4, 5, 7, 13,
   14, 17, 18–19, 21, 23, 24, 26, 36–8,
   39, 42, 43, 55, 57, 61, 68, 70, 76,
   77, 83–5, 87, 99–122, 134, 141,
   142, 147, 191, 195, 208, 209–10,
   212, 219–20, 221–5:
   Songs of Innocence and Experience
   102, 103, 104, 117, 118; Book of
   Thel   61, 106–14, 117, 118, 209;
   Marriage of Heaven and Hell   7,
   23, 76, 87, 101, 115; Europe, A
   Prophecy   19, 102; Book of Urizen
   36–7, 102, 195, 222, 223; The Four
   Zoas   3, 37–8, 102, 104–6;
   Milton, A Poem   57–8, 76–7, 113,
   141; Jerusalem   102, 113, 210
Blavatsky, H.P.   175
Bloom, Harold   185
Byron, George Gordon, Lord   48,
   90, 124, 125: Manfred   124

cabala, see Judaism   56, 218
Chaucer, Geoffrey   11

Chrysippus, see Stoicism   111
Clement of Alexandria   85–6
Cohn, Norman   55, 217
Coleridge, Samuel Taylor   1, 7, 14,
   15, 43, 44, 124, 140, 157, 197, 204,
   208: The Eolian Harp   43
Collison, Henry   173, 194
consciousness, see self, self-
   consciousness
Cottrell, Alan   46
creation, myth of   28, 34–5, 36–8,
   119, 145
Cronin, Richard   32, 47, 49

Darwin, Charles   11–12, 182, 184,
   198
deconstruction   26
Donoghue, Denis   181
double, Doppelgänger   62, 63,
   146, 151, 154, 155
dualism, see Gnosticism,
   Manichaeism, Zoroastrianism
   87–9, 95, 118–19, 126, 213

ego, see self, self-consciousness
Eliade, Mircea   116–17, 212
Eliot, T.S.   71
Ellmann, Richard   166, 176, 187,
   188, 189, 193, 194, 227
esoteric thought, see visionary,
   visionary line   1, 5, 55–7, 79, 86,
   95, 114–15, 165, 167, 168–9, 171–
   89, 211, 217

faith, see religion, faith
Felkin, R.W.   170–1, 172, 173, 193
Fludd, Robert   56, 86, 89
Freud, Sigmund, see unconscious
   22, 28, 61, 208

Genesis, see creation myth   28, 36,
   54, 84
German literature   123–4, 125,
   150

gnosis, Gnosticism 2, 18–19, 36, 55, 56, 77, 114–15, 117, 118, 119, 122, 134, 189, 207, 210, 213, 217, 218–20, 221–5
Godwin, William 84
Goethe, J.W. von 1, 4, 14–15, 23, 25–6, 36, 46, 61, 76, 109, 112, 123–5, 130–5, 136–41, 142, 144, 146, 147–8, 149, 150, 157, 210: *Das Märchen (The Green Snake and the Beautiful Lily)* 46, 149, 162, 163; *Dichtung und Wahrheit* 109, 112; *Faust* 1, 4, 25, 36, 46, 61, 76, 123–5, 130–5, 136–41, 144, 146, 147–8; Goethean science 1, 14–15, 23, 147, 183, 210–11
Greek thought, Hellenism 29–30, 34, 136–8: levels of style, 'Olympian ideal' 29, 33
Green, Martin 171

Hartman, Geoffrey 8, 17
Hermetic thought, Hermes Trismegistus 56–7, 66, 115, 120, 168, 169, 189, 202, 207, 208, 209, 228, 230
Hill, Christopher 55, 218–19
Holmes, Richard 150

image 5–8, 27–8, 68, 71, 77, 99, 104, 176, 181, 194, 195, 204, 210
initiation, *see* esoteric thought 3, 24, 43, 50, 54, 64–5, 69, 71, 79–80, 82, 114–17, 120, 138, 142, 145, 149, 150, 157, 160, 193, 197, 220

James, D.G. 4
Jeffares, A.N. 199
Johnson, Samuel 4, 54
Jonson, Ben 11
Judaism, Jewish thought, *see* cabala, Lucifer 28–30, 34, 56, 74, 81, 92, 120, 187

Keats, John 1, 2, 3, 29, 43–4, 47, 48, 49, 83, 203: *Fall of Hyperion* 43–4
Kermode, Frank 58
Kircher, Athanasius 227–30

Klopstock, F.G. 87, 88

Latitudinarians 119
Lawrence, D.H. 13, 70
levels of style, *see* Greek thought, Hellenism
love 44–6, 62, 69, 70, 93, 145, 151, 152, 157, 171
lyric, *see* music and poetry
Lucifer, Luciferic 28–31, 39–42, 47, 83, 85–90, 92–5, 120, 121, 142–3, 149, 151, 154, 155–7, 162, 166, 167, 176, 177, 179, 180, 181, 183–4, 191, 193, 203–4, 205–7, 210, 213, 214

Maeterlinck, Maurice 149
Manichaeism 35, 115, 126, 134, 148, 217
Marlowe, Christopher 76, 81, 82, 134
Mesmer, Anton 143
metaphysical poetry 47
Michael, Michaelic 76, 85, 187, 200–1
Milton, John 2, 5–12, 14, 24, 30, 39, 43, 44, 53–95, 104, 115, 117–18, 134, 147, 165, 168, 181, 183, 187, 189, 202, 206–7, 210, 213, 217–20: *Comus* 206–7; *L'Allegro, Il Penseroso* 8–11, 181; *Paradise Lost* 30, 53–95, 104, 117–18, 219; *Samson Agonistes* 6
Morton, A.L. 219
music and poetry, lyric 7, 39–40, 41, 70–1, 77, 99, 102–3, 149, 160–4, 211
mythology 3, 16, 26, 27, 28, 40, 42, 54, 69, 72, 82, 101, 103, 126, 138, 149, 203, 213, 221

Newton, Isaac 16, 19, 119
Newton, John Frank 125–6, 128, 133

occult, *see* esoteric thought

Palmer, Samuel 202
Paracelsus 101

Parmenides 108
Pater, Walter 39
Peacock, Thomas Love 125, 128, 133
Pehnt, Wolfgang 40, 41

Raine, Kathleen 115
Ranters 55, 115, 217–20
religion, faith 2–3, 6, 35, 42, 44, 46, 84, 213–14, 222
Reuss, Theodor 171
Richter, Helene 151
Robinson, Henry Crabb 120, 121
Rosicrucians, *see* esoteric thought 56, 58, 86, 89, 115, 135, 149, 150, 164, 168, 169, 172, 178, 193, 219

Sartre, Jean-Paul 5, 27
Schiller, Friedrich 149, 150
science 2–3, 5, 11–15, 16, 22, 26, 38, 45, 56–7, 60, 118, 119, 133, 135, 147, 148, 167, 202, 205, 208, 223
self, self-consciousness 21, 24, 29, 30, 34, 43, 45, 58, 70, 73, 74–5, 76, 77, 80, 82–3, 86, 91, 93–4, 100–1, 104, 111, 117, 134, 139, 140, 165, 176, 179, 211
Shakespeare, William 11, 15, 55, 82, 115, 199–200
Shelley, Percy Bysshe 1, 2, 4, 5, 7, 14, 23, 26, 30–4, 35, 36, 38, 39, 43, 44, 45, 46–50, 73, 77, 83–5, 89, 121, 124–30, 131, 133–7, 141–8, 149, 150, 151, 152, 154, 155, 157, 158, 192, 203, 210, 211, 212, 214, 217: *Alastor* 126–7, 140, 152, 154; *Mont Blanc* 26, 127–30, 131, 133, 136, 140, 142; *The Two Spirits* 158; *Skylark Ode* 33; *Ode to the West Wind* 47, 50, 192; *Prometheus Unbound* 4, 26, 30, 31, 36, 39, 45, 61, 89, 136, 141–7, 149, 151, 154, 155, 157, 158; *Peter Bell the Third* 16; *Epipsychidion* 39; *Adonais* 46–50; *Witch of Atlas* 31–4; *The Triumph of Life* 73, 178, 182; *Defence of Poetry* 5, 23, 148; *Essay on Love* 44; Goethe translations 124
Spengler, Oswald 185, 186, 188
Spenser, Edmund 2, 16, 210
Steiner, Rudolf 4, 24, 26–7, 29, 40–2, 70, 71, 82–3, 85–9, 94, 114, 134, 146, 147, 149–64, 167, 170, 171, 174–6, 178, 179–83, 186–201, 210, 211, 226, 227, 229: *Philosophie der Freiheit* 40; *Die Pforte der Einweihung* 40, 149–64, 171
Sterne, Laurence 13
Stoicism 111–12, 120
Strindberg, August 149, 211
Swedenborg, Emanuel 115, 221
Symbolist movement, *see* image

time, imaginative 102, 103–4, 222
Tynan, Kathleen 166

unconscious 22, 27, 61, 175, 176, 178, 188, 208, 226, 227
Underhill, Evelyn 172

visionary, visionary line, *see* esoteric thought 1, 2–3, 15, 16, 17, 30, 44, 58, 65–71, 75, 95, 100, 102, 115, 117, 147, 169, 171, 210, 214

Waddington, C.H. 208
Waite, A.E. 172
Warnock, Mary 23
Wordsworth, William 1, 2, 5, 14, 15, 16–24, 25, 39, 83, 99, 124, 178, 205, 212–13, 214: *The Borderers* 18, 212; *The Prelude* 18, 20–1; *The Excursion* 16; *Ode, Intimations of Immortality* 17; *Ode on the Power of Sound* 39

Yates, Frances 56
Yeats, William Butler 1, 3, 4, 7, 26, 28, 53, 165–201, 202, 204, 208, 209, 210, 211, 214, 226–30: 'Ego Dominus Tuus' 175; *The Player*

Yeats, William Butler—*continued*
Queen 175; *The Phases of the
Moon* 181–2; *The Second
Coming* 186; *Sailing to
Byzantium* 190–2, 202, 204;
Byzantium 191–201, 209, 210;
Per Amica Silentia Lunae 178;

A Vision 167, 174, 176, 177, 178,
179–89, 190, 192, 193, 196, 197,
208, 211, 226–30

Zoroastrianism, *see* Ahriman 35,
125–6